The Great Palace

BRITISH BROADCASTING CORPORATION

The Great Palace

The Story of Parliament   Christopher Jones

Published by the British Broadcasting Corporation
35 Marylebone High Street, London W1M 4AA

ISBN 0 563 20178 9

First published 1983
Reprinted 1984
© Christopher Jones 1983

Set in 11/13 pt Bembo by August Filmsetting, Warrington
Printed in Great Britain by Balding & Mansell Limited, Wisbech

Contents

Introduction

The Palace of Westminster is one of the most famous buildings in the world. Yet, paradoxically, it remains far too little known by the people on whose behalf it exists. It is remarkably hard for visitors to get into the place, except into the very limited Strangers' Galleries in the House of Lords and the House of Commons, and it is quite impossible for an ordinary individual to see beyond the so-called 'line of route' – the route through parts of the Palace that groups of schoolchildren or constituents are guided along on weekday mornings by Members of Parliament or by official guides. The MPs who have the time – or the inclination – to take their constituents round have probably not paid much thought to how or when or by whom this extraordinary place was built; why it is still a Royal palace; and what goes on behind some of those elaborately decorated walls or beyond those endlessly long corridors.

Every British citizen has the traditional right to come to Westminster to ask to see his Member of Parliament, but he will be lucky to get beyond the Central Lobby, unless his Member is prepared to take him off for a cup of tea or a drink to one of the many cafeterias or bars scattered around the place. For the countless thousands of tourists who flock round Westminster, its doors remain firmly closed. During the summer months when the Houses are not sitting, one of the saddest sights in London is the rickety group of no less than five 'No admittance' notices hung, by tatty bits of string, on the main public entrance to the Palace, and the steady tide of disappointed tourists being turned away by the endlessly patient and amiable policemen. The tourists, whose faces light up with the pleasure of instant recognition when they first see the Clock Tower, have to be content with sticking their cameras through the wrought-iron railings, or listening to the doubtful history blaring from the loudspeakers of the river boats that take them on day trips from Westminster Pier.

There are, of course, excellent reasons for keeping the Houses of Parliament for the politicians and those who work with and for them – although it is, perhaps, significant, that visitors are still always known by the unwelcoming and cold word 'strangers'. Security, in such a place, however, must be tight and efficient; it would inevitably attract cranks and oddities who could make its work impossible. Mere gawpers and gapers cannot be allowed to interfere with the work of government. Yet the spirit that is said to have moved the Duke of Wellington to advise that the present Palace should be built with its face securely to the Thames and its back to the mob, does still seem to be there.

After working in the Palace of Westminster for a quarter of a century I am, of course, still a Stranger there myself. Like all journalists, I am only tolerated, and technically I daily break the strict rules of the House that its proceedings may not be reported. Yet, after some twenty-five years reporting its activities for the BBC, its fascination both as an institution and as a building remains as great. It took some two years negotiating with senior officials and Members in both Houses before my colleagues and I were allowed to make the television series which this book accompanies.

The book and the BBC television series are an attempt to show the British Parliament as an active, working and modern institution; not without blemishes and inefficiencies; but with an immense wealth of history and tradition which are used to temper and direct the work and day-to-day lives of MPs and Peers.

In the preparation of both the book and the series I have, of course, had a great deal of unstinted help from many people both in the Palace of Westminster and in the BBC. Members, officers and officials in both Houses, from the most senior politicians to junior members of the staff, have all given their time without stint in the lengthy filming sessions involved, and I am deeply grateful to them.

We were granted facilities that no other journalist or television team has ever been given before, and we were able to see not only the grand and gilded State Apartments of Mr Speaker, but also the busy below-stairs life that makes such an enormous place work smoothly and efficiently; we saw the great national archive of more than three million state documents at one end of the building in the Victoria Tower; we saw what makes the great bell of Big Ben strike the hours in the Clock Tower at the other end; we saw the Prime Minister at work in her room; we saw the housemaids dusting sideboards and tables. In the thirteenth century the chronicler, Matthew Paris, called the king's palace at Westminster 'the Great Palace'. We saw the Great Palace at work.

My sincere gratitude, too, to my many BBC colleagues: to the members of the BBC Parliamentary staff with whom I have worked for the last twenty-five years; the enthusiastic and ingenious director of the television series, Alan Scales; to our brilliant cameraman, John Goodyer and his assistant cameraman, Andrew Godfrey; our stills photographer, Tully Chaudry, who was responsible for so many of the photographs in this book; our resourceful picture researcher, Vanessa Whinney; John Gau, our executive producer; Liz Gathercole, our production assistant; and our endlessly patient secretary, Nora Sale.

To the British Parliament, my deep gratitude and respect.

RTA TVR:CORPVS:EADWARDI:REGIS:AD:ECCLESIAM:S͞C
PETRI AP

CHAPTER ONE
A Miracle

The miracle of Thorney Island St Peter, tradition says, came to Thorney Island, where Westminster now stands, and blessed the chapel the monks had built there. The saint promised the Thames fishermen great draughts of salmon provided they paid their taxes

It all began with a miracle: St Peter himself, so legend says, came to Thorney Island, beside the River Thames, to bless a small chapel that some holy men, in the reign of King Sebert, had built there on a lonely and mysterious spot. There might have been a ford there, leading from the Roman roads that came up from the Channel coast through Kent to the settlement of Londinium further down the river. Perhaps, the Romans built a temple to Apollo on Thorney Island and it may have been on the site of its ruins that, two hundred years after the Romans left Britain, the seventh century Christian King Sebert founded the church.

The island was a desolate, marshy place, full of thorn bushes and quagmires; a place only suitable for men who had retired from the world. It was formed by the River Thames and two branches of the Tyburn; its scrub lands covered thirty acres, and it was here, says the legend, that St Peter came on a stormy night when the tide was up and the river was running fast. The dark-cowled figure called the ferryman, Edricus, to row him over to Sebert's tiny chapel on the island, and Edricus grudgingly agreed. He followed the mysterious figure into the little chapel, and as they passed through the small door the candles inside sprang into flames, and choirs of angels sang St Peter's praises. For this, the terrified Edricus now realised, was the great Apostle himself, who had come to dedicate his church and his island in his own name and to the glory of God. As a practical man and as a fisherman who had once known an even greater miracle, St Peter ordered Edricus to cast his nets into the Thames, and the ferryman brought up 'such a draught that the nets were ready to break with the vast quantity of salmon'. Then the saint ordered Edricus and his successors to give one tenth of their catch to the church on Thorney Island, for if they paid their taxes, promised St Peter, (in words which politicians are using at Westminster to this very day) they would never want for this world's goods.

From the monks' point of view – and they were certainly established on Thorney Island by 785 – this story was, quite literally, a Godsend. It meant that their church would become a place of miracle-working and therefore of pilgrimage; and pilgrims, of course, brought money with them. Monks had to be both holy and practical.

The Burial of Edward the Confessor The Bayeux tapestry recalls the burial of Edward in the newly-built Abbey of St Peter at Westminster. Later the same day in January 1066, Harold was crowned King in the Abbey

The great Abbey church of St Peter on Thorney Island still stands commemorating the legend. The monks prospered and continued to build on 'the awful place that is called Westminster', which had been made more awful by the ravages of the Danes in the ninth century until it was finally made safe by King Edgar and St Dunstan, who restored the buildings in 960 and established a dozen Benedictine monks there.

It was the Danish King Canute who first set up a Royal palace at Westminster in the first half of the eleventh century. There, sitting beside the muddy shore of the tidal Thames, he is reputed so famously, and so ineffectually, to have commanded the waves to obey him.

'He passed by the Thamys,' wrote John Norden, five hundred years later, 'which ran by that Palace, at the flowing of the tide; and making staie neere the water, the waves cast forth some part of their water towards him. This Canutus conjured the waves by his regal commande to proceede no further. The Thamys, unacquainted with their new god, held on its course, flowinge as of custome it used to do and refrained not to assayle him neere to the knees.' The point, of course, being not that the wise Canute was so vain as to think that he could command the waves, but that his courtiers were flattering fools to suggest that he could.

Seven years after Canute's death, the holy Edward the Confessor became king in 1042, and he built his great Abbey at Westminster – in which he was buried eight days after it had been consecrated in the Christmas of 1065. Around the Abbey, the monks had laboured to make the desolation of Thorney Island bloom and prosper, and among their drained and cultivated fields, Edward's triumphant successor, William the Conqueror, began to build a new and grander palace for himself than the one in which Edward had died. Yet like Canute before him, William could not command the waves, and fourteen out of the fifteen ships which he had requisitioned to bring stone from Caen, in France, to his new palace were sunk in a great storm in the Channel – and the one that survived slipped up the Medway to the monks at Canterbury after its Master and the Abbot had made a little private deal on the side.

It was William's son, William Rufus, who became king in 1087, who really began the work that has never ended – making Westminster a truly Royal palace, fit for the greatest in the land, and a fitting place from which that land should be governed. Westminster at that time was not the permanent seat of government, which was still wherever the King happened to be with his seal. William Rufus first planned the greatest glory of the Palace of Westminster – Westminster Hall; he began it in 1097, and he held his Whitsun feast there in 1099. It was by far the largest and grandest hall in England; probably in all the known world. As men slaved over the King's work, they grumbled at their oppression; a bad harvest in 1097 was made worse by men being forced to raise the great walls at Westminster and to continue with the Conqueror's plans, which his son had now inherited, for enlarging the Tower of London into a massive fortress.

'Men from many shires were sorely oppressed in building the wall round the Tower,' it was reported, and they were so worn down both there and at Westminster, that 'many men periched of want'. When the Hall was completed there were signs in the Heavens of prodigies and tokens; the Thames flooded and 'drowned divers towns', and 'the devil was seen walking in many likenesses' wrote a London alderman.

So Westminster became a truly Royal palace. It became, too, the place where the Royal treasure was kept, and that meant it was the centre of the entire kingdom. The King's gold and jewels and magnificent ornaments and plate had been kept behind the sturdy walls of Winchester Castle, but now they were being carted, together with masses of documents, back and forth between Winchester and Westminster each spring and autumn. A subsidiary treasury had, therefore, to be set up at Westminster, and by the time John was sitting, restively, on the English throne in the early years of the thirteenth century, the treasury had settled firmly at Westminster. 'Where thy treasure is, there shall thy heart be also,' it was said.

John's artistic son Henry III certainly spent a good deal of that treasure on extending and beautifying the Palace of Westminster. He had come to the throne as a child in 1216 – he was crowned, for a second time, when his title was confirmed in 1220 – and he created one of the greatest splendours of Westminster, the Painted Chamber. This, although it was much knocked about and damaged over the centuries, lasted six hundred years until the Victorians rebuilt the entire Palace and finally destroyed it.

Henry built his Painted Chamber on existing foundations, which ran parallel to the present St Stephen's Hall, and were at the very centre of his Palace. His craftsmen began work on the paintings in 1236, and they continued for nearly sixty years, sometimes having to repair damage done by both a fire and by a mob which had burst into the Palace. The Chamber was as grand and as colourful as craftsmen and King could make it. 'That famous Chamber,' wrote two awe-stricken Irish monks, in 1322, fifty years after Henry's death, 'on whose walls all the war-like scenes in the Bible are painted with wonderful skill, and explained by a complete series of texts beautifully written in French, to the great admiration of the beholder.' On one wall was 'a great story' from the Bible, above plaster painted to represent a green dado. There were many Biblical scenes: the stories of Joab, Abner and David; of Elijah and Elisha; of Judas Maccabeus and many, many more, in vivid colours of scarlet and green and blue and gold. There was a great fireplace, built by Robert of Beverley from plans drawn by Master John of Gloucester, and Master William the Painter got £2.3s.10d. for painting the Tree of Jesse above it. The King lay in a splendid canopied bed, its posts painted green with gold stars, and apparently complained about the draughts, as he squinted through a little window, into his private chapel of St Luke.

There Henry III, and kings after him, lived in regal splendour, with their queens, who had their own grand apartments and adjoining private chapel. The King had two painted wardrobes, in one he hung his clothes and in the other 'where the King washes his head' Master William was commissioned to paint a picture of 'the king who was rescued by his dogs from his seditious subjects' – prophetic, that, for in the spring of

1267 Master William had to be compensated by the King for loss of his equipment when a mob broke into the Palace and wrecked everything they could lay their hands on.

Inevitably, with all that magnificence in the King's and Queen's apartment, the money eventually ran out. On 28 August, 1297, when Henry's son, Edward I, was now in Royal possession of those splendid chambers, Master William got a final payment of 54s.7d. and was told to stop work unless informed otherwise by the Chancellor of the Exchequer, Philip of Willoughby. The Chancellor of the Exchequer, in the inescapable tradition of his office, said no.

It was in Henry's chapel, beside his Painted Chamber, that one of the most significant figures in parliamentary history was married. Henry's sister, Eleanor, quietly and privately married Simon de Montfort, the man who is credited with creating the foundations of the modern British Parliament.

Simon de Montfort, Earl of Leicester, was born and brought up in Normandy, the son of Count Simon IV of Montfort l'Amaury. He was twenty-one when he came to England, and thirty when he married Henry's sister, in 1238. His heavy-handed behaviour as governor of Gascony earned him enemies who gained the King's ear, and he quarrelled with Henry over the influence of the Royal favourites. Simon became the leader of the barons whom Henry now felt himself strong enough to challenge. War became inevitable as the King wriggled out of the Provisions of Oxford which, in 1258, had given those barons domination over the throne. On 14 May, 1264, de Montfort defeated and captured the King and his son, Edward, at the Battles of Lewes. In December 1264, de Montfort summoned a Parliament in the King's name, which met at Westminster in January 1265, but by 4 August de Montfort was dead, cut to pieces on Evesham battlefield by the King's

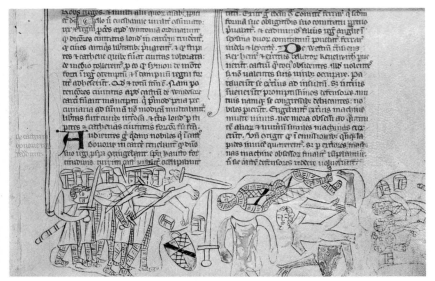

The death of Simon de Montfort Simon de Montfort, the Norman-born Earl of Leicester, called the first truly representative English Parliament in 1265. It met at Westminster and all British Parliaments are descended from it. De Montfort was killed in a battle against Henry III's forces at Evesham later in the same year

victorious forces. When he died he was seen either as an ex-communicated traitor to the King, his brother-in-law, or as a saint. The Franciscan monks prayed for him as 'the guardian of the English people', and in a eulogy after his death another monk wrote of de Montfort: 'He was indeed a mighty man, and prudent and circumspect; in the use of arms and experience of warfare, superior to all others of his time: commendably endowed with knowledge of letters: fond of hearing the offices of the church by day and by night: sparing of food and drink, as those who were about him saw with their own eyes; in time of night watching more than he slept, as his more intimate friends have often related.'

Simon de Montfort, the creator of the British Parliament and the perfect parliamentarian.

THE BEGINNING OF PARLIAMENT

Parliament: the word comes from the French, *parler*: to speak or talk. Monarchs have always felt the need to talk to their subjects and to seek advice and consent despite their own ideas about their divine rights and powers as governors of the realm. It was, after all, generally easier to rule by some sort of consent from, at least, the barons and landowners, rather than by dictatorial imposition of the Royal will without explanation or formal agreement. The Anglo-Saxon kings had adapted the principle in a rough and ready way in the Witenagemot, a group of the great and wise in the land, who advised the monarch, although they neither made laws nor, until Danegeld was thought up as a land tax raised to buy off the Danish invaders, did they impose taxes. When William the Conqueror took the throne in 1066 he developed a mixture of the Witenagemot and the Norman feudal courts as his *Curia Regis*, the King's Council; it was from this council that the House of Lords, the courts of law and the Privy Council eventually evolved.

The Conqueror descended, in great state, upon the sittings of his *Curia Regis*: 'Three times every year he wore his crown, as often as he was in England; at Easter he wore it at Winchester; at Whitsuntide at Westminster, and at Christmas at Gloucester, and then there were with him all the powerful men over all England, archbishops and bishops, abbots and earls, thegns and knights.'

There was no representative of anything less than a knight to act on behalf of the ordinary mass of the people, or even of the merchants and men of affairs who increasingly influenced the life of the kingdom. Not until the French-born Simon de Montfort won his place in British parliamentary history when, in the King's name, he called knights of the shires and burgesses from the towns to sit in Parliament in 1265.

It was, of course, not even remotely democratic – de Montfort made sure none of his opponents were there. The top clergy came (although the Archbishop of Canterbury, uncertain of de Montfort's real power, thought it prudent to stay away), but only five earls and eighteen barons turned up. To these were added summonses calling two knights of each shire, two citizens from the cities and two burgesses from the boroughs, plus delegates from the Cinque Ports. Altogether he called 120 prelates; twenty-three earls and barons, two knights from each of thirty-seven shires in England, two citizens or burgesses from York, Lincoln and a couple of dozen towns and cities, and four representatives from each of the Cinque Ports.

'Henry, by the grace of God King of England, Lord of Ireland, and Duke of Aquitaine, to the Venerable Father in Christ, Robert by the same grace Bishop of Durham', began the writ sent from Worcester on 14 December, 1264. 'Whereas, after the great peril of the disorders recently experienced in our kingdom, Edward our dearest first-born son was delivered as a hostage to assure and strengthen the peace of our kingdom; and whereas, now that the aforesaid disorders have – thank God! – been quieted, we must treat with our prelates and magnates to make salutary provision for his release, and to establish and consolidate full assurance of peace and tranquillity for the honour of God and the advantage of our whole kingdom . . .'

The summons to the knights, citizens and burgesses went out from the Royal palace of Woodstock, to which the King had now moved from Worcester, on Christmas Eve, 1264. Their names were tacked on, in three short paragraphs, to those of the prelates and magnates, rather as though they were an afterthought. 'It was commanded to each sheriff throughout England that they should summon two knights, of the more lawful, trustworthy and discreet knights, of each county, to the King at London in the aforesaid octave (of St Hilary) in the form above said.

'Letters are also written in the preceding form to the citizens of York, the citizens of Lincoln and to other boroughs of England, that they should send in the preceding manner two of the more discreet, lawful and trustworthy of their citizens or burgesses.'

They came to London from all over the country. Precisely how many came, or where they came from, or where they met when they got to the King's court at Westminster, is not certain. Perhaps they met at St Paul's for some of their debates and discussions or went to the Chapter House of Westminster Abbey or even to the Great Hall of the Palace itself.

They sat for two months – from 20 January to 20 March, 1265. After the recent battles with the King at Lewes, they agreed on the terms for peace and the release of the young Prince Edward. 'In which Parliament,' it was recorded by a chronicler, 'on St Valentine's day it was made public in the Chapter House at Westminster that the Lord King had bound himself, on oath, by his charter that neither he nor the Lord Edward in time to come would do injury to, nor cause to be injured, the Earls of Leicester (de Montfort) and Gloucester, nor the citizens of London or any of those who adhere to them, on account of anything done in the former time of disorder in the kingdom; and he

Henry III swears to keep the Magna Carta Henry III, a profligate and untrustworthy king, was brought by his barons to Westminster Hall in 1252 and forced to swear an oath that he would uphold the liberties of the Magna Carta. Lighted tapers were thrown to the ground as the Archbishop of Canterbury prayed that the souls of any man who broke the charter 'might thus be extinguished and stink and smoke in hell'. Henry duly swore, but inevitably broke his oath within months

ordered expressly that the charters of liberties (Magna Carta) . . . should be kept inviolate.'

The attempts of those knights, burgesses, prelates and nobles to obtain peace did not succeed. The Earl of Gloucester broke from de Montfort and joined the King's cause; at Evesham, the freed Prince Edward was at the head of overwhelming forces which not only did injury to de Montfort, but also brought him to a bloody death.

However Prince Edward, when he became Edward I, with a wisdom that had escaped his father, called the first Parliament that was most truly the predecessor of our present system at Westminster. Thirty years after de Montfort's Parliament, on 13 November, 1295, the Model Parliament met at Westminster. It earned the title 'Model' because it is from this meeting that all future Parliaments were developed. Two knights from each shire, two citizens from each city and two burgesses from each borough were all elected, rather than simply nominated by the local lord; there were representatives too, of the lesser clergy, and they all sat with the bishops, barons and nobles at Westminster. The King wanted money, so he called representatives of all sections of society who were in a position to supply it – or, just as important, to withold it, unless they felt they had some sort of control over his spending.

Once this great principle of financial control had been wrested from the King, it was eagerly consolidated by Parliament and built up over the centuries.

During Edward's reign, prominent women were summoned to add their voices to his council; but whether they actually came themselves or sent proxies, no one knows. Writs, though, were certainly sent to the Abbesses of Shaftesbury, Barking, St Mary at Winchester, and Wilton, in their capacity as owners of great convent estates.

Edward I called sixteen Parliaments in the thirty-five years of his reign, which sat in the Painted Chamber, or in the adjacent White Chamber (which, in due course, became the House of Lords), and sometimes in the Chapter House or Refectory of the nearby Abbey. It was inevitable that factions formed: the knights, citizens and burgesses found they had their own interests to promote, plus power and influence to make their wishes felt. The nobles and prelates gathered closely together to protect their positions and, little by little, they divided into two separate groups which sat in two separate Houses. By 1332 the Lords and Commons were meeting apart; by 1363 the Commons had its own Clerk, a man called Robert de Melton from the court of Chancery who was paid 100 shillings a year, for life, plus any perks he could get; and by 1377, the Commons was so entirely separate from the King and the Lords that it had its own Speaker – that is, the man who spoke to the King on their behalf, and had the absolute right to do so. 'The Commons' it was certainly called by then but not yet the 'House of Commons'. That title would take nearly another hundred years to develop.

Parliament made up of Lords and Commons acting together, developed its powers rapidly under the Plantagenet kings. The two Houses refused to supply Edward II with money unless he righted their grievances, and by 1327, before the assembled citizens of Westminster and London, they deposed him, in a great ceremony in Westminster Hall.

'The archbishops and bishops, earls and barons, abbots and priors and all others from the cities and boroughs together with the whole commonalty of the land' were there. Edward was at Kenilworth, but sent his crown and sceptre as token of his resignation. Nine months later he was murdered in Berkley Castle, and it was under his son, Edward III, that the Commons established its own, separate identity in Parliament.

Edward III, a boy king when he succeeded his murdered father in 1327, called one or more Parliaments during every one of the fifty years of his reign. The Commons increasingly assumed rights and powers of its own as it held its debates away from the ears of the King and his court.

Edward presided, presumably without much pleasure, over the Good Parliament of 1376, which took measures against corruption at court and against his mistress, Alice Perrers, who was particularly singled out for censure by the Commons. In the next year, though, all the good of the Good Parliament was promptly undone by the bad of the Bad Parliament which reinstated Alice Perrers and imprisoned the Speaker. The Merciless Parliament of Richard II in 1388 engineered the judicial murder of the King's favourites – it was also known as 'The Parliament that Wrought Wonders' by those who agreed with what it had done.

The Reformation Parliament of 1529 – or the Black Parliament to those who wept to see the old order and Church go – carried out the wishes of Henry VIII. For the six years of its sitting, the Commons of the Reformation Parliament eagerly supported the King in the destruction of the Church's power and the religious revolution that he brought about. In the process, the Commons, while allowing itself to be used by Henry to legalise his depredation of Church land and properties, wrested the initiative from the Lords; the Upper House knew that the Lower House was doing the King's bidding, and so had to comply. So compliant were the nine Parliaments that Henry called in thirty-five years, that they freed him from the obligation to pay his debts; allowed him to demand forced loans; made him supreme Head of the Church and denied the authority of the Pope; changed the Royal succession; condemned to death by Acts of Parliament two of his wives, Anne Boleyn and Catherine Howard, and others of whom the King wanted to be rid; and changed the laws of treason according to his dictat.

Yet the Commons, paradoxically grown more powerful while ruthlessly used by Henry, still had no regular place in which to hold its meetings. The Lords and Commons had their first meetings together with the King in his Painted Chamber when they were summoned, then the Commons usually moved across to find a meeting place in Westminster Abbey. After 1352 they sometimes met in the great octagonal Chapter House, and then later moved into the now-destroyed Refectory. No doubt they watched with interest as, in 1476, William Caxton, newly back in England from Bruges, set up the country's first printing press just outside the Chapter House where they were meeting – although few enough of them would have been able to read the books he produced. Perhaps they got the point when the monks had the wall of their Chapter House painted with the scene of the Last Judgement, with the saved – the sheep – on the Lord's right hand, and the damned – the goats – on the Lord's left. If the Members had looked hard at the painting they would have found that the pictures of the damned goats looked remarkably like some of their number; they would have been looking at the country's first political cartoon.

It was there that the Commons were meeting, sitting on the monks' cold stone seats round the walls, with their Speaker in the Abbot's central seat, when news came to them, on 21 January 1547, that the terrifying King Henry VIII was dead. It was the last time they were to sit in the Chapter House. Soon they were to move out, to an even more splendid Gothic building just across the Old Palace Yard from the Abbey. The smell of candlegrease from the votive candles was in the air; the lingering scent of incense remained; the altar was still there, and the crucifix was still upon the altar, as the Commons moved into their first permanent home: the Royal Chapel of St Stephen's, Westminster.

CHAPTER TWO
Westminster Hall

The Great Hall which William Rufus and his knights saw when they reached the banks of the Thames at Westminster, after their long ride up from the Kent coast, had taken two years to build. It had almost certainly been started in 1097 and, by using what was virtually slave labour, it had been completed astonishingly quickly. In all probability it replaced a hall in the Royal Palace that Canute had established at Westminster earlier in the century, and the craftsmen had simply built round the existing hall. The result was that they could not get their measurements quite right, so they built the two long walls, on the east and west sides, four feet out of alignment. In the rush to complete the building, some of their stonework was less than first-rate. Eight hundred years later, Sydney Smirk, a Westminster architect, said, rather stuffily, that he was 'unable to speak in terms of any commendation' of the way that the Norman craftsmen had cut and set the stone.

Yet the walls that those craftsmen built are still standing today, although much repaired and refaced. They were massive walls, over six feet thick, and decorated with chequer work; they were 20 feet high, and enclosed a Hall that was over 239 feet long and more than 67 feet wide. Between the twelve round-headed windows on each side ran an arcade of arches, and inside the Hall two rows of pillars supported the wooden shingle roof. It was undoubtedly immensely grand and impressive, although the extravagant William said it was 'not half large enough; too big for a chamber, and not big enough for a hall.'

To the south of the Hall, the yard from Canute's palace remained; it is still known as Old Palace Yard. To the north of the Hall they created a new square; and this has retained to this day the name by which it was known in 1099, New Palace Yard. William himself saw little of the splendour he had created. The following year he was dead – mysteriously shot through the head by an arrow while out hunting.

William's younger brother, Henry, succeeded him to the throne, and in 1102 called his first council in his great Hall, which was thronged by 'all the chief men of England both clergy and laity'. It was in Henry I's reign that the Hall began to be used as law courts, a function that it retained for over 700 years. Of course, it was also used for great celebrations and banquets, with makeshift kitchens tacked on to the outside walls, and an open drain carrying away the filth of the Hall – and of its occupants – down its entire length. Henry II had the drain covered over, and his son, King John, held his coronation banquet in the more salubrious Hall in 1199. In 1212, John celebrated Christmas at Westminster – and took a bath which cost him sixpence.

The Court of the Exchequer
The Court sitting in Westminster Hall in 1460

Henry III was still a small boy when his father, John, died, but as a grown man he brought his new Queen Eleanor, to the Hall, in 1236 for her coronation feast. A great fire blazed in the centre of the Hall on that cold January day, and the High Marshal of England cleared a way through the throng with his wand of office for the Royal couple. The barons of the Cinque Ports sulked because they thought they had been slighted, but the citizens of London supplied 'the abundance of divers liquors', and in the kitchens citizens of Winchester cooked the 'dainties of the table', with 'quantities of game and varieties of fish'. Jesters vaulted under the feet of the waiters. A year later, the King entertained a very different class of subjects by inviting 6,000 poor people, the weak and the aged, to feast with him in his Hall.

Henry, though, was to know very much less happy times in his Hall. His duplicity and cunning, and his endless demands for money, drove his people to despair and his great men to revolt. Finally, in 1253, the Lords spiritual and temporal gathered together in Westminster Hall and drew up in a threatening circle round the terrified King. Each man held a lighted taper in his hand, and the Archbishop of Canterbury called down a terrible curse from Heaven on anyone – meaning, of course, the King – who should infringe the rights of the citizens or ignore the provisions of Magna Carta, which the barons had extracted from the King's father in 1215. The tapers gutted in the draughts of the Hall, and each baron and bishop raised his hand as the Archbishop's great curse was pronounced and then, instantly, the Hall was plunged into darkness as each man threw his taper 'stinking and smoking, on the ground, and the dire malediction uttered that the souls of everyone who infringed the Charters might "thus be extinguished and stink and smoke in hell" '. Not surprisingly, the King swore the oath demanded of him: 'So may God help me, I will inviolably observe all these things, as I am a man and a Christian, a knight and a crowned and anointed King.' Once the drama of that night was forgotten, Henry broke his oath, and was once more brought back to the Hall by the barons, trembling and frightened – 'Am I a prisoner then?' – to be stripped still further of Royal prerogatives.

Henry's son Edward I, like his father before him and the kings of England who followed down the centuries, held his coronation banquet in the Hall. In 1274, when Alexander, King of Scotland, came to join the English king in the celebrations, the Scottish knights simply turned their horses loose as they dismounted outside the Hall, and gave them to anyone who could catch them. Unwilling to lose face, the four hundred English knights had to follow suit, and New Palace Yard became a bedlam of bolting horses and frantic citizens trying to catch them. The fountains poured out wine 'like rain water' and the feast was gargantuan: over 400 sheep, 450 pigs, 16 fat boars, over 270 flitches of bacon and nearly 22,500 capons and other kinds of bird.

The Hall survived the roistering of this and other banquets. It survived, too, a fire in 1315, and the Royal coats of arms, which flew from standards at either end of the Hall, periodically had to be refurbished or renewed. The painted walls had to be spruced up, and in 1385 the Clerk of Works received orders from the King – Richard II – to commission thirteen stone statues for the Hall, one for each king from Edward the Confessor to Richard himself. They were 'ordained by the King and his Council to stand in the great hall' and they were made by Thomas Canon for £2.6s.8d. each – although only six of them were actually set up.

Richard, the son of Edward, the Black Prince, had come to the throne as a boy in 1377, and he had been brought to the Hall, still the Norman hall of William Rufus, on St Swithin's day of that year from the Tower of London. He had been clad 'in white garments' with a 'great multitude of princes, nobles, knights and squires'. The next day, the ten-year-old king sat in the marble chair in his Hall and then walked, with the Archbishop of Canterbury and his nobles, down a red carpet that stretched from the Hall to Westminster Abbey, for his coronation. The Hall was to be his greatest glory and a memorial unequalled by any other English king – it was also to see his ruin.

In spite of all the turbulence of his reign, the Peasants' Revolt of 1381 and his own growing despotism, Richard's court became the most magnificent in Europe. He surrounded himself with people of learning and taste; with artists and musicians; painters and sculptors; with dancing masters and makers of extravagant fashions. There had to be a suitable place in which to parade all this gaiety and opulence, and Westminster Hall was, by then, three hundred years old. Richard decided to rebuild it as his most stunning achievement. The Clerk of Works at the time when Richard first began to think about the changes, was Geoffrey Chaucer. Chaucer held the post for two years, from 1389 to 1391, and as a young man he had, like other young men in the King's service, slept two-by-two in the Hall. Some years later he was mugged and robbed of £10 just outside the Hall.

John Godmanston had become Clerk of Works when, on 21 January, 1394, he was told to 'repair the Great Hall within the Palace of Westminster, to take masons, carpenters and other workmen, and set them to the said repairs; and also to take such stone as should be necessary for the work; and to sell to the King's use the old materials of the Hall together with a certain old bridge over the Thames . . .' Godmanston must have been an efficient man, for only three days later, Master Gamylston of Retford, mason, was told to buy lead in Nottinghamshire and Derbyshire, and to hire horses, carts and carters to bring it to London. Orders were also issued to bring lead from the High Peak, and for ships to carry stone from Yorkshire. The rebuilding had begun.

Like the other great rebuilding of the Palace of Westminster, which was to come nearly five hundred years later, this one involved the co-operation of two men of genius: Hugh Herland, the master carpenter, who built the great hammer-beam roof of the Hall, and Henry Yevele, the mason, whose new walls and buttresses were to bear the massive weight – some 600 tons – of the oak roof.

Herland came from a family of carpenters who had been in Royal service for many years. In 1375 he became 'disposer of the King's works touching the art and mystery of carpentry' and was paid 12d. a day by the Clerk of Works at Westminster and the Tower. He received a Royal patent in 1378 as 'master carpenter and disposer of the king's works of carpentry' (still at 12d. a day), but it was not until 1394 that he began his greatest work – the roof of Westminster Hall. Four years later, in gratitude for what this splendid craftsman had then achieved, the King awarded Herland an annual pension of £18.5s. as a reward for his 'long, good and gratuitous service'. He continued to enjoy this Royal generosity until his death in 1406.

Henry Yevele, his partner in rebuilding the Hall, died six years before Herland, in 1400. He lived only just long enough to see his greatest work completed. Yevele had come to London from Derbyshire at the time of the Black Death – perhaps he still had connections in the area and so was able to make arrangements for materials for the rebuilding of the Hall to be provided by people he could trust.

The Master Mason Henry Yevele, the Derbyshire mason who rebuilt Westminster Hall for Richard II in 1399. From a misericord in St Katherine's Church, Regents Park, London

He quickly made his mark in the City as a mason, and on 25 June, 1360, he became 'disposer of the King's works of masonry' at Westminster and at the Tower, at a fee of 1s. a day and an annual robe 'of the suit of the serjeants of the household'. He was allowed to work outside the Royal palaces and castles, and was responsible for the rebuilding of the great naves of Westminster Abbey and Canterbury Cathedral. When the King wanted his Royal Hall to be rebuilt, it was the 'King's chief mason' who was given the task. Yevele had already been exempted from jury service and other duties some years before because of his official work and 'his great age', but in 1394 he was still sprightly enough to control and command when the rebuilding of the Hall began. The strain must have been tremendous. The Hall was barely finished when he was laid in his tomb on 21 August, 1400. He had designed it himself, and it bore the proud inscription: 'Freemason to Edward III, Richard II and Henry IV'.

When they began their work on the Hall, the two craftsmen almost immediately ran into trouble. On 7 June, 1394, Richard's wife, Queen Anne, died and Richard, beside himself with grief, fled to Ireland and stopped building work on his palaces. It was months before word came for work to start again, and Herland could begin the massive task of finding, cutting and transporting the oak for his roof, and Yevele could begin organising the supply of stone. Richard Washbourn and John Swallow, Gloucestershire masons, won a contract for stone that was to be cut 'according to the purport and pattern and mould made by the advice of Master Henry Yeveley'. They had to work to a time limit; half the stone was to be ready by the feast of St John the Baptist, 1395; the other half by Candlemas, 1396. Some of the stone was paid for at a rate of twenty shillings for each corbel; some at a rate of 12 pence for every foot. Swallow's work must have satisfied Yevele, because the Gloucestershire mason later joined with another man and won a contract to build twelve windows in the Hall at £8 each.

While the masons chipped and shaped, Hugh Herland had been busy on the first stages of the roof. In effect, he prefabricated the entire, tremendous structure, and then brought it down the Thames, piece by piece, to put it together at Westminster. Herland set up a workshop at a place called The Frame, near Farnham, Surrey, and there he gathered together the massive trunks of the oak trees he needed. These came from the Royal forests at Odiham and Aliceholt, in Hampshire, and the two hundred oaks needed for the rafters were bought from the Abbot of St Alban's park at Bervan, near Northaw, Hertfordshire. Still more was ordered from Stoke D'Abernon in Surrey, and then, at Farnham, the sawyers and carpenters slaved away, at 6d. a day, to cut it all up into the vast jig-saw that Herland had arranged in his brilliant mind. He designed angels, each carrying the King's coat of arms on a shield, to be placed, wings outstretched, at the point at which each of the arches springs from its horizontal beam. For carving two of these angels, presumably the patterns for the others, Robert Brusyngdon was paid 26s. 8d. each; but for the rest he and other carvers received only 20s. or 15s. each. 'And he set the cherubim within the inner house, and the wings of the cherubim were stretched forth.'

The enormous task of moving hundreds of tons of solid oak (the old tradition, incidentally, that the roof was built from Irish oak is entirely without foundation) began at The Frame. The sheriffs of Hampshire, Berkshire and Surrey were each asked – they would have known what would happen if they refused – to send thirty strong wains, or carts, to The Frame to carry the oak to the Thames at Hamme, near Chertsey. Throughout the dust and heat of that June summer of 1395, the great wains, each drawn by sixteen horses, toiled back and forth between The Frame and the river; ninety carts dragging the oak sixteen leagues to the loading point for the barges. Nearly five hundred loads of oak were sent that month down to Westminster; it cost £19.1s.4d. to drag twenty-six half-beams and twenty-six wall-posts to Hamme in two carts, each taking sixteen horses, in fifty-two journeys at 7s. 4d. a time. Little by little the oak was brought down to the Royal palace to wharves where, centuries later, stone for the Victorian palace would be unloaded.

With the lead that had already been bought to cover the outside of the roof moulded into shape by the King's plumbers, the roof gradually began to emerge. The scaffolding that was needed to get it up was paid for in the accounts of 1395–96, and the huge trusses were in place by 1397. By 1399 the entire roof was completed. An enormous spider's web of English oak, 69 feet wide – too wide for individual beams to stretch across so the brilliant system of curved arches was used to span that great space. It has withstood centuries of fires and bombings, of death-watch beetle, of repairs and battering, of neglect and ignorant manipulation. It cost King Richard approximately £10,000 to build and, in his memory, the craftsmen carved his badge of a white hart round the walls.

The life of the court went on, of course, as the Hall was being built, and when Richard married again in 1397, this time Isabella of France, coarse woollen cloth known as wadmole was bought to make a temporary roof in the Hall for the 'pantry, ewery, scullery, dresser and cellar' at the new Queen's coronation banquet. Later that year, however, work which was being carried out in the Hall made it impossible for Richard to hold his Parliament. He had planned it as a dramatic occasion on which he intended to condemn to exile or death the Earls of Arundel and Warwick, the Duke of Gloucester and the Archbishop of Canterbury. As he could not use his Hall, he ordered 'a long and large hous of tymber . . . that was callid an Hale' to be built in New Palace Yard. It was open all round – the Parliament met in September, so the weather was probably reasonable – so that 'all men might see and heare what was both sayde and done'. The King's company of Cheshire archers threateningly faced the crowd that gathered to watch, and when the Parliament was over and the King's work done, the timber and the 103,000 tiles from the roof were sold off. The timber was sold for £30 to a sharp-witted dealer who promptly sold it back to the King's Clerk of works for a profit.

By the time the Hall was finished, the King's despotism and arrogance had grown so great that his subjects had been driven to desperate measures. In August 1399, far away from Westminster, Richard surrendered to the forces of Bolingbroke at Flint Castle. Two weeks later, Parliament reassembled in the fine new Hall, still bright from the paint that had been used to decorate the walls. There was only one empty chair – the King's. Richard was in the Tower, and the Archbishop of York read his renunciation of the throne. The Archbishop of Canterbury proposed that the renunciation should be accepted and that Richard should be deposed. Henry of Lancaster rose and twice made the sign of the cross, upon his forehead and his breast, and then staked his claim to the Crown of England. There was a great roar of 'Aye' from the people packed into the Hall. Thus, Henry IV was declared King of England in the Great Hall at Westminster.

Richard had been subjected to a form of trial before he was deposed, so carrying on the established tradition of using the Hall as a court of law. Over the centuries the Hall has seen the trial of the greatest in the land: of kings and commoners; of saints and martyrs, of thieves and rebels and fakes and liars. Sometimes those who were summoned were sent to their terrible deaths on Tower Hill or in Old Palace Yard; sometimes they had to stand, with their ears and hands lopped off, in the stocks in New Palace Yard; sometimes they had to parade, placards round their necks proclaiming their crimes, through the bustle of Westminster Hall. For the Hall was always a-bustle. It had wooden divisions separating the courts at the south end which had to be taken down and then put up again whenever there was a great occasion in progress. Round the walls there were stalls that sold books and ribbons and trinkets, and lawyers constantly bustled through the Hall. When Peter the Great of Russia was brought to see the Hall in 1697 he asked who were the men in wigs and black gowns. Lawyers, he was told. 'Lawyers!' exclaimed Peter. 'Why, I have but two in my whole dominion, and I believe I shall hang one of them the moment I get home.'

All the lawyers in Christendom would not have saved the great men the English state wanted dead and who were brought to trial in the Hall over the centuries. In 1305 the Scots patriot, William Wallace, stood trial in the Hall beneath its old Norman roof. He had fought against the English King Edward I, to whom he claimed he owed no allegiance but, beaten and betrayed, he was brought to Westminster for judgement. 'He was,' it was recorded later, 'of a tall, almost gigantic, stature, broad-shouldered, large-boned, with long muscular arms, yet thin in the shanks and unencumbered by much flesh or fat round the reins.' Wallace

The Law Courts in Westminster Hall For 600 years Westminster Hall was used as the nation's principal law courts. The Court of King's Bench sat in the south-east corner *(top left)*; Chancery in the south-west corner *(top right)*; and Common Pleas along the west wall *(bottom right)*. Booksellers and drapers had their stalls round the walls, all of which had to be taken down when one of the many state trials was held in the Hall. St Thomas More, Charles I and Guy Fawkes were among the many who were tried and condemned to death there

continued his defiance of the King during the proceedings, and he heard the dreadful sentence which was handed down impassively. He was immediately dragged to Smithfield and torn to pieces with unimaginable savagery. The King looked on, unmoved.

Hugh Herland's roof was little more than a century old when one of the greatest Englishmen who has ever lived was brought to trial – and his inevitable death – beneath the flock of carved angels. On 1 July, 1535, Sir Thomas More, former Speaker of the House of Commons and Lord High Chancellor of England, stood trial for treason. Only weeks earlier, John Fisher, Bishop of Rochester, had stood in the same Hall accused, like More, of treason against Henry VIII. Fisher was feeble from age and rough treatment in the Tower, but still strong enough to defy Henry's demands of acknowledgement as head of the Church in England. Fisher went on his way to his death from the Hall, to share, centuries later, the Church's crown of canonisation, and the same feast day as More.

More, like Fisher, had suffered the rigours of the Tower for months before he was brought to the Hall. He was haggard and deeply weary as he stood, leaning on his staff, facing his judges. One of the charges brought against him was that he had encouraged Fisher in his opposition to the King's divorce from Katherine of Aragon and subsequent marriage to Anne Boleyn. Anne Boleyn's father, uncle and brother were among the judges sitting at the south end of the Hall to hear the case.

More was given a chair, and gazed about the Hall where once his own father had sat as a judge, and where his King and former friend, Henry, had rushed about, playing tennis. More told the court he was loyal to his King, but that, above all, he was loyal to God and his conscience. Perjured evidence was brought against him, and it took the jury a mere quarter of an hour to return the inevitable verdict. 'I verily trust,' said More, as he heard the death sentence, 'and shall therefore right heartily pray, though your Lordships have now here in earth been judges to my condemnation, we may yet hereafter in Heaven merrily all meet together, to our everlasting salvation.' He was beheaded on Tower Hill on 6 July, 1535, and his head was put on a spike on London Bridge.

Another defender of the Catholic faith stood trial in the Hall some seventy years later. He was no saint but a deluded zealot who was to become the most famous villain – perhaps the most famous hero – in British history. The man's name was Guy Fawkes, and he was accused of trying to blow up King James I and Parliament on 5 November, 1605.

In the House of Commons *Journal* – its minutes book – of that date, the Clerk scribbled a hasty note down the side margin of one of the pages, alongside a list of Members who had been appointed to sit on a rather tedious committee. The Clerk's note said: 'This last night, the upper house of Parlyam(en)t was searched by S(i)r Tho. Knevett, and one Johnston serv(an)t to Mr Thomas Percye was there apprehended who had placed 36.barrelles of gunpowder in the Vawt under the house w(i)th a purpose to blowe K (the King) and the whole company, when they should there assemble. Afterwards div(er)se other gen(tlemen) were discov(er)ed to be of the plott.'

Johnston was, of course, Guy Fawkes. He had been found in a room under the House of Lords, with the gunpowder buried beneath piles of firewood — it had been rowed across the river from Lambeth — and a slow fuse which was supposed to give him fifteen minutes to get away after he had lit it.

Nearly three months after the plot had been discovered, on 27 January, 1606, Fawkes, who had once been a 'very tall and desperate fellow', stood before his accusers in the Hall, broken by the rack in the torture chamber of the Tower. A dock had been built in the Hall to contain him and the seven other conspirators who had been involved in the mad scheme to blow up King and Parliament and in this way, somehow, bring Catholicism back to England. They had been betrayed as they stored their gunpowder at Westminster. Their tortures had been terrible, but when Fawkes was brought before the King himself immediately after his arrest, he said defiantly that, 'a desperate disease requires a desperate remedy'. Their gunpowder was to 'blow the Scots back to Scotland', he told James I of England and James VI of Scotland.

The Gunpowder Plot
Guy Fawkes and Robert Catesby, two of the seven plotters who planned to blow up James I and Parliament on 5 November 1605. When Guy Fawkes was caught lighting the slow fuse, he claimed his name was Johnston

The Lord Chief Justice, Sir John Popham, and a special commission sat in the Hall to hear the case. Stands were built round the walls and touts did a roaring trade selling tickets for the trial at ten shillings each. One MP was furious when he arrived at the Hall to find that his seat was already taken by a man of 'the baser sort' and he sent for the Keeper of the Hall to protest. He was told to sort it out with the Lord Chancellor.

In the crowded Hall, the Lord Chief Justice read the charges against Fawkes and against his companions: that they 'traitorously among themselves did conclude and agree, with Gunpowder, as it were with one blast, suddenly, traitorously and barbarously to blow up and tear in pieces our said sovereign Lord and King, the excellent virtuous and gracious Queen Anne, his dearest wife, the most noble Prince Henry, their eldest son and future hope and joy of England . . . and all of them, without any respect of majesty, dignity, degree, sex, age or place, most barbarously and more than beastly, traitorously and suddenly to destroy and swallow up.' Once again, the result of the trial was inevitable. Three of the men died outside St Paul's on 30 January, 1606. Fawkes himself was so weak from torture and illness that he had to be helped up the ladder to the scaffold, 'but yet with much ado by the help of the hangman went high enough to break his neck with the fall'. He, and his three companions, died in Old Palace Yard, within sight of the House of Lords that they had tried to blow up. Today, Old Palace Yard is used as a car park for members of the House of Lords.

Forty years later the son of our sovereign Lord and King and the excellent and virtuous and gracious Queen Anne — although 'not their eldest son and future hope and joy of England' — sat in the same spot in Westminster Hall also accused of treason. Charles I, King of England, stood trial in his own Hall in 1649, and was taken from it to his execution half a mile away in Whitehall.

Charles knew the Hall all too well. He had made a dramatic, and foolish, appearance in it on a cold January day in 1642 when he had marched through the Hall with a troop of soldiers, and passed through a door in its east wall and up the steps into the House of Commons. There he tried to arrest five Members who, he claimed, were guilty of treason against him. The men in question had got wind of his intentions and had fled, but it was this supremely tactless assault on the position and role of the Commons that eventually led, almost exactly seven years later, to Charles being brought back to the Hall to stand trial.

The years of the civil war between the Parliamentary forces and the Royalists had led to the King's capture in 1648 and Parliament's decision to put the King on trial. On the morning of 20 January, 1649, Oliver Cromwell watched from a window at Westminster as the barge bringing Charles to the Hall drew up alongside the steps down which, years before, the five members had fled from the King. One hundred and thirty-five commissioners had been appointed by the Commons to sit in judgement upon the King, although less than half of them turned up throughout the week-long proceedings. John Bradshaw, a provincial magistrate, was their president, and he sat, wearing a bulletproof hat — marksmen were stationed on the roof in case of a rescue attempt — in the centre of the front row of the commissioners. They were drawn up in rows beneath the great south window of the Hall, Bradshaw on a chair of scarlet velvet, with the clerks at a table covered in a Turkey carpet, and beyond them lay the crossed sword of justice and the Mace — ironically, the symbol of the King's authority. The King himself sat in a wooden dock, dressed in a dark cloak, the blue sash of the Garter across his chest, a silver-topped cane in his hand; there was a gasp of horror from his friends when the silver crown fell off the top, for they saw it as a bad omen. Throughout the trial Charles kept his hat upon his head. He refused to remove it since he refused to do the court the courtesy of acknowledging its authority. Charles gazed round the court and at the crowds who had flocked into the newly built galleries along the walls, and he listened, without any effort to disguise his contempt, to the hectoring of Bradshaw and the endless speeches of Cook, the Solicitor General. He recoiled with horror at the abominable scene when a Scotswoman, Lady Anna de Lille, shouted at the 'rebels and traitors' who were trying the King. One of the commissioners, Hewson, called for hot irons and, in front of the King, branded Lady de Lille on the head and shoulders. 'His Majesty,' noted a spectator, 'then seeing her flesh smoake and her haire all of a fire for him by their hot irons, much commiserated her, and wished he could have been able to requite her.' Charles, however, was able to do nothing except ineffectually defy the court and deny its legal right to try him. When other women shouted from the galleries that Oliver Cromwell was a traitor, the soldiers were ordered to turn their muskets on them and shoot if they repeated the insult.

The trial dragged on for a week. When Hewson, who was to escape to France after the Restoration and there starve to death, came from the commissioners' seats and shouted, 'Justice, justice upon the traitor', and spat in his face, Charles wiped away the spital and said: 'Well, sir, God has justice in store for both you and me.' The commissioners' version of justice was dealt out in Westminster Hall when, on 27 January, 1649, after another rambling and self-righteous speech by Bradshaw, the Clerk announced the predictable sentence. First of all he read out a list of the King's alleged offences, and then 'for all of which treasons and crimes this court doth adjudge that the said Charles Stuart, as a tyrant, traytor, murtherer and publique enimy to the good people of this nation, shall be put to death by the severing of his head from his body'. The commissioners all stood to show their unanimous agreement. Charles tried to speak, but was prevented from doing so. 'I am not suffered to speak,' he said bitterly. 'Expect what justice other people may have.' Then he was taken out of the Hall, through the crowds and between lines of soldiers. The men puffed tobacco and little explosions of gunpowder in his face, and, on the orders of their officers, shouted: 'Justice, justice. Execution, execution.' One soldier who shouted 'God bless you, Sir', was beaten by his officers. Charles was executed outside his own banqueting hall in Whitehall two days later.

Tradition says that the commissioners signed the death warrant, with Cromwell's signature coming third, partly in the Oriel Room, in the

The Trial of Charles I
The trial of Charles I in Westminster Hall lasted for a week in January 1649. Charles would not remove his hat since he refused to recognise the right of the court to try their King. Bradshaw, the chairman of the Parliamentary Commissioners who tried him, also wore his hat; it was bullet-proof in case any of the king's supporters should try to rescue him

ancient cloisters that had been built between St Stephen's Chapel and Westminster Hall, and partly in the Painted Chamber. Caught up in the hysterical excitement of the occasion, the commissioners flipped little blobs of ink at each other from their quill pens.

In later years Cromwell twice came to the Hall in the grandest state and had himself declared King in all but name. In 1653 he was named the Lord Protector in an elaborate ceremony in the Hall. On this occasion he drove up to the door in a coach and then, wearing a plain black coat to show that the period of military rule he had imposed on the country was now over, he took a chair of state which had been set up for him on a rich carpet. The next time he came in state to the Hall, the chair had become the throne itself, complete with the sacred coronation stone, the Stone of Scone, within it. This was 'The Happy Inauguration' of 26 June, 1657, when Cromwell declined the title of King, but accepted Royal power. He sat in the King's Hall beneath a Royal cloth of state, and the Speaker gave him a sword and sceptre 'of massy gold'. Trumpets sounded and, after taking the oath, Cromwell walked out of the Hall with his train carried by two boys and a Peer of the realm.

Cromwell's final association with the Hall was squalid and macabre. When Charles II was restored to the English throne in 1660, he had the bodies of Cromwell and the other leading regicides exhumed, and their skulls cut from their skeletons. Cromwell's skull was then stuck on a spike on the roof of Westminster Hall, and there it rattled and rotted for twenty-five years until it was blown down in a storm and picked up by a sentry. Eventually the Lord Protector's skull was sold to a London pawnbroker for £100 by a man called Sam Russell, a drunken music hall

'Be gone you rogues' In 1653 the Commons infuriated Cromwell by trying to prolong its own life. He came with soldiers and drove the Members out of their Chamber. 'In the name of God, go,' he shouted at them. Noticing the Mace on the table, Cromwell demanded: 'What shall we do with this bauble?' and told the soldiers to take it away. Cromwell then ordered the door of the Commons Chamber to be locked

comedian, who claimed to be a descendant of the sentry who had retrieved it.

Between these dramatic events, the bustling life of the Hall and its courts and market stalls went on. The clerks and lawyers and litigants who thronged the place, and the carpenters who had to put up the law courts and take them down again for each great occasion, went off to eat and drink in Heaven, Hell and Purgatory – once debtors' prisons among the taverns and the cockpits around the outside walls of the Hall, which had been turned into eating houses. There is still a canteen – known as the Policemen's Canteen – on the spot where, for centuries, Hell flourished.

Samuel Pepys courted the pretty girls who sold ribbons and books and trinkets in the Hall, and he was annoyed when the place became a dump for furniture rescued from the Great Fire of London in 1666 – there were no pretty girls left to sell him a shirt or some gloves. Pepys himself appeared before one of the courts in the Hall accused of piracy, Popery and treachery in the hysterical atmosphere whipped up by the scheming of that arch-liar Titus Oates. In 1679 Pepys and his friend Sir Anthony Deane hurried from the Tower of London, where they were being held, to become the first two persons to apply for a writ of Habeas Corpus under the act which had just been passed. They did not succeed, but Pepys found comfort back in the Tower in a fat buck which the King himself had shot, and eventually he was let free.

By an ironic twist of fate Oates was finally tried in the same Hall from which, by giving false evidence, he had sent men to their deaths. The Hall had only just been cleared after the coronation banquet of Catholic James II when Oates, on 8 May, 1685, faced the feared Lord Chief Justice Jeffreys on charges of perjury. In addition to the fine of 2,000 marks, he was sentenced to stand in the pillory outside Westminster Hall, and to be whipped from Aldgate to Newgate and then from Newgate to Tyburne. He uttered 'hideous bellowing and swooned several times with the greatness of the anguish' during the first flogging, but survived to spend three years in prison and to be granted a pension of £300 when the Protestant William of Orange came to the throne.

The rickety wooden partitions that were provided for the law courts had, by the middle of the eighteenth century, become elegant Gothic-style structures, which had to be taken down and put up again many times for the last great trial to be held in Westminster Hall. It was also by far the longest. This was the trial of Warren Hastings, and it lasted, on and off, for seven years – from 1788 to 1795.

In fact, the court just sat for 142 days during those seven years, since it met only when Parliament was sitting. Every time it did meet, it was a major social occasion. Charles and Fanny Burney bustled off to sit with the fashionable audience in the Hall; Mrs Fitzherbert was in the Royal box with the Queen and four princesses; Joshua Reynolds was observing the gathering with an artist's eye; Mrs Siddons savoured the drama of it

The Impeachment of Warren Hastings in Westminster Hall The trial lasted for seven years – from 1788 to 1795. It is the longest trial in British history, although the court sat for a total of only 142 days. Hastings was accused of corruption during his years as Governor-General of India but was eventually found not guilty of all sixteen charges against him

all. Tier upon tier of commissioned boxes surrounded the Hall, and the Royal box was draped with silk; the Commons sat on green benches, of course; the Lords on scarlet. The place was bitterly cold during much of the hearing, so J. H. Oldham was ordered to supply 'a very capital dome Warming Machine with large Pillars and Capitals, brass festoons and ornaments and a fluted Crown top, the whole very strong and of large Dimensions'. Gurney's shorthand writers took the evidence down in long, black-covered notebooks, and Warren Hastings himself observed it all with thin, frail and distant disgust.

Hastings was the former Governor-General of India and had, by pursuing Draconian policies, fallen foul of the parliamentary power of Burke, Fox and Sheridan. Burke led the attack against him, in his most oratorically thunderous style: 'I impeach Warren Hastings in the name of our holy religion, which he has disgraced; I impeach him in the name of the English constitution which he has violated and broken; I impeach him in the name of the Indian millions whom he has sacrified to injustice; I impeach him in the name and by the best rights of human nature, which he has stabbed to the heart. And I conjure this high and sacred court not to let these pleadings be heard in vain.'

The ladies fainted right away at such tremendous stuff, and so great was the public enthusiasm when Sheridan was due to speak – under the delighted gaze of his wife – that seats were sold for £50 each. Eventually, of course, the dandies of the day got tired of the case, and moved on to other novelties, but Warren Hastings and his lawyers had to plough on, year after year, bringing evidence from India and collecting witnesses before they died of old age. Seven years after Warren Hastings first stepped into that temporary dock in Westminster Hall, he was cleared of all sixteen charges.

The trial ruined both accused and accusers. It had cost the innocent Warren Hastings £97,000, although the East India Company eventually came to his rescue. Burke, whose summing up speech at the end of the trial had lasted, altogether, for nine days, was accused by some MPs of turning the whole thing into a farce; and although he was officially thanked for his part in the impeachment by the Commons, he applied for the Chiltern Hundreds. A year later Burke was dead, but Hastings lived on to the age of eighty-six. The public, of course, paid for all the drama; it cost nearly £4,000 to prepare and furnish the court and over £2,500 to light and heat it.

One other state trial was to be held in the Hall; another impeachment, but this time it was a brief affair involving a minor figure compared with the great men who had stood accused before him. In 1806, Henry Dundas, Viscount Melville, was impeached for syphoning off public money into his own account as Treasurer of the Navy. The trial lasted fifteen days and, in spite of the eloquence of the reformer and brewer, Samuel Whitbread, Dundas got away scot-free. In preparation for the hearing, the staff had dusted down the fittings used for the impeachment of Warren Hastings and put them up again, at a cost of £8,000. 'I never knew what earthly magnificence was till yesterday when I was present at Lord Melville's trial,' wrote Lord Campbell. 'Ye Gods! the Peeresses' box. A glory seemed to play round their countenances and to shoot in vivid flashes to the extremities of the Hall.'

In spite of this glory, the trial was a dull affair compared with earlier dramas, and the last impeachment brought under British law.

Fourteen years later, in 1820, new courts were built alongside the Hall and the lawyers and the judges moved out. The new buildings were constructed by Sir John Soane amid the inevitable arguments on their cost and style – 'an unpleasant excrescence' one MP called the elegant edifices. These survived the fire of 1834, and remained the nation's principal courts until the Law Courts in the Strand were opened in 1883 and Soane's were pulled down.

The Hall itself remained, largely unused and largely ignored. Seventeen thousand pounds were spent on restoring it after the 1834 fire and at this time the tradition began of kings and queens and great statesmen lying in state within its walls. Yet much of the building's splendour is now gone in spite of being perfectly preserved, monitored and maintained, with hidden rods of steel helping to hold up its wonderful roof. When the small leathery bodies of beetles fall from the iron-hard oak beams onto the stone-flagged floor below, each is mapped and recorded in the exact position in which it was found. Every five or six years – no more – there is a grand ceremony in the Hall and blue carpets are run out and trumpeters and Yeomen of the Guard and arc lamps and cameras appear. Apart from this flurry of activity, it remains empty except for scatterings of tourists, footsore at the end of their long tramp through the Palace of Westminster, and secretaries hurrying from their offices to the canteen in what was once Hell. The Hall is weighed down by its own tradition; too grand to be used; too heavy with history for anything but the most solemn ceremonies.

Right:
A carved angel,
Westminster Hall

Left: *The Law Courts, Westminster Hall, 1809*
In the eighteenth century elegant Gothic law courts had been built at the south end of the Hall. They had, however, to be taken down when the Hall was used for a Coronation Banquet

Right: *A carved angel, Westminster Hall* Twenty-six angels, each costing about 15 shillings, were carved as decorations for the great oak hammerbeam roof at the reconstruction of Westminster Hall by Richard II. They hold the king's coat of arms, which were originally painted in heraldic colours, between their wings

Right: *Westminster Hall*
There has been a Royal hall on this site since the days of King Canute. William Rufus built his Hall there in 1099 (it was much the same size as the present Hall), and Richard II rebuilt it in 1399. St Thomas More, Guy Fawkes and King Charles I were among the many famous people tried and condemned to death in the Hall. It is 240 ft long; 68 ft wide and 92 ft high.

Far left: *Geoffrey Chaucer* Clerk of Works to Richard II at Westminster

Left: *The Court of King's Bench* One of three law courts which met in, or around, Westminster Hall from the fourteenth century

Below: *New Palace Yard and Westminster Hall, c. 1760* Coffee houses and taverns – known as Heaven, Hell and Purgatory – surrounded the Hall

Above: *The miracle of the Thames salmon* St Peter, says tradition, came to Thorney Island – Westminster – and promised the fishermen great draughts of salmon, provided they paid their tithes

Left: *Edward III* A Victorian reconstruction of a painting in St Stephen's Chapel

Above: *Richard II loses his throne* Richard II was deposed in Westminster Hall in 1399, the year he completed its reconstruction

Far left: *A painted angel, St Stephen's Chapel* A reconstruction of the painting which was destroyed by fire

Left: *The Crypt Chapel, Westminster* The Chapel of St Mary Undercroft

Below left: *Interior of St Stephen's Chapel* An early nineteenth–century reconstruction

Right: *Latimer preaching before Edward VI at Paul's Cross, 1548* A 1910 painting by Ernest Board

Below: *St Stephen's Chapel* A Victorian reconstruction of a cross section of the Chapel

Left: *The Gunpowder Plot,
5 November, 1605* The King
sits in Parliament
surrounded by Lords and
Commons, while below
Guy Fawkes and the
conspirators, accompanied
by the devil, are discovered
by soldiers

Right: *Oliver Cromwell*
The bust, in the Lower
Waiting Hall of the Palace
of Westminster, between
the Commons Library and
the Commons Dining
Room, is attributed to
Bernini

Left: *Where the gunpowder
was stored* The cellars
beneath the House of Lords
where Guy Fawkes stored
36 barrels of gunpowder in
his attempt to blow 'The
Scots back to Scotland.'
A pictorial reconstruction
of 1820

Right: *The execution of
Charles I (by Weesop, an
eyewitness)* Charles was
executed outside his Ban-
queting Hall in Whitehall.
The executioners wore
masks to disguise them, and
the King's supporters
afterwards dipped their
handkerchieves in his blood

Right: 'The birds have flown' In January, 1642, Charles I became the only monarch ever to enter the House of Commons when he came to try to arrest five members whom he accused of treason. He stood by the Speaker's chair, and Speaker Lenthall, on his knees, refused to say where the five members were. 'I see the birds have flown,' said Charles

Below right: *The death warrant of Charles I, 1649* On the back a later hand has written: 'The bloody warrant for murthering the King.' Cromwell's signature is the third one down in the left-hand column

Top right from l–r: *The old House of Commons Table* The Table is said to have been designed by Sir Christopher Wren. Later moved into the Commons Lobby where it was stained by the blood of Spencer Percival, the Prime Minister who was shot dead in 1812; *The King's Champion* Henry Dymock, who made the traditional challenge to mortal combat against anyone who doubted the King's rightful succession, at George IV's Coronation Banquet, 1821; *The Champion's golden cup* The King three times drank the health of the Champion from a golden cup which was then presented to the Champion

Above left: '*The ASSASS-INATION of the RIGHT HONble SPENCER PERCIVAL, Chancellor of the Exchequer*' 'Who was murder'd by a pistol shot in the lobby of the House of Commons by an assassin John Bellingham a Merchant of Liverpool on Monday evening May the 11th 1812'

Left: *The Painted Chamber, 1817* Originally the King's great chamber in the old Palace of Westminster. Its walls had once been covered with brilliant Biblical paintings, but they were later whitewashed and tapestries hung on them instead

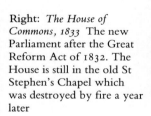

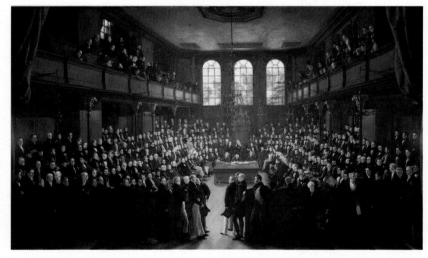

Right: *The House of Commons, 1833* The new Parliament after the Great Reform Act of 1832. The House is still in the old St Stephen's Chapel which was destroyed by fire a year later

Right: *Chance, the London firemen's dog* The mongrel mascot of the London Fire Engine Establishment was at the great Westminster fire of 1834.
'Stop me not, but onward let me jog,
For I am the London firemen's dog'

Previous page: *Thursday, 16 October, 1834* 'Drawn on stone by William Heath from a sketch taken by him by the light of the flames.' Soldiers keep back the vast crowds. Commandeered carts take away valuable state papers to safety; men pump the fire engines to keep the flames from spreading across to Westminster Abbey (see left)

Left: *View of the Houses of Lords and Commons* Firemen on the roofs try, unsuccessfully, to stop the spread of the flames which destroyed both Houses

Left: *The ruins from Cloister Court* The Oriel Room (on the right of the picture) was said to be the place where the death warrant of Charles I was signed

Right: *Westminster Hall is saved* Fire engines were dragged into Westminster Hall – which was being repaired at the time – and poured water into the roof to stop it catching fire. It was the only part of the original Palace to survive

Right: *After the fire* The ruins of the old House of Commons; the Gothic design, which had been much changed over the years, was now once again visible

Left: *Tally sticks* The ancient system of accounting by cutting notches in pieces of stick. When they were burnt in the House of Lords furnace the flues overheated and started the fire which destroyed the Houses of Parliament

Left: *Inside the ruined House of Commons* Only the walls of the old St Stephen's Chapel were left after the fire. They were later pulled down in the Victorian rebuilding of the Palace

CHAPTER THREE

The Beautiful Chapel

The Royal Chapel of St Stephen's beside Westminster Hall, was two hundred years old, and its painted saints, angels and stars still bright, when members of the House of Commons took their seats in the stalls where the vicars and canons had once chanted their daily office. One of the last people to hold the office of Dean of St Stephen's had been appointed by the dead king – Dr John Chambers had been Henry VIII's physician. Now, Henry's ten-year-old son, the sickly King Edward VI, gave the splendid Royal Chapel to the Commons; or rather his mouthpiece, the Protector Somerset, did. It was a flamboyant gesture on the part of Somerset. His aim was to show the nation that the new ideas of the Reformation could sweep aside even such a holy and impressive place as St Stephen's and make it into a mere meeting hall. The Commons, in fawning gratitude, in the same year it was given the Chapel, sent one of its Members, a man named Storie, to the Tower of London for speaking ill of the great Somerset – the first time that the Commons had ever assumed the right to punish one of its own number. Much good it did Somerset; four years after his bequest, he was tried for his life in Westminster Hall, just beyond the walls of St Stephen's, and lost his head on the scaffold.

The Chapel was the most English of buildings, the very brightest achievement of British craftsmen and the greatest flowering of English Gothic. But it had had its origins not in this country, but in France. On 26 April, 1248, Henry III had accompanied his cousin, the saintly Louis IX of France, in the ceremonies which marked the consecration of the French king's superb new chapel at his palace in Paris. Louis had built his chapel, La Sainte Chapelle, as a jewel-encrusted setting for his superb collection of holy relics which were the wonder of the Christian world. For the astounding sum of 135,000 livres Louis had bought the Crown of Thorns itself, and around it and in the gilded tabernacle above the high altar, he arranged his other treasures: a large piece of the True Cross; part of the spear that pierced Our Lord's side on the Cross; the robe which He had worn when the soldiers mocked Him as He was scourged; the shroud in which His body had been wrapped. All these Henry would have seen as they were carried in magnificent procession through La Sainte Chapelle. At his Royal cousin's invitation, he took one of the holy relics in his own hands to carry to the altar. In Henry's eyes La Sainte Chapelle was the ultimate in Royal status; he would, he said, like to carry it away in a horse and cart.

However, all that Henry, given his interminable problems with his restive nobles in England, could carry away with him was a deep envy of his French cousin, and a determination to outstrip him in religious grandeur if he possibly could. It was left to his son, his grandson and his great-grandson to carry out that dream.

The achievement of that dream was constantly interrupted by the nightmares of affairs of state and financial short-comings. Edward I, when he succeeded his father in 1272, knew of the glories of La Sainte Chapelle, and he knew, too, of his father's determination to exceed its wonders. England might not have the great collection of relics of the Passion, but it did have an undoubted Royal saint, Edward the Confessor, who was buried in Westminster Abbey just beyond the King's palace.

On 28 April, 1292, twenty years after he came to the throne, Edward began to build his Chapel of St Stephen's. He was long dead by the time the craftsmen finished it seventy years later, and during that time the actual construction work went on for only twenty years. It constantly had to be stopped and restarted as the Royal finances ebbed and flowed. The final burst of painting the walls and glazing the windows took up fifteen years – from 1348 to 1363.

On that April day, seven hundred years ago, when work began Stephen of Knill, Clerk of the Works to the King at Westminster, noted in the weekly diary he kept that work started on 'the foundation of the King's chapel in his palace, in honour of God, the Blessed Virgin Mary and the blessed Stephen'. First things first: the master mason, Michael of Canterbury, built himself a lodge from which to supervise his workmen, and he also put up a workshop. He had come fresh to Westminster from building in Cheapside one of the twelve memorial crosses that King Edward had had erected along the route taken by the funeral cortège of his beloved Queen Eleanor of Castile, who died in 1290. Master Michael brought with him, as his foreman, another Michael, and a whole troupe of Kentish men to do the King's work, among them Adam of Lamberhurst, Roger of Tonbridge and Henry of Faversham.

The King had always had his own private chapel at his Westminster palace and there were also several other chapels scattered around the sprawling building, of which there had always been one dedicated to St Stephen. The new building was to be ninety feet long, only twenty-eight feet wide, but the vaulting of its painted roof soared nearly a hundred feet above the tiled floor.

Master Thomas of Houghton, one of the King's engineers, brought his 'engine' to drive piles deep into the unstable Thames mud and to make a firm foundation for the walls and for the turrets which were to be built at each corner. Stone came from Boulogne and Caen in France; freestone from Taynton in Oxfordshire, and marble for the long shafts running up the inside walls from the Isle of Purbeck. Timber was cut and brought from the Royal forest at Pamber; glass from the glassmakers at Wells; iron was brought by ship from Spain.

For five years the work went on. Gradually the walls began to rise, and the people at court and the gawpers beyond the Palace, saw that the King's new chapel was to be a two-storied building. The lower, smaller and darker section was for the Palace servants and the more lowly officials; the upper storey, high, light and magnificent, was for the King and his courtiers. The door from the outside led only into the bottom part of the chapel; the only way into the upper, main part of the building was by narrow staircases leading from the court galleries.

However great a King may be, he needs money, and Edward I, in spite of his skills as an administrator and at dealing with men, rapidly ran out of it. He needed money to finance wars with Scotland and France, so even his chapel had to be put aside. In September 1297, Master Michael of Canterbury and Master Robert of Colebrook gathered the stones that the masons had already carved and built a shed with a thatched roof over them to keep out the weather, and then returned to their homes. There the stones lay for over twenty years before the ineffectual Edward II could find enough money to continue his late father's work. Master Michael of Canterbury was back again in 1320 in a new robe that cost the Treasury 20 shillings. He tore the thatch off the shelters above the stones and set the men back to work. His son, Master Thomas, later took over from him and ordered wall-shafts from Adam the Marbler. Master William of Hurley made a smooth-topped deal table so that his fellow craftsmen had somewhere to draw the designs of the complicated niches that were to contain the statues of saints. Up went the walls, and once again in 1324 machinery was brought from the Tower of London to be used to hoist the Reigate stone into position on the walls. The King had built a new gallery to enable him to slip, unnoticed, from his private apartments nearby into an extra-private chapel he wanted constructed against the wall of St Stephen's where he could look down onto the altar, seeing but unseen.

Once more the money ran out and wood prepared for the building had to be stacked away safely until work could be started again. Edward II was murdered in 1327, after he had been deposed in Westminster Hall, and it was another five years before his son, Edward III, found time from these dramatic upheavals to turn his attention to the half-built chapel. With gaps here and there, the work went on with the new King's approval. The workmen went on a spree with a sixpenny bonus they got when the great east end behind the altar was completed; they laboured on until, in 1348, the roof was up.

As they looked up at their handiwork, the craftsmen must have stared with astonishment at their splendid achievement. The roof was made of wood, carved and painted to look like stone. Between its curved ribs it was painted deep sky-blue and spattered with thousands upon thousands of gold stars. Soaring high above the Purbeck marble altar those stars glittered down on a chapel brilliant with colour. Every inch that could be decorated was painted in scarlet, green and blue.

They used peacocks' feathers to paint the angels on the walls and they caught squirrels in the Royal forests and used their tails to paint the hosts of saints round the altar; white down was plucked from the breasts of the King's swans to paint the golden stars. Thousands of leaves of real gold and silver were used to ornament the mouldings on the walls and pillars. Thirty glaziers were hard at work, under half a dozen masters, filling the tall, broad windows with coloured glass and, below them, as they worked, the chief glazier, Master John of Chester, earned his one shilling a day by painting his coloured patterns for them to follow on to white-topped tables. Silver, azure, vermilion, verdigris, white and red lead and ochre were lavished on the walls. Beneath each of the ten great windows – five along the north and south walls – were eight brilliantly coloured paintings; and there were angels with spread wings, holding drapery that was painted with doves, eagles, elephants and castles. Royal and noble shields of arms jutted from the walls; coloured glass, lit from behind, twinkled among the angels. To the left of the altar was a fine painting of the Holy Family, with the Magi bringing their gifts. On the other side of the altar, the shepherds watched over their flocks by night, and a boy played the pipes. Edward III himself, of course, was there, painted upon the walls he had finally seen built, dressed in armour and being presented by St George to the court of Heaven. His Queen, Phillipa, was there, too, with their ten sons and daughters around them; and guarding it all were statues of two great serjeants-at-arms and angels swinging thuribles suspended from bronze wires.

It was all vastly expensive – although when one set of stalls turned out to be unsuitable for the chapel, the king's officials shrewdly sold them off to the nuns at Barking for £33.6s.8d. The man who had carved those stalls, though, had been well paid in the first place; he insisted on 2s. 6d. a week at St Stephen's, 6d. more than when he had worked for the King at Windsor Castle. But the men who built the chapel for their King struck some hard bargains on his behalf. They bought in bulk, so they got twenty carved angels for 6s. 8d. each; three carved kings at £2.13s.6d. each; a coupe of serjeants-at-arms for £4 each. All in all, something like £9,000 was poured out over the years to create this the most magnificent of Royal ornaments.

Of course, with a little imagination and organisation, some of that money could be recovered – and it was. The King had his own private chapel within his private chapel; it was known as the King's Pew, built against an outside wall, with windows looking down on the altar. It contained a miracle-working statue of Our Lady – or perhaps this was in a small chantry chapel at ground level in St Mary Undercroft, where ordinary people could see it and the King retained his most private chapel immediately above it. This was a statue in which, it was said, the 'Kings of England always had great trust'. Naturally, the people trusted it too and it was credited with great miracles. With its fame came many donations, as they contributed towards the upkeep of the shrine in the

The Beautiful Chapel
St Stephen's Chapel – 'the beautiful chapel', a chronicler called it, was the King's private chapel at his Royal Palace of Westminster. It was begun by Edward I at the end of the thirteenth century and finished by his grandson, Edward III, seventy years later. It was the most magnificent Gothic building in the country. The upper Chapel of St Stephen could be entered only from the Royal apartments; the lower chapel, St Mary Undercroft, was for the Royal household. St Mary Undercroft still exists as the Crypt Chapel of the Houses of Parliament

hopes of miracles to come or in thanks for miracles achieved. Its treasures became vast – second only to the great treasure of the shrine of St Thomas of Canterbury. A hard-headed London merchant left money to the Chapel of the Pew because, he said, God obviously liked being worshipped in the Pew otherwise he would not have allowed so many miracles there; leaving money to the Pew was a good investment to get himself out of Purgatory and into Heaven more quickly.

In 1348, an event took place in the Royal Chapel which was to shape British parliamentary life – and parliamentary life throughout the world where the British writ has run. Edward III turned the chapel into a college of vicars and canons, partly in honour of St Stephen and partly in honour of Our Lady and in gratitude for the protection she had given him. 'I finished the beautiful chapel which was left unfinished by my progenitors', said Edward when he established the college. It had a dean, twelve canons and thirteen vicars who conducted the services and sang the daily offices, and to do so they sat in stalls facing each other across the chapel. At the west end of the chapel they built a great screen, with double doors at its centre.

When MPs moved into St Stephen's in 1547, they found this arrangement of choir stalls for the monks and a screen near one end of the chapel still in place. So they simply took over both stalls and screen for their own purposes. They sat in the choir stalls and made speeches at each other across the chancel of the chapel; they have been sitting in those same straight lines facing each other ever since. A House of two distinct sides, which inevitably fostered and encouraged the two-party system in British political life. It had no place for subtle shades of opinion symbolised by more flexible arrangements of seats. If MPs had continued to sit in the octagonal pattern of the Abbey Chapter House, perhaps the political history of Britain might have been very different indeed.

Political debates, of course, lead to votes in the House, and when MPs moved into their new home, they made ingenious use of the screen which the monks had left behind. What was easier than for the people who wanted to vote 'Aye' to walk through the right-hand door of the screen; those who wanted to vote 'No' to walk through the left-hand door of the screen? 'Ayes to the right, Noes to the left', calls the Speaker of the House to this day when Members go off to vote in a Division.

So MPs took over the 'beautiful chapel' for their own, undoubted home, but Reformation or no Reformation, they could not quite forget that it was a chapel. The altar, with its crucifix, was still there, so they bowed towards it every time they went in or out of their Chamber. To this day, although their House is on an entirely different site which has no ecclesiastical history, MPs turn and bow towards the end of their Chamber, as they go in an out; bowing, in other words, to the place where the crucifix once stood. They had to have somewhere to put Mr Speaker's chair; what more natural than to put him on the altar steps, where he could see and be seen? Mr Speaker still climbs steps today to get up into his chair. In the House of Lords, which has no ecclesiastical connection of this kind, the Woolsack, from which the Lord Chancellor presides, is at floor level.

Around the Speaker still, the benches rise in tiers, precisely as the monks' stalls did over four hundred years ago, with the benches at the end of the House furthest from the Speaker's chair running at right-angles to the other benches – precisely as the stalls of the Dean and Precentor did when they stood there to chant their daily rituals.

From that day when the Tudor Commons took over the chapel, little has changed. Some twenty years after they had moved, the Member for Exeter, John Vowell, described the scene in 1571: 'This House is framed and made like unto a theatre, being four rows of seats one above another, round about the House. At the higher end, in the middle of the lowest row, is a seat made for the Speaker, where he is appointed to sit; and before him sitteth the Clerk of the House, having a little board before him to write and lay his books upon. Upon the lower row, next to the Speaker, sit all such of the Queen's Privy Council and head officers as be knights or burgesses of that House; but after, everyone sitteth as he cometh, no difference being there held of any degree, because each man in that place is of like calling, saving that the knights and burgesses for London and York do sit on the right side, next to the Councillors.' Four hundred years later, that is an instantly recognisable description of the Commons as it is today. Hardly a thing has changed, except the special places for the knights and burgesses from London and York have gone. Every man still 'sitteth as he cometh', since no one, not even the Prime Minister, has any right, other than by tradition, to any particular seat. That description could be inserted straight into a modern guidebook.

Since the atmosphere of a chapel still hung about the place when MPs first settled down to work there, they naturally felt it only right and proper to start their day's work with a prayer; they and their predecessors had, for generations, been coming to St Stephen's for a special mass at the beginning of each parliamentary session. Now, in these Reformation days of Edward VI, there was no mass; instead, the Clerk of the Commons, at the beginning of each day, fell on his knees and recited the litany, and the House, on its knees, responded. The Speaker added an elevating word or two, 'such as he should think fittest for the time' and for years either the Speaker or the Clerk led the day's devotions. By 1650, a hundred years after it had moved into the chapel, the House decided that, 'The Governor of the College of Westminster do take care that some fit and able person or persons to attend *de die in diem* to pray in Parliament, and that they give their attendance accordingly.' Nine years later, the first Speaker's Chaplain was appointed, and his successors ever since have begun each day's House of Commons sitting with the same prayer: 'Almighty God, by whom alone Kings reign and Princes decree justice, and from who alone cometh all counsel, wisdom and understanding; we Thine unworthy servants here gathered together in Thy name do most humbly beseech Thee to send down Thy heavenly wisdom from above, to direct and guide us in all our consultations. And grant that, we having Thy fear ever before our eyes, and laying aside all private interests, prejudices and partial affections, the result of all our counsels may be to the glory of Thy name, the maintenance of true Religion and justice, the safety, honour and happiness of the Queen, the publick wealth, peace and tranquillity of the Realm, and the uniting and knitting together of the hearts of all persons and estates within the same, in true Christian Love and Charity one towards another.'

Prayers are always said in private, with no Commons' officials or Strangers present, and with the Chaplain and the Speaker kneeling on footstools by the Table. Members who are present turn with their backs to the Speaker, facing the walls. Some would say they do this because Members would find the sight of each other at prayer too risible to contemplate; others would say – and they would be right – that they turn because it was impossible, in the days when they wore swords, for them to kneel straight down on the floor in front of them without getting mixed up with their weapons.

The difficulties of dress troubled Members as soon as they moved into their new Chamber. It was the fashion in Tudor times for men to wear enormous pantaloons stuffed with wool and hair, which simply could not be squeezed into the pews recently vacated by the monks. So Members ordered that holes, two inches square, should be cut in the walls for posts which would take scaffolding on which, since they could not sit down, they could, presumably, lean – or perhaps they could discreetly take off all that padding and hang it on the bars.

So Members of Parliament settled down to make history in their new House. They began to knock the place about a good deal trying, as they still do, to secure more space and fresh air and more comfort for themselves. They watched the tedious hours drift by on a sun-dial set high in one of the windows – and when that one was blown out in a gale they ordered a new one, which served until Charles II's clockmaker made them a new clock in 1673. Somehow, they settled on the idea that green was the right colour for their Chamber – a great deal of it had been used in decorating the Chapel – and they have kept that colour ever since. When the carved monks' pews eventually went, they covered their new, backless and comfortless benches with green serge, and the Speaker's chair had touches of green and gold about it. 'To Robt. Streeter paynter for paynting green in oyle one end of the seats & a dorecase & some other things in the House of Commons in February last', runs one account, from the seventeenth century.

In the atmosphere of the Reformation MPs looked with horror on the Popish paintings, and statues and ornaments that were everywhere. Whitewash was slapped on liberally and large tapestries were hung to hide such idolatries. Later they put up large areas of wooden wainscotting and the memories of the beauty of the original chapel began to fade. Only hundreds of years later were they to be seen, briefly, by an earnest antiquarian clambering around with a lantern beneath the seats. Fire and Victorian insensitivity did the rest.

The Royal Coat of Arms replaced the Biblical stories on the east wall behind the Speaker's chair, but during the Long Parliament from 1640–60 under Cromwell, that drab administration abolished the Royal Arms and the House resounded to the tremendous events of the Commonwealth. Yet the Chamber still looked much the same, even if the Members themselves dressed in duller and more worthy clothes. The Royal Arms went back in 1663 after the Restoration.

Parliament, though, had long memories, so there was great alarm when there were reports in the ominous month of November in 1678, of people hearing 'knocking and digging in the earth, in some cellars near adjoining to' the Houses of Parliament. It was all much too like 5 November 1605, when Guy Fawkes had been found trying to light the slow fuse to thirty-two barrels of gunpowder beneath the House of Lords. Sir Christopher Wren, appointed Surveyor of the King's Works in 1669, was ordered to inspect the cellars underneath the Chambers of the Lords and Commons. He reported to the Lords that 'the vaults and cellars under and near this House are of such a nature, that there can be no assurance of safety; and the only remedy at present is that the cellars of the houses near this House and the Court of Requests (a building at right-angles to the House of Commons) may be cleared, and a passage made out of one into the other, so that soldiers and sentinels may walk day and night there, and have a trusty officer over them.' £49 was spent converting the cellars into a guard house, and that is why the cellars of the Houses of Parliament are still ceremonially searched by Yeomen of the Guard before each State Opening. Guy Fawkes was not responsible for this particular episode, for it was a disagreeable professional liar, Titus Oates, who had put about the story of an entirely fictitious Popish Plot which was supposed to involve Jesuit plans to murder the King.

Sir Christopher Wren had not only looked at the cellars of the Houses of Parliament during the Popish Plot scare; he had also looked all over the Palace and especially at the Commons. What he had found filled him with alarm. The place was falling down. The vast piles of parliamentary records that had been stored in the roof of the Commons were threatening to bring the House down about its Members' ears, and they had to move out while the building was shored up and the records moved. By 1692, the inevitable House of Commons committee found 'the walls and timber so much decayed they are of the opinion the Building is in a dangerous condition and not capable of further repair'.

With admirable speed and something not far short of vandalism, Wren set to work. He managed to reduce one of the greatest glories of Gothic ecclesiastical architecture to something resembling a dissenting chapel of the most stringent kind. The roof was drastically lowered; three round-headed windows appeared behind the Speaker's chair where once the great east window had been above the altar, and around the walls he put up galleries supported by cast-iron pillars and decorated with Grinling Gibbons' carvings. It all cost far too much: £4,600, which was £2,000 above the estimate. The MPs were also provided with 'New Backs to all the Seates', a 'new clock with carved workes and ornaments', and 'A particular clossett for Mr Joddrell' (he was the Clerk of the House), and finally 'The passage from Westminster Hall to the Parliament Staires made more lightsome'.

The Act of Union with Scotland in 1707 made the overcrowded Commons still more uncomfortable. Wren tried to squeeze in the extra forty-five Members who now came down from Scotland by widening the side galleries he had put in a few years before. This, though, like all the other tinkerings with the Chamber, did not really solve the problem that the Commons has always faced, and never solved — how to fit several hundred Members into a room less than half the size of the one that they really needed. They were, in spite of Wren's skill and Gibbons' decorations, still wretchedly uncomfortable. A satirical poem of the period summed up their discomfort precisely:

> *No satin covering decks th' unsightly boards;*
> *No velvet cushion holds the youthful lords;*
> *And claim illustrious tails such small regard?*
> *Ah! Tails so tender for a seat so hard.*

What is more, it was intolerably stuffy. Wren tried to improve the ventilation, but without much success, so in 1715 the Speaker invited Dr J. T. Desagulier, a Fellow of the Royal Society, to 'propose a method to

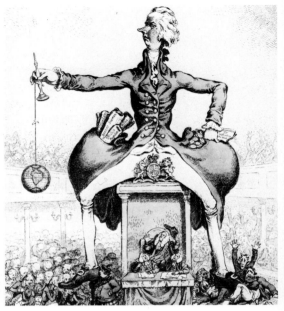

evaporate the unhealthful breathing in the House of Commons'. Dr Desagulier was one of a long line of dubious scientist who tried, over the years, to get rid of the hot and unpleasant air from the Commons, and they all, not surprisingly, failed utterly. In 1723 he persuaded the Board of Works to pay him £105 for 'remedying the inconveniency arising by the hot steam and want of fresh air in the House of Commons when sitting late and in full house'. His system was based on large fires producing hot air, which then rose through a series of flues and chimneys. Dr Desagulier and the House, though, had reckoned without Mrs Smith, the housekeeper, who lived in rooms above the Commons' ceiling. Mrs Smith, 'not liking to be disturbed in the Use of those Rooms, did what she could to defeat the Operation of those Machines'. Which meant that she simply refused to light the fires decreed by the doctor, and that was that. Mrs Smith managed to defeat both science and the British constitution.

The Commons did, however, take one practical step. They passed what must be one of the first 'no smoking' orders ever enforced. 'Ordered that no Member of the House do presume to smoke tobacco in the gallery, or at the Table of the House, sitting as Committees.'

It was all rather squalid. The place was dirty and it smelt, there were rats about and it was grubby with bits and pieces of biscuits and fruits scattered around by Members. A Lutheran pastor, who visited England towards the end of the eighteenth century, was decidedly unimpressed:

'I now for the first time saw the whole of the British nation assembled in its representatives, in a rather mean looking building that not a little resembles a chapel. The Speaker, an elderly man dressed in an enormous wig with two knotted curls behind and a black cloak, with a hat on his head, sat opposite me on a lofty chair. The Members have nothing

Above left: *St Stephen's Chapel* In 1707, Sir Christopher Wren drastically altered St Stephen's Chapel to try to make more space for MPs. He filled in the great Gothic windows, and put in smaller, round-headed lights. Below was an entrance known as Solomon's Porch

Above: *The Giant Factotum* William Pitt, the giant of eighteenth-century politics, astride the Commons which he dominated for so long. He plays cup and ball with the world. Pitt was a great drinker; he used to be sick in Solomon's Porch *(see picture left)*, while keeping the door to the Commons open with his foot so he could listen to the speeches

particular in their dress. They even come into the House in their great coats and boots and spurs. It is not at all uncommon to see a member lying stretched out on one of the benches while others are debating, some crack nuts, others eat oranges or whatever is in season. Two shorthand writers sat not far from me, who endeavoured to take down the words of the speakers; and thus all that is very remarkable may generally be read in print next day. The shorthand writers are supposed to be employed and paid by the editors of different newspapers, and are constant attendants in Parliament; and so they pay the doorkeeper a fee for the session. I have seen the members bring their sons, while quite little boys, and carry them to their seats along with them . . .'

Beneath the House of Commons, in the under-chapel of St Mary's, the thoughtless destruction of the fourteenth century building went on. Cromwell, inevitably, was said to have stabled his horses there, but gradually the vaulted roof of St Mary Undercroft sheltered piles of coal for the fireplaces in the Commons above. Wine was stocked there, and eventually part of the undercroft was made into a dining-room for Mr Speaker, with holes knocked in the wall for kitchen chimneys to go through. Yet this unregarded place – not a crypt, whatever it may now be called, because it is not below ground – has survived better than the fine upstairs chapel of St Stephen's above the stone ribs and ancient bosses of the undercroft roof. It is still used as a chapel where Members may pray or where they may be married or have their children baptised.

Undoubtedly, some of the bottles stored in the undercroft were sent up to quench the enormous thirst of the young William Pitt. During the famous debate of 21 February, 1783, when Fox was defending the Peace of Paris, Pitt had to go outside the door behind the Speaker's chair, which was known as Solomon's Porch, to be violently sick from drinking too much port. He kept the door open with one hand so he could hear Fox's speech, and then tottered back into the Chamber, to answer him, point by point. A sensitive clerk was so overcome by this astonishing behaviour that he got a violent attack of neuralgia. Pitt found this, he said, a providential division of labour: he enjoyed the wine but the clerk got the headache!

In spite of those formidable Abbesses who had, somewhere in its history, sat in Parliament, and in spite of the equally formidable Mrs Smith who refused to let Members have a bit of fresh air when they wanted it, the House of Commons was, of course, entirely a man's world. Ladies of spirit occasionally made sorties towards it – the Duchess of Gordon once sat in the Strangers' Gallery dressed as a man – but on the whole, they knew their place. That place was certainly not in the Chamber, or anywhere near it. In 1778 they caused a riot when they refused to withdraw from the galleries when they were ordered to do so and, led by the Duchess of Devonshire, they clung to their seats and refused to budge. Some of the gentlemen thought it a tremendous lark and helped them to hold on, so it took two hours to quell the uproar.

They paid the price in due course; from then until 1850 ladies were forbidden to come even into the Strangers' Gallery, although they do not seem to have been much missed. 'I was in hopes that long speeches would have been knocked on the head when the ladies had been excluded from the galleries', said a doorkeeper, miserably, 'because they often used to keep the members up'. But the ladies were still there, even though illegally and invisibly, listening to their speeches, as every MP knew very well.

After Wren had put in the false ceiling at the end of the seventeenth century he had obviously created a large space between that ceiling and the roof of the old chapel – a space as big as the House itself. The roof was now topped with what looked like Kentish oasthouse wind vanes, in yet another attempt to get fresh air into the place. Into that dank and dark space beneath the roof and above the Commons ceiling the ladies used to creep. In the middle of the floor was a large, glowing, octagonal grille. Through it rose the shimmering heat and fumes from the great chandelier in the Commons below. There the ladies were allowed to come, after a small arrangement had been made with the doorkeeper who complained he only made £10 a year out of it, to watch their lords and masters in the chamber beneath the chandelier. The only light for the ladies was a farthing dip stuck in a tin candlestick. The prevailing gloom meant that the formidable Irish MP, Daniel O'Connell, coming up one evening expecting to find his wife there, grabbed the wrong lady and gave the Dowager Duchess of Richmond a smacking kiss.

'In the middle of the garret', recalled Miss Maria Edgeworth, who visited the Commons in 1822, 'is what seemed like a sentry box of deal boards, and old chairs placed round it; on these we got and stood and peeped over the top of the boards. Saw large chandelier with lights blazing immediately below; a grating of iron across veiled the light so that we could look down and beyond it. We saw half the Table and the Mace lying on it, and papers, and, by peering hard, two figures of clubs at the farther end; but no eye could see the Speaker or his chair – only his feet; his voice and terrible "Order" was soon heard. We could see part of the Treasury Bench and the Opposition in their places – the tops of their heads, profiles and gestures perfectly.'

The Commons which Miss Edgeworth saw in 1822 was still on the same site, and restricted within the same area, as the House which MPs had moved into in Edward VI's time. So much had happened here: King Charles I had arrived here on a January day in 1642 in his fatal attempt to arrest the five Members whom he accused of treason against the Crown; Cromwell, who had engineered the King's downfall and execution in the name of Parliament, brought his soldiers, in April 1653, to clear the Members from their own Chamber, and told his men to take the Mace – 'this bauble' – from the House. Here the British political system had developed in the eighteenth century and Pitt, father and son, Fox, Sheridan, Burke, Canning, Peel and Gladstone thundered their great

The Ladies' Gallery above the old House of Commons
Ladies were never allowed into the old House of Commons. They used to bribe the door keepers to let them into the roof over the Chamber and then peer down through a ventilator above the massive chandelier that hung just above the Table of the House

speeches in this cluttered, dingy place. The law courts, which carried out the behest of Parliament, clustered in Westminster Hall and in makeshift buildings round about it – it was all hopelessly inconvenient and ramshackle. Things were made even worse when, on 1 January, 1801, the Act of Union with Ireland came into effect, and a hundred Members were suddenly added to the 550, or so, who were already sitting there. They were turbulent Members, too, who were to make the next hundred years at Westminster some of the most rip-roaring the place had ever known.

MPs, when they were not arguing about Parliamentary reform in the 1820s and 1830s, were arguing about building themselves a new House of Commons. The Marquis de Chabannes, with no greater qualific-ations than his grand-sounding name, was called in for yet another attempt to make the place smell less dreadful; he was paid £200 for a ventilating machine, but it had little effect. The architect, Sir James Wyatt, who was made Surveyor-General in the year that the union with Ireland was decided upon, had the hopeless task of trying to expand the House to seat the new Irish Members. Wyatt was a great knocker-down of buildings – he had done terrible damage to Salisbury Cathedral and destroyed the Chapter House at Durham – and had well earned the nickname of 'the Great Destroyer'. As his workmen tore down the wainscotting in the Chamber, they found beneath it the original wall paintings which had then been covered for nearly five hundred years. Frantic antiquarians tried to record them before Wyatt's men knocked them to dust and carted them off to the rubbish heap. John Carter, an eccentric draughtsman to the Society of Antiquaries, loathed Wyatt and all he stood for. He tried, 'by the light of a lanthorn, and lying nearly full length under benches' to make drawings of what was being discovered by the workmen before it was destroyed. Another draughtsman and antiquarian, J. T. Smith, also tried to preserve some sort of record of the wall paintings; but although Smith arrived at the first light of dawn as the work went on – he had to be out of the House by nine o'clock in the morning – Wyatt destroyed so fast that Smith could not keep up with him.

Committees sat, of course, trying to decide what to do. They knew things could not go on in the Commons as they were. Parliamentary reform was a major topic of discussion and had been for years. How could they make the House of Commons a practical, efficient place from which to run an increasingly sophisticated society which was moving into an era of industrial expansion on a scale that the world had never before known? They had to deal with a vast quantity of legislation that was now needed for the great building of harbours, roads, bridges and, above all, the railways, yet they had hopelessly inadequate facilities.

William Cobbett, who was elected for Oldham in 1833, wrote strongly of his disapproval of the conditions he found then: 'Why are we squeezed into so small a space that it is absolutely impossible that there should be calm and regular discussion, even from that circumstance alone? Why do we live in this hubbub? Why are we exposed to all these inconveniences? Why are 658 of us crammed into a space that allows to each of us no more than a foot and a half square, while, at the same time, each of the servants of the King, whom we pay, has a palace to live in, and more unoccupied space in that palace than the little hole into which we are all crammed to make laws by which this great kingdom is governed?' Why indeed? The principal answer is that in Parliament things move remarkably slowly; it had been like that for centuries, so why change it now? Or, if it must be changed, then it must only be changed after a vast amount of due care, discussion, committees and speech-making. So plans for a new House were drawn and redrawn; first they were in the classical style, with round-headed windows and arches, and then they had to be Gothicised, and the windows and arches made pointed, to meet the growing fashion of reviving mediaeval architecture. No one could agree what should be done, or how it should be done. Suddenly, one windy evening in October 1834, the MPs' minds were made up for them: by fire!

CHAPTER FOUR
'*Most Terrible Conflagration*'

Chance, the mongrel dog, twitched his moist black nose. His sharp-pointed ears pricked up, and he gave a low, knowing growl. Somewhere, not very far away, there was a fire. He had been going to fires for years, ever since, as a young puppy, he had learned to run safely between the galloping legs of the fire brigade's horses and to dodge the iron-rimmed wheels of the fire engines. Now he was well known, a famous mascot of the London Fire Engine Establishment, and he got as big a cheer as the firemen themselves when he turned up at a fire. He growled a little louder as he lay beneath the scarlet and brass engine in the fire station. The man on duty, brass buttons undone in his navy uniform tunic, told him to shut up and went back to reading the latest funny piece by that new young writer, Charles Dickens, in the *Monthly Magazine*.

Chance, with his long experience and animal instinct, was right. The most spectacular fire that London had seen since the Great Fire of 1666 was beginning to light up the early evening sky just above the Palace of Westminster: the Houses of Parliament were on fire. Before that night was out, both the House of Lords and the House of Commons would be smoking ruins and four hundred years of British history would be obliterated.

All day long on that windy Thursday, 16 October, 1834, there had been a faint smell of burning in and around the House of Lords. The Lords' home was once the White Chamber of the mediaeval palace, built by Edward II in 1308 as a private apartment for his new French bride, Isabella. The Lords had moved into it from the Painted Chamber in 1801, and they had found it agreeably comfortable, and of a suitable size. On that autumn day in 1834 neither the Lords nor the Commons was sitting – they had not sat for some three weeks – so Mrs Wright was doing her daughter-in-law a good turn by standing in for her as the Housekeeper and earning a little pin-money, as all the other officials did, by letting visitors in to have a look round.

Mrs Wright had been worried all day about that smell of burning. Twice, at least, she had sent the young Reynolds lad, who was doing odd jobs about the place to help his father, Richard Reynolds, the House of Lords fire lighter, to tell the two men stoking the furnace near the Lords that they were overheating it. They had ignored her, and sent the lad packing. Mrs Wright did not like the look of those two; she had heard that one of them, a surly man named Cross, had been sentenced to seven years' transportation to Australia, but he had somehow managed to wriggle out of it and had done only three years in an English prison.

In the late afternoon a couple of respectable-looking men rang the bell at Mrs Wright's door and asked if they could see round the House of Lords. They gave their names as Mr Snell and Mr Shuter, and handed her a tip for her trouble. It was, noticed Mrs Wright, just about four o'clock and they all went off on their tour of inspection. What they saw, what they felt, and what they smelt when they got to the Lords gravely alarmed all three. The smoke in the Chamber was so thick that they could hardly see the throne at the other end from the door where they stood. They could barely make out the great tapestries of the Spanish Armada that hung on the walls and they had to feel for them to make sure they were there. As they stood beside Black Rod's box – the cubicle where that official of the House sat during debates – the worried Mr Snell turned to Mrs Wright and said: 'Bless me, how warm it is in here, I feel it through my boots'. Mrs Wright agreed that the House was 'in a complete smother', but she was sure that everything was quite safe as there was a stone floor so it could not catch fire. The workmen were below, she explained, and anyway, the place always got hot like this. Reassured and apparently not curious, the three went away. Mrs Wright locked the door and put the key in her pocket.

She was sitting comfortably in her daughter-in-law's rooms a couple of hours later when the peace of the empty Palace was shattered by screams. It was Mrs Mullencamp, wife of the doorkeeper. 'Oh God', she shouted, pounding on Mrs Wright's door, 'the House of Lords is on fire'. Mrs Wright rushed through the corridors of the Palace searching desperately for help, but when she met Mr Weobley, the Clerk of the Works, he seemed too terrified to act. So, throwing respectability to the winds in such a dire emergency, Mrs Wright rushed out into the street 'without bonnet and shawl', as she admitted later, where she and her maid stood bellowing for help. The fire blazed away from 6.30 in the

Below left: *Devil's Acre*
The nineteenth-century slums around Westminster were some of the worst in London. Devil's Acre, within sight of the House of Parliament and the Abbey, was a haunt of coiners, thieves and prostitutes

Below: *The Westminster Slums* 'And Behold the Stables, and Pigstyes and Privies all were removed.' Rowlandson's satirical comment on the attempts by the authorities at Westminster to clear up the slums that made it one of the most unhealthy and dangerous places in London

evening of the 16 October, until 3 o'clock on the morning of Friday, 17 October, while all London came to watch and thrill at the spectacle.

The astonishing thing was that a fire had not occurred many years before. During its long history the Palace had suffered many minor fires, yet the authorities had irresponsibly let the jumble of buildings grow until they became like a massive bonfire ready, at any moment, to blaze up. Bits and pieces had been added endlessly to the Palace over the years; often the additions were made only of wood and tarred paper or tarred sailcloth; chimneys and flues were everywhere, running through holes in wooden walls. Not so many years before it had been officially reported that the area of the Palace near the place in which the fire started had ceilings and walls lined with deal which were a fire hazard and 'the public houses and coffee-houses on the south side of New Palace Yard . . . are particularly dangerous, as they have several chimnies and coppers; the roofs are . . . some of them, covered with sail cloth pitched . . .'

When the inevitable fire broke out, all London was agog. Word swept through the town quicker than the fire itself swept through Westminster, and soon the area round the Palace was dense with the mob of sightseers. The thieves and beggars came out from the rookeries of Seven Dials, a couple of miles away, to see the fun and make good pickings. The whores and pimps from the hundreds of brothels within easy strolling distance of Westminster came to pick up some trade; the coiners left their furnaces and the fakers their printing presses in the stews around Westminster Abbey; the starving and diseased and destitute crept out of the foul and stinking slums that jostled close to the splendours of Whitehall and Westminster. The prisoners banged their tin plates on their doors in Bridewell and demanded to know what all the excitement was about. Their light-fingered brethren were already hard at work, lifting what they could either from honest men's pockets in the crowd or from the great mountains of books and papers and furniture and pictures and carpets and curtains that were being carried out of the blazing buildings. Police Inspector May, Superintendent of 'A' Division, had his men there keeping a sharp watch on the looters and thieves. 'There were vast gangs of light-fingered gentry in attendance', said *The Times*, 'who doubtless reaped a rich harvest, and did not fail to commit several desperate outrages, which were, however, much checked by the exertions of the police.'

The opportunists were there, spinning a pretty penny by guiding people who did not know the area round the backstreets of Westminster so they could get a good view of the fire. The cabbies were doing a roaring trade, although they spent most of their time stuck in the great mob of people. 'A great number of gentlemen's vehicles and hackney carriages were . . . to be seen driven to and fro, and another glaring instance of the reckless conduct of those ruffians, cab-drivers, presented itself', said a *Times*' correspondent – and *Times*' correspondents seem to have been remarkably numerous, too.

Suddenly, through the noise and the shouting and roar of the flames, there came the clanging bells of the fire engines. The crowd cheered as Chance, the famous mongrel, led the engines into the fight against the fire. They had arrived just one hour after Mrs Wright had rushed into the street to raise the alarm. Charles Dickens himself, then a journalist working as a parliamentary reporter, noted how gallantly the mongrel Chance behaved that night – as gallantly as one of the MPs who turned himself into a sort of amateur fireman for the occasion.

The MP, 'and the celebrated fireman's dog, were observed to be remarkably active at the conflagration of the two Houses of Parliament', wrote Boz. 'They both ran up and down, and in and out, getting under people's feet, and into everybody's way, fully impressed with the belief that they were doing a great deal of good, and barking tremendously. The dog went quietly back to his kennel with the engine, but the gentleman kept up such an incessant noise for some weeks after that occurrence, that he became a positive nuisance.'

That gentleman might have been Mr W. Hughes Hughes, MP, who claimed later, in letters to the newspapers, that he was the only Member actually present when the fire broke out. What a spectacle he and the crowds saw. 'The progress of the fire exhibited a *tableau vivant* of not inferior interest', said a rather condescending observer. 'The wind blew briskly from the south-west, but became more southerly as the night advanced; the moon was near the full and shone with radiance; but occasionally vast masses of cumulus clouds floated high and bright across the skies and, as the fitful glare of flames increased, were illuminated in a remarkably impressive manner, which gave great interest to the busy scene that was passing below.' The same reporter continued: 'An immense multitude of spectators assembled at Westminster to witness the ravages of the fire, the lurid glare of which was distinctly visible for many miles around the metropolis. Even the River Thames, in the vicinity of the spot, was covered with boats and barges full of persons whom curiosity had attracted to the scene; and the reflection of the waving flames upon the water, on the neighbouring shores and upon the many thousands thus congregated, composed a spectacle most strikingly picturesque and impressive.'

Picturesque and impressive it was. Columns of smoke rose, now black now white in the brilliant moonlight, now scarlet from the flames beneath, and shot high into the air among the turrets and towers of the Palace. The fire made such a roaring and crackling that rumours rushed through the crowd that a store of explosives had been set off. Beams from the ancient rooms crashed down into the flames beneath; scraps of burning sailcloth from the makeshift additions to the Palace swirled up into the draughts caused by the heat and spread the fire into the other parts of the Palace. Within an hour of the alarm being raised at 6.30 p.m., the House of Lords was gutted, and at 10 o'clock that night its walls crashed inwards with a tremendous roar. By 7.30 p.m. the House of

Commons had caught fire. Lord Duncannon, who had rushed to the scene with Lord Melbourne, the Prime Minister, scrambled onto the roof of the Commons with a group of firemen and soldiers, to try to save it. They were too late. Duncannon sent the others down to safety, then waited just long enough to see that things were hopeless, and got down only moments before the roof of the Commons' Chamber collapsed into the flames below.

More and more fire engines came galloping from all parts of London to help in the fight to control the fire. All three regiments of Foot Guard were marched to the scene, some in the full splendour of their scarlet uniforms and bearskins, with their weapons, but others in undress. Then came the Horse Guards, cantering down from their barracks in St James's Park, taking up their stand to help keep the vast crowds at bay. Guardsmen lined the high stone parapet of Westminster Bridge and looked down on the throng of boats that blocked the Thames, now at low tide; each boat full of gaping spectators who could get a much better view of the full destructive power of the fire than the people crowded into the narrow streets. Desperately, the soldiers and policemen and firemen ran the hoses down to the river to try to get enough water to control the flames, but the tide was so low that it was an impossible task. Other firemen ran hoses over the roofs of nearby houses to stopcocks, so that water could at last be brought to play on the fire. The main water supply was tapped in New Palace Yard in a frantic effort to help overcome the flames.

Inside the burning building were constitutional treasures of enormous value, and with huge enthusiasm and cheered on by the crowd, officials of both Houses, policemen and soldiers set about saving as many papers as they possibly could. Luckily, many of the most precious documents were not in the Palace itself. Some were across the road in the Jewel Tower, which was undamaged, and others were in the Chapter House of Westminster Abbey which, like the rest of the Abbey, escaped unscathed. Bundle after bundle of papers were hurled from the windows of the burning building into the street below, where they were gathered up and dumped in coaches and cabs, commandeered on the Prime Minister's orders. From there they were taken either to newly-built offices in Downing Street, or stacked among the pews in St Margaret's Church, just across the street from the burning House of Commons. So many documents were piled into the church that next Sunday's charity sermon and service had to be cancelled because there was no space left for the congregation. In the excitement and confusion and chaos of the night, some papers inevitably went astray. There was a rumour that the death warrant of Charles I was lost – a tale that turned out to be totally false. Precious documents, though, certainly did get lost, and some turned up as wrapping paper on the counter of a butter merchant in the Walworth Road not long afterwards.

DREADFUL FIRE!

And total destruction of both Houses of Parliament.

On Thursday evening, between six and seven o'Clock, a fire broke out in the House of Lords. The flames spread very rapidly, and great alarm immediately prevailed. Detachments of police soon arrived from the different station-houses, out of the different offices, &c. where they were deposited, and put into all sorts of vehicles—hackney-coaches, cabs, waggons, &c. which were put in requisition for their conveyance to places of safety. Many of them were placed in of Commons fell in, three firemen and one of the Life Guards were buried in the ruins; but they were got out alive. Many persons were seriously injured; but we have not heard of any loss of life. Tower, at the south end of the building, totally destroyed. The Painted Chamber, totally destroyed. The north end of the Royal Gallery abutting on the Painted Chamber destroyed from the door leading into the Painted Chamber, as far

Dreadful fire! 'On Thursday evening (16 October 1834), between six and seven o'clock, a fire broke out in the House of Lords. The flames spread very rapidly, and great alarm immediately prevailed.' Within a few hours, both Houses of Parliament were destroyed, but Westminster Hall was, by great exertion, saved. The fire was caused by over-stoking a furnace beneath the House of Lords

23rd October, 1834. Mr Editor.

It having been stated that some well-dressed persons were picking up the Papers & Records in the Street at the time of the Fire at the House of Lords & Commons insinuating that they were carried off by them I beg to send you an account of two of those Gentlemen so that such a statement may not mislead the Public, with regard to them.

At 11 o'clock on the night of the Fire, as Sir Thomas Phillipps (who spent his time & his fortune in preserving Records & ancient MSS.) was returning home from a party he saw the blaze from a Distance, & on the coachman informing him of the cause, he hastened down to the spot, fearing the Augmentation Office Records might be in danger. On arriving he had the good fortune to get within the rank of Police Constables, & then saw what, to him, was a greater vexation than the loss of the two Houses, namely a multitude of records lying in the Street over which Men, Carts, Wagons & Horses were continually tramping. Sir Thomas Phillipps instantly drove off to the House of Mr Cooper in Circus Road, St. John's Wood, to inform him of the fact. Mr Cooper had just gone to bed, but Sir Thomas Phillipps waited to carry him back to the Record Office, & these two gentlemen were most active in endeavouring to save the scattered and perishing documents from total destruction from 12 o'clock till half past 3 or 4, employing also Soldiers to collect them together as well as using their own individual exertions to pick them up.

If these therefore are the well-dressed *Gentlemen alluded to in the above Paragraph the Public may rest assured that nothing has been lost through them.*

Sir Thomas Phillipps also came down the next morning & employed himself again in endeavouring to save such remnants as could not be seen during the night, and as many of the Records had been crushed & jammed between the stones of the newly made portions of the road, they

were discovered in the Morning & preserved, in which duty, Mr Black of
the Record Office was also most active and diligent.
        I have the honour to be Sir,
                Your most obed. Servt.
                      SPECTATOR.

It goes without saying that Spectator was the touchy and self-congratulatory antiquarian, Sir Thomas Phillipps himself.

While Sir Thomas was scrabbling for precious papers among the cobblestones, and somehow managing to avoid being crushed by fire engine wheels and horses' hooves – which injured quite a few of the onlookers – the scene around him grew more tremendous by the minute. 'The spectacle was one of surpassing though terrific splendour', said *The Times.* 'The conflagration viewed from the river, was peculiarly grand and impressive. On the first view of it from the water it appeared as if nothing could save Westminster Hall from the flames. There was an immense pillar of bright clear fire springing up behind it, and a cloud of white, yet dazzling smoke, careering above it, through which, as it was parted by the wind, you could occasionally see the lantern and pinnacles, by which the building is ornamented. At the same time a shower of fiery particles seemed to be falling upon it with such unceasing rapidity as to render it miraculous that the roof did not burst into one general blaze.'

The Dean of Westminster, Dean Ireland, thought much the same thing. His successor, Dean Stanley, recorded the events of that night:

'On the night of the fire which consumed the House of Parliament in 1834, when thousands were gathered below watching the flames, when the waning affection for our ancient national monuments seemed to be revived in that crisis of their fate – where, as the conflagration was driven by the wind towards Westminster Hall, the innumerable faces of the vast multitude, lighted up in the broad glare with more than the light of day, were visibly swayed by the agitations of the devouring breeze, and one voice, one prayer seemed to go up from every upturned countenance, "Oh! save the Hall!"': on that night two small figures might have been seen standing on the roof of the Chapter House overlooking the terrific blaze, parted from them only by the narrow space of Old Palace Yard. One was the Keeper of the Records, Sir F. Palgrave, and the other was Dean Ireland. They had climbed up through the hole in the roof to witness the awful scene. Suddenly a gust of wind swept the flames in that direction. Palgrave, with all the enthusiasm of the antiquarian and of his own eager temperament, turned to the Dean and suggested that they should descend to the Chapter House and carry off its most valuable treasures into the Abbey for safety. Dean Ireland, with the caution belonging at once to his office and his character, answered that he could not think of doing so without applying to Lord Melbourne, the First Lord of the Treasury.'

At that very moment, Lord Melbourne, the Prime Minister and First Lord of the Treasury, was listening to the cry to save Westminster Hall which Dean Stanley had reported in a carefully censored version. The cry came from the Chancellor of the Exchequer, Lord Althrop. 'Damn the House of Commons, let it blaze away; but save, oh save the Hall', he bellowed above the noise. 'The exclamation was natural and even praiseworthy; but some sticklers for privilege may deem it one of those unpardonable breaches of it for which nothing can win a pardon but a retirement from office', rumbled *The Times* the next day, presumably trying hard to be funny.

Yet save, oh save, the ancient Westminster Hall they did. They saved it with a prodigious effort, directed by the Prime Minister himself. Men on the fire engines slaved for hours on the long wooden bars that they had to force up and down to send the water up into the roof ninety feet above them. Soldiers, policemen, passers-by and aristocratic politicians, manned the pumps, as sparks flew on to the roof and threatened to catch it alight. Men hurriedly pulled down adjoining, ramshackle buildings to make a fire break round the Hall. First one and then another of the fire engines was trundled inside the Hall itself so that water could be pumped up to the inside of the roof to dampen and cool it to stop the sparks, that were raining down on it from the adjoining House of Commons chamber, setting it on fire. The hoses were not long enough to reach from inside the Hall to the mains in New Palace Yard, so the engines had to be linked in series, one to the other, to get the water to the nozzles. Scaffolding that was being used inside the Hall to repair the roof was pressed into use as men climbed it with hoses to damp down parts of the roof that had now begun to smoulder. Outside, more jets were brought to play on the slates: in the eighteenth century the government had sold off the lead sheeting that had, up to then, been used to cover the roof in an unsuccessful attempt to make a little money. Had the lead still been in place on the night of the fire it would certainly have melted and set the oak beams beneath it ablaze.

Parts of the scaffolding in the Hall were torn down to make a battering ram to break open a door leading out of the Hall. Beyond the door was found a great cache of Parliamentary papers which were promptly man-handled to safety. The Hall was saved; it was a little the worse-for-wear, but it survived.

The firemen and all the other volunteers could not, however, save the houses of Mr Ley, Clerk of the House of Commons, or the castellated house of Mr Speaker Manners-Sutton, which looked out over pleasant lawns to the river. Mr Speaker's house was very badly damaged, and so, too, was his State dining-room in what had once been the undercroft chapel of St Mary beneath the House of Commons. Mr W. Hughes Hughes, MP, made himself busy supervising the rescue of portraits of earlier Speakers from his house – they had to be cut out of their frames because they were too big to get out of the doors – and Mr Hughes

Hughes and some soldiers tied Mrs Speaker's jewellery and valuables in the sheets off her bed and got them to safety. Mr and Mrs Speaker were not there; they were on holiday in Brighton.

With daylight, when the flames were out and the place a steaming shambles, came the task of adding up the damage. The Office of Works issued its report that day. 'The Painted Chamber, totally destroyed. The house, libraries, committee-rooms, housekeeper's rooms, &c are totally destroyed (in the Commons); the official residence of Mr Ley (Clerk of the House) – this building is totally destroyed. All the rooms from the oriel window to the south side of the House of Commons are totally destroyed. Westminster Hall: no damage has been done to this building.' This claim for the Hall was not quite accurate, but it was near enough.

With the inspection of the damage, came the inevitable questions. How did it happen? Who was responsible, and who would have to pay the penalty? Why had the fire engines not arrived more promptly on the scene and once they *had* arrived why were they not better organised? How many people had been hurt? The answer to that last question was: surprisingly few. When the House of Lords fell in fairly early on in the fire, four of five firemen were buried in the ruins and were dug out by rescuers; people were scalded by water pouring down onto them through the flames and burnt by molten lead from the roofs. The foolhardy Earl of Munster had to be saved from the fire by a man named M'Callam and in the process M'Callam was hit by a falling rafter and rushed to Westminster Hospital. A party of Foot Guards was rescued in the nick of time when they were trapped in a blazing turret. The assistant Serjeant-at-Arms climbed up through a window with some firemen to rescue the Commons' Mace and got out with only seconds to spare. The casualties were carted off to hospital, on shutters. 'George Simmonds, a mechanic, run over by a fire engine: broken thigh and otherwise bruised; Michael Penning, a fractured arm caused by falling off timber; John Hamilton, fireman, not expected to live; Charles Boylan, labourer, fractured skull; Thomas Rowarth, fireman, fractured skull; John Slater, severely hurt by hot lead.'

In the excitement of the fire, and the inquests and investigations that followed it, rumours began to grow and flourish. It was said that the soldiers, policemen and firemen had been drunk. The soldiers were supposed to have broken into Mr Speaker's cellar and stolen and drunk his wine. The firemen were said to have gone off to the many pubs that surrounded the Palace and could not be persuaded to leave to fight the fire. Rumours spread of suspicious people who were said to have been seen skulking about not long before the fire with matches, and there were said to have been people with Irish accents around.

It is certainly true that the exhausted firemen did have to be winkled out of the pubs next day to deal with one or two flare-ups, but they had fought valiantly throughout the night and were only trying to get a little rest. As for the rumours about the behaviour of the soldiers, their commanding officer angrily wrote to the newspapers denying the allegations against them. They had not stolen a drop of Mr Speaker's wine, or anything else.

Mr W. Hughes Hughes, MP, naturally saw everything they had done, and strongly approved of their conduct:

'I say deliberately that I did not once witness an act on the part of either firemen, soldiers, or police, which I could have wished to alter, much less that I could atribute to inebriation or wantonness. It is true that between 11 and 12 o'clock, when everything had been accomplished which it was possible for activity and zeal to effect, beer was given to the men, and exhaustion, in some instances, caused it to have an effect which the same quantity would not have produced at another time, but I repeat my unqualified admiration of the firemen, soldiers and police, until there remained literally nothing for them to do.'

There did remain, however, something for the Superintendent of the London Fire Engine Establishment, James Braidwood, to do. He wrote to *The Times* to explain why his engines had taken such a long time to get to the fire, and why they were so disorganised when they finally arrived. *The Times* had severely criticised the Establishment for its lack of efficiency. 'Where the completest co-operation is necessary all is confusion and contradiction', the newspaper had reported on the night of the fire. Superintendent Braidwood retorted that he had 'every reason to be satisfied with the zeal and alacrity displayed by the foremen, engineers and firemen belonging to the Establishment'. He listed the way that the twelve engines he had sent to the fire had been deployed. 'Though I regret the extent of the fire and the loss that has been sustained by the country', wrote Braidwood, 'I have the satisfaction of feeling that no exertions were spared either by myself, or the men under my command, to arrest the progress of the flames'. No doubt Braidwood wrote nothing but the truth, for it was not until the tide turned, and the great floating fire engine could be hauled by steam boat up the Thames to Westminster from the docks, that the fire was brought under control. As the night of the fire had worn on, the Blues had trundled down an engine from the Knightsbridge Barracks and another had been brought up from Elliotts' brewery in Pimlico. A messenger had galloped off through the night to ask the Navy at Deptford for help, and two parties of Marines rushed up two more engines in the early hours of the morning. Two thousand gallons of water, it was estimated, plus a ton of water a minute from the floating engine, were pumped on to the fire. Superintendent Braidwood rushed around trying, rather hopelessly, to organise the fight against the biggest blaze London had seen for two hundred years.

But how did it all begin? One of the spate of rumours was that a man had been seen with a box of matches somewhere near the place where the fire broke out. A medical gentleman, a Dr Jones, residing in Carlisle Street, Soho, had found a quantity of matches under a tree in the corner

Tally Sticks They had been used for centuries as a way of keeping official accounts. Millions of them had been stacked up and when old ones were used to stoke the furnace of the House of Lords, the flues overheated and started the great fire of 1834

of the Speaker's garden. Dr Jones, without explaining what he had been doing in the Speaker's garden in the first place, handed the matches over to Police Constable Farrell, No. 48L, who told a sentry of the Second Batallion of the Grenadier Guards, who told an officer — who did nothing. That, rather surprisingly, turned out to be precisely the right thing for the officer to do.

It was certainly not the mysterious matches — if they ever really existed — that caused the fire. It was caused by totally unmysterious tally sticks. Tally sticks had been used since the Conquest as a simple but efficient system of accounting. Notches were cut in a stick according to a code and the stick was then split down the middle. One half was kept by the Treasury, the other by the debtor. When the debtor came to pay his due the two halves of the stick were put together, and if they tallied and the amount of money he had brought was correct, then the debt was paid. The system had officially been abolished in 1783, but its use lingered on until 1826 — many of the people watching the fire and speculating on its cause would have been very familiar with the sticks. Vast piles of them had mounted up over the centuries, and although they had stopped being used eight years before the fire, the backlog was so great that they were still being burnt up. Sometimes they were made into a great fire on Tothill Fields, not far from Westminster; sometimes they were burnt in New Palace Yard; sometimes they were used as kindling in the dozens of fireplaces in the Palace of Westminster; sometimes simply dumped in the furnace that heated the House of Lords, to be destroyed.

Precisely how these innocuous pieces of stick came to burn down an ancient Royal palace was a problem fit only for a Committee of the Lords of the Privy Council to investigate. Six days after the fire, on 22 October 1834, the Committee sat. First, it dealt with the problem of 'numerous persons under sentence of death at Newgate', then it got down to finding out how the fire that had burnt their House had started. The Committee sat in secret, but *The Times* managed to get an exact transcript of what was said — even if it did get the names of the witnesses wrong. Those witnesses, quite obviously, lied through their teeth. Mr Weobley, the Clerk of Works, who rather preferred to be called by his grander title of Labourer in Trust, (the man whom the housekeeper had found petrified with fright when the fire was first discovered), said it was certainly not his fault. He had told the workmen stoking the House of Lords' furnace not to put on too many tally sticks at a time; just small handfuls, so the thing did not overheat. Joshua Cross, the old lag who had somehow managed to escape transportation, swore virtuously that he had stuck strictly to instructions. Richard Reynolds, the fire lighter in the Lords, swore he had seen Cross and his mate throwing on the tallies in quantities. Certainly not, said Cross, just a few at a time, and then well damped down. The Attorney General rose to question him.

The Attorney General: Now, Sir, answer me this question and be careful how you answer it: did you at any period of the day of Thursday, 16 of October, perceive anything unusual, or feel any extraordinary degree of heat in the House of Lords?

The witness hesitated.

The Attorney General: Now, Sir, recollect yourself.

Witness: I do not recollect feeling anything extraordinary in the heat of the House during that day.

The Attorney General: Nor at any time?

Witness: Nor at any time.

The Attorney General: You are quite certain of that fact?

Witness: Yes.

Poor Cross, to have to put up with this sort of questioning. The Lord Chancellor himself tried to get more information out of him, and cross-examined him 'very severely'. He did extract the information that Cross had 'been transported for a felony during an early period his life'.

Next there was a flurry because the Lords of the Privy Council had heard a rumour that news of the fire had been available a hundred and fifty miles from London less than four hours after it had broken out – a clear impossibility in their estimation. A Mr Cooper, a 'respectable tradesman of London', was reported to have heard about the fire when he was staying at the Bush Inn at Dudley, Worcestershire, at 10 o'clock that very same evening. Yes, he told their Lordships, he had heard about the fire from a man with his slippers on in the Commercial Traveller's room at the Bush. Mr Cooper had gone to Birmingham from London by the Comet coach, and then on from Birmingham to Dudley and he was sure he could remember it all quite clearly. The Privy Council pondered and discussed this but eventually came to the conclusion that Mr Cooper, respectable tradesman of London though he might be, had got himself into some sort of muddle. Perhaps their Lordships and Mr Cooper were not too sorry to put up something of a red herring. Mr Cooper was a partner in the firm of Hall and Cooper, ironfounders, of Drury Lane. The flues of the furnace that had caused the fire had not been swept for over a year in a money-saving cut back on maintenance. Mr Cooper's firm was working on the repair of the flues at the time of the fire. So perhaps both the Lords, because of their economies, and Mr Cooper's firm, because of the work it was doing, had something to be discreet about when it came to apportioning the blame.

In the end, no one, it seemed, was to blame. Everyone involved managed to lie or wangle himself or herself into a snug position of publicly washing guiltless hands. 'It would be very difficult to point out a case of fire which could be more clearly traced than this has been to its cause, without suspicion of evil design', said their Lordships. Joshua Cross, the ex-convict, had simply piled on the tally sticks too high. That was all.

Not quite all, because there was still money to be made out of the fire, if you knew how to do it. The Speaker, Manners-Sutton, thought he did know how. In spite of the efforts made by the soldiers to save his goods and chattles, he had lost many of his possessions, and he had made the dreadful mistake of not insuring himself. Mr Speaker tried to get the government to pay him £9,000 compensation, a very substantial sum, on the grounds that it was the carelessness of the government's servants that caused the fire, but the government absolutely refused to pay. To make matters worse, a valuable marble fireplace, worth between two and four hundred pounds, which had somehow been rescued by the soldiers from the Speaker's house, was now being ruined by sightseers climbing over the rubble and chipping bits off as souvenirs.

Then Bellamy, the sharp-witted caterer who looked after the food and drink in the Palace, whose eating house and bar had gone up in the first few minutes of the flames, wanted compensation. He, however, had prudently kept up his insurance, and he got most of the £1,500 he claimed. Lesser men tried to make lesser sums out of the disaster. A clerk got £20 for a cornelian ring and a manuscript which he had left on his desk. A messenger, who had to live mostly on tips he could make from Members and from the public, claimed 10s. 6d. for a dress hat, 10s. for a pair of court shoes and 12s. for a pair of buckles to go with them.

The fire had certainly been a theatrical sight for everyone who witnessed it, and a money-making theatrical manager promptly turned it into a stage spectacle. *The Times* reported it on 25 October, 1834 (nine days after the fire).

'Victoria Theatre – The manager of this theatre has used most extraordinary exertions to be first in the field with an exhibition of the late fire at both Houses of Parliament. On Thursday night (that is, a week after the fire) he produced a panoramic view, exhibiting not only a splendid and most accurate representation of both Houses of Parliament, as well as Westminster Abbey, Westminster Hall and Westminster Bridge, previous to the breaking out of the fire, but a faithful sketch of those buildings in each successive scene, from the first appearance to the extinction of the fire, as well as a most correct view of the ruins as they now stand. The spectator in this pictorial display is supposed to stand on the Surrey side of the river, and those who select that point for viewing the scene cannot restrain from being impressed by the correctness with which the artist has sketched it. Mr Marshall, we understand, is the person to whom this praise is due.'

Augustus Welby Pugin, who was to have so much influence on the Palace that replaced the one destroyed in the fire, would have admired the theatre manager's enterprise – and the theatricality of the fire itself. Pugin had already done some stage designs for a ballet at Covent Garden and he would certainly have seen the dramatic potential when he went to Westminster to watch the fire among the jostling crowds. He was, he wrote later to a friend, fortunate enough to witness the 'late great

conflagration' almost from the beginning till 'the termination of all danger as the Hall had been saved which is to me almost miraculous as it was surrounded by fire.'

'The old walls stood triumphantly midst the scene of ruin while brick walls and framed sashes, slate roofs etc. fell faster than a pack of cards. In fact the speed of the spread of the fire was truly astonishing, from the time of the House of Commons first taking fire, until the flames rushed out of every aperture could not have been more than five or six minutes and the effect of the fire behind the tracery was truly curious and awfully grand. What is most to be regretted is the Painted Chamber, the curious paintings of which I believe are totally destroyed.' Pugin obviously did not know very much about the history of St Stephen's Chapel and the House of Commons, otherwise, as an obsessive champion of mediaeval Gothic architecture, he would have been in deep misery at its destruction.

Also at the fire – although they seemed not to have met each other there – was Charles Barry, who was to create the new Palace of Westminster. The evening coach from Brighton was rumbling through the shabby streets on the southern banks of the Thames when Barry, who was one of its passengers, saw a red glow in the sky. An urchin shouted that the Houses of Parliament were on fire, and Barry hurried from the coach office in the City back to Westminster, and pushed his way through the crowds to watch. He knew there would have to be a new Palace to replace the one that had been destroyed. The young architect, who was already establishing a name for himself in the world, began, that night, to make his plans.

Above left: *Sir Charles Barry* Barry was born, in 1795, the son of a 'respectable stationer' in the shadow of the old Palace of Westminster. He won a competition for rebuilding the Palace after the fire of 1834 and, although his estimates of both cost and time were hopelessly wrong, his design resulted in one of the world's most famous buildings

Above: *Augustus Welby Northmore Pugin* An eccentric genius who died, quite mad, at 40. He was an obsessive Catholic convert, dedicated to recreating pre-Reformation Gothic architecture and values. In a frantic burst of energy lasting seven years, Pugin designed everything at Westminster, from the Royal throne to screws in the doors

CHAPTER FIVE
The Great Work

'The new Palace of Westminster was', said Earl de Grey, the first President of the Institute of British Architects, the 'most difficult and most magnificent work ever attempted.' It was certainly the largest building ever planned and built as one single enterprise in Great Britain. It was the subject of endless squabbles between the architect and politicians. It cost at least three times as much to build as Parliament had bargained for and although it was expected to take six years to complete it was some thirty years before it was finished – the craftsmen went on strike for over a year; and for a long time the architect would not speak to the man appointed over his head as his principal collaborator.

Yet the New Palace was built and designed with a dash and aplomb – perhaps even recklessness – that would be impossible today. It broke new technological ground in building and was a dazzling achievement for both its architect and its builders. It set entirely new standards in the arts and in interior decoration. It was built with all the confidence expected of a great imperial power, and became the seat from which the greatest empire the world has ever seen was ruled. It survived bombing and fire and massive social changes to keep its place as a symbol of national solidity and durability.

The arguments that dogged every stage of its building began almost as soon as the ashes of the old Houses of Parliament had been cleared away after the October fire of 1834. There were a few suggestions of moving Parliament away to a more suitable site – perhaps St James's Palace, or the recently refurbished Buckingham Palace, which William IV immediately offered to the nation. His motive was not altruism as he did not like his palace much, in spite of the vast amount of money that had been spent on recent improvements. Sites at Charing Cross or in the City were suggested, but nothing came of these ideas. Parliament's historic ties with Westminster were too strong to think seriously of anywhere else.

First, of course, Parliament itself had to go on, fire or no fire. Temporary Houses were fitted up with tremendous speed: the Commons took over the old House of Lords where the Lords had sat since 1801 and the Lords, much to their annoyance, were crowded back into the cramped and uncomfortable space of what had been, before it was finally destroyed in the fire, the Painted Chamber. By prefabricating the timber and iron-work elsewhere and doing the ornamental pieces in papier mâché, and having the men work all night by guttering flares, the elegant and comfortable temporary Houses were ready by February 1835 – just three months after the fire. The Commons found its

temporary House so comfortable, and became so used to it, that it was loathe to move out when the permanent new Chamber was eventually completed, fifteen years later.

Then came the competition for the designs of the New Palace. A commission was set up to organise it with the condition that the plans were to be in the Elizabethan or Gothic styles. The arguments over this choice of styles were furious; many people wanted the Houses of Parliament to be in a classic mode of Greek or Roman origin, with rounded heads to the windows and arches. The Gothic-style supporters insisted, quite wrongly, that their preference had originated in England and was particularly suitable for Westminster, with the Abbey only

Below: *The Competition for the New Palace* Parliament decided to have a competition for the design of the New Palace, which had to be in either Gothic or Tudor style. Among the ninety-seven entries (Barry's winning design was No 64), was this unsuccessful one by Lewis Nockalls Cottingham

yards away and with the enormous mass of Westminster Hall to be absorbed into the new building.

The Gothic supporters won the day and the commission set about laying down the detailed conditions for a competition for designing the New Palace. The members of the commission were all amateurs, which was a deliberate decision to avoid any suggestion of professional jealousy in their selections. The men who made the final choice of the design were the Hon. Thomas Liddell, who had dabbled in designing new Gothic buildings; Charles Hanbury Tracy, who had designed the great Gothic house at Torrington; and George Vivian, another amateur architect. They gave the competitors from 24 August, 1835, when the site plans were first available, to 1 December (originally it had been 1 November) that year to provide their designs. There were ninety-seven entries and the winner was entry number sixty-four, which bore the Charles Barry symbol of the portcullis. The design, said the commissioners, 'bears throughout such evident marks of genius and superiority of talent, as fully to entitle it to the preference we have given it'.

There were immediate and bitter complaints about the choice of Barry's design. Thirty-four of Barry's furious rivals presented a petition to Parliament to have the whole competition scrapped and re-run. Barry had, in any case, been tipped to win; his designs for the Travellers' Club in Pall Mall were considered to be highly successful, and there had been hints that there was some sort of arrangement between him and the commissioners – an allegation which, not surprisingly, the commissioners absolutely and angrily denied. They had no idea, they said, which plan was which. Each had to be submitted without a name, and identified only by a symbol.

The disgruntled and jealous unsuccessful architects were turned away by Parliament. Sir Robert Peel, the former Prime Minister, defended Barry; it would destroy the whole principles of public competition if the design was rejected now, he said. The great mistake that both Parliament and the commissioners did make, however, was not to ask for even the roughest estimates of how much any of the plans submitted in the competition would cost to carry out. To ask for such estimates would,

The Temporary Houses

Far left: *The House of Lords* After the fire of 1834, both Houses moved into temporary Chambers which were ready within six months. The House of Lords moved to the old site of the Painted Chamber, and complained that the new House was too small for them

Left: *The House of Commons* The Commons moved into the old Court of Requests, where the Lords had sat since 1801. The temporary Chamber was bigger and more comfortable than the old House, and they were reluctant to move out of it when Barry's Chamber was ready in 1850

Below: *Against the Rules* Charles Robert Cockrell broke the rules of the competition with his design which was not in the Gothic style but was based on the Palace at Greenwich

they thought, delay the submission of the designs, and put the competitors to unnecessary expense. Of Barry's plans, the commissioners, hopeful but totally erroneously, said that 'we have sufficient evidence to lead us to the belief that . . . no Design worthy of the country of equal magnitude can offer greater facilities for economy in execution'. When the first estimates were made they were officially put at £707,104, based on Barry's measurements, and it was expected that the new Palace would take six years to build. Although that estimate did not include the cost of furnishings and generally setting the place up, no doubt many MPs thought it did. Those who survived to work out the final cost when Barry died in 1860, and when the major work was pretty well completed, found that the total cost of both building and their furnishing was some £2,400,000.

Once the competition was won and the ensuing arguments more or less sorted out, Barry together with his designer, Augustus Welby Pugin, set furiously to work to produce a mass of drawings that would turn the plans into a reality. Barry's great achievement in his design had been to see the vast new Palace as one; a unified, continuing building, grand and spacious for ceremonial occasions, but practical and efficient for everyday use. He designed one long spine of Lords' and Commons' Chambers, running along the line of the river, and took into his plans, with great tact and success, the huge mass of Westminster Hall and the site of the old House of Commons, which was now to be an elaborate entrance to the realigned Chambers.

Barry planned that the necessary facilities that went with the legislature – libraries, refreshment rooms, committee rooms and so on – would be set along the river bank in a frontage which, including the Terrace, was eventually to be eight hundred feet long. At each end of this formally arranged mass of buildings, broken with a raised section in the centre, he placed his two great towers – the Clock Tower to the south and the King's Tower, which became the Victoria Tower, to the North. This plan is, basically, what Barry eventually built, but not without many changes along the way – some changes were imposed

Right: *The ceiling and the chandelier, Central Lobby* The ceiling is 75 ft above the floor. It contains more than 250 carved bosses, and the Venetian mosaics include the emblems of England, Ireland and Scotland. The brass chandelier by Jon Hardman, of Birmingham, weighs three tons. It is raised and lowered by an electric motor in the roof above the lobby.

An early Barry design Barry constantly modified his plans and made changes without authorisation, much to the annoyance of MPs. In the set of plans below drawn after the addition of the Central Tower had been forced on Barry by the ventilating expert, Dr Reid, the design of all three towers had still to undergo radical changes before their final details were settled. In these early plans the roofs of the two Chambers rose above the east front of the Palace, and great changes had still to be made on both the design and placing of the Clock Tower which had already been drawn up by Pugin for a country mansion in Lancashire

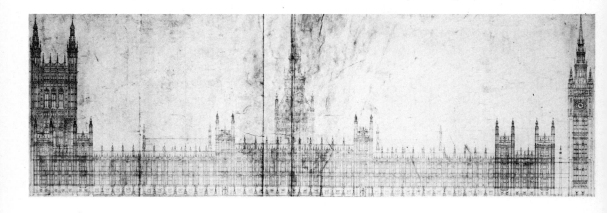

Left: *The Central Lobby*
The crossroads of the Palace of Westminster. All visitors come here to see their MPs, or to go to the Strangers' Galleries in either the Commons or the Lords. The Latin text in the floor (designed by Pugin) is from Psalm 127: 'Except the Lord build the house, they labour in vain that build it'

Below left: *Above the Central Lobby* The impressive interior of the spire above the Central Lobby, which is rarely seen and contains only the motor for raising and lowering the chandelier

Below: *The central spire* The spire was not included by Charles Barry in his original plans for the new Palace, but the ventilating expert, Dr David Reid, insisted it should be built as a shaft to expel 'vitiated air.' It was, in fact, never used for anything at all

Right: *The Royal Gallery*
It was designed by Barry
as part of the great
processional routes for the
monarch at State Openings
of Parliament; leading from
the Royal Staircase and the
Royal Robing Room to the
Parliament House – the
House of Lords – itself. It is
110 ft long and 45 ft wide

Below right: *The Royal
Gallery* 'The Death of
Nelson at Trafalgar, 1805.'
One of the two massive
paintings by Daniel Maclise
in the Royal Gallery.
On the other wall is the
meeting of Wellington and
Blücher at Waterloo in
1815. On two occasions the
President of France has
been invited to address
both Houses at a joint
meeting in the Royal
Gallery!

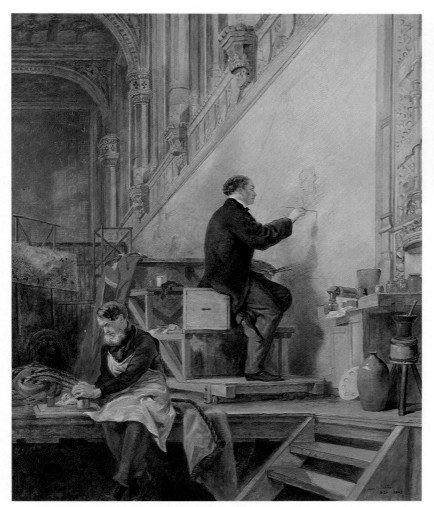

Left: *Daniel Maclise painting 'The Death of Nelson' in the House of Lords* Both paintings are 45 ft long by 12 ft high. They are painted in a process using water-glass. Maclise was paid £3,500 for each picture and they took him some six years to complete

Above: *'The Death of Nelson'* (detail)

Below: *'The Meeting of Wellington and Blücher at Waterloo'* (detail)

Right: *Queen Victoria
opening Parliament,
4 February, 1845* The
ceremony was in the
temporary House of Lords
which was built after the
fire

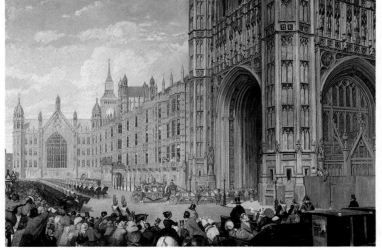

Right: *Queen Victoria
arriving at the Victoria Tower
for the State Opening of
Parliament, 1861* The
Victoria Tower, which had
not long been completed,
was originally going to be
called the King's Tower

Left: *The New Senate House* One of the more eccentric ideas, by Joseph Michael Gandy, for the new Houses of Parliament after the 1834 fire

Below, far left: *Sir Charles Barry* The architect of the Palace of Westminster. He won the competition for the Palace out of nearly a hundred competitors. This statue stands at the foot of the main staircase of the Palace. He is holding plans for the Victoria Tower

Below left: *Augustus Welby Northmore Pugin* The eccentric genius who was responsible for all the interior decorations at Westminster. His picture appears in the stained-glass window of the tomb he built for himself at the Church of St Augustine at Ramsgate, which he also built and designed

Above right: *Pugin designs* Some of the many thousands of designs drawn and painted by Pugin for decorations at Westminster

Middle right: *Encaustic tiles* Pugin virtually recreated the art of making encaustic – inlaid – tiles for decorations at Westminster. These designs are in St Stephen's Hall

Below right: *In the House of Commons Library* Ink wells, penholders, letter racks and calendars were all designed by Pugin. He designed every detail in the Palace – even the screws in the doors

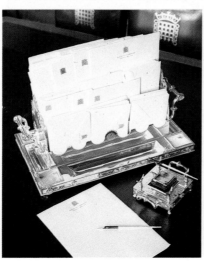

Above: *The Palace nears completion* Both the Victoria Tower and the Clock Tower were built without external scaffolding. Building materials were brought to docks beside the Palace at a spot where the Embankment Gardens now stand

Left: *The Chamber of the House of Commons, 1858* MPs refused to use the Chamber Barry had designed for them in 1850 until he had changed the design of the roof. He refused ever again to go into the Chamber unless he was forced to do so

Right: *The Royal Robing Room* The room in which the Queen puts on the Imperial State Crown and the velvet train when she comes to the State Opening of Parliament. The elaborate decorations are by Pugin; the paintings by William Dyce

Left: *The Chair of State in the Royal Robing Room* The Chair is embroidered with Queen Victoria's monogram; behind it, the Cloth of State. Both were embroidered by the Royal School of Needlework in 1856

Above: *The Prince's Chamber* Henry VIII and five of his six wives. Katherine of Aragon is on his right. The pictures were painted by students of the Royal College of Art

Right: *The Prince's Chamber* Henry VIII's mother, Elizabeth of York; his brother, Arthur Prince of Wales and his first wife, Katherine of Aragon

The House of Lords The most elaborate part of Barry's design. The Chamber is 80 ft long and 45 ft wide. At the far end the Throne; in front of it the Woolsack, stuffed with wool from Commonwealth countries, on which the Lord Chancellor sits

Pugin's decorations in the House of Lords The entire Chamber is an elaborate re-creation of heraldic designs and coats of arms

Left: *The Throne, House of Lords* Barry designed the Throne; Pugin its elaborate decorations. The five orders of chivalry are in the canopy above it; Privy Councillors may sit on the red hassocks on the steps of the Throne when the House is sitting

Right: *The Throne, House of Lords* The Royal Coat of Arms, and Victoria's monogram, above the Throne and one of the angels

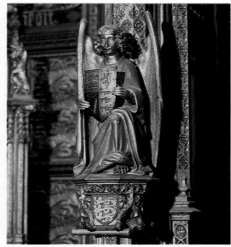

Below: *The House of Lords* The entrance from the Peers' Lobby. At the far end of the Chamber is the Throne

Right: *The Peers' Lobby* The massive solid brass doors into the House of Lords

upon him by Parliament, some he simply made on his own account without seeking, or getting, permission. Barry's son, the Reverend Alfred, wrote later that his father's 'tendency to alteration grew on him in later years', but with so many masters trying to control what he was doing, it was inevitable that Barry would eventually simply shrug his shoulders and get on with things in his own way. He was, after all, building a palace covering eight acres of very difficult, unstable and watery ground. It had within it eleven courtyards; residences for a living-in population of something like two hundred people – the Speaker's House, alone, has sixty rooms; the Parliament House of the Lords; the House of Commons, with both Houses built on one enormous floor without a single step in it; an underground park for Members' carriages – although this was never used for that purpose; the biggest and most accurate clock in the world; a Palace fit for Royal ceremonial, with all the back-stairs facilities that it would need.

Barry's first plans had no rooms at all for either Ministers or Members in either House, and even today Ministers' rooms are often converted dining-rooms or drawing-rooms or libraries where once officials of the Lords and Commons lived in great style. Where the Prime Minister now makes some of the most important decisions of the day, the Clerk of the House once took his ease in his private drawing-room. The Serjeant-at-Arms and a few other officials still have official residences in the Palace, but their style is a great deal less grand than Barry designed for their predecessors.

So the work on Barry's winning plans finally began. First, the preparation of the awkward site involved the building of a great coffer-dam to hold back the Thames and make way for the river frontage of the Palace. The first iron-shod pile of the dam was driven in on 1 September, 1837 – just three years after the fire. A steam engine pumped out the river water, and then, once the coffer-dam was dry, on 1 January, 1839, the work of building the New Palace of Westminster began.

Idlers on Westminster Bridge could look down over its high stone sides onto the enormous area of complicated scaffolding, wooden huts, workshops, steam engines, stonemasons' yards and piles of equipment. Beyond the site, where Embankment Gardens were eventually laid out, was a wharf where barges and boats brought their loads of stone and timber and cast iron. On Westminster Bridge itself, stalls sold tools and equipment to the men – at one time, nearly 1500 of them – who flocked to what Barry called 'his great work'. It was great indeed. One of Barry's most daring and brilliant plans was to build the Palace on one enormous raft of concrete, to stabilise it above the uncertain ground of Thorney Island. Behind the layers of 'fine wrought Scotch granite' that formed the river frontage, the concrete was poured down to form the 'Barry raft' on which the Palace was constructed. It was over ten feet thick in places, and the precise recipe for the concrete and the precise height from which it had to be poured to compact it and make it firm, were included

Left: *St Stephen's Hall* The site of the original House of Commons. Barry rebuilt it as the main entrance hall of the Palace

Overleaf: *Barry's pocket plan of the Palace of Westminster* He carried this plan in his coat-tail pocket throughout the building of his 'great work'

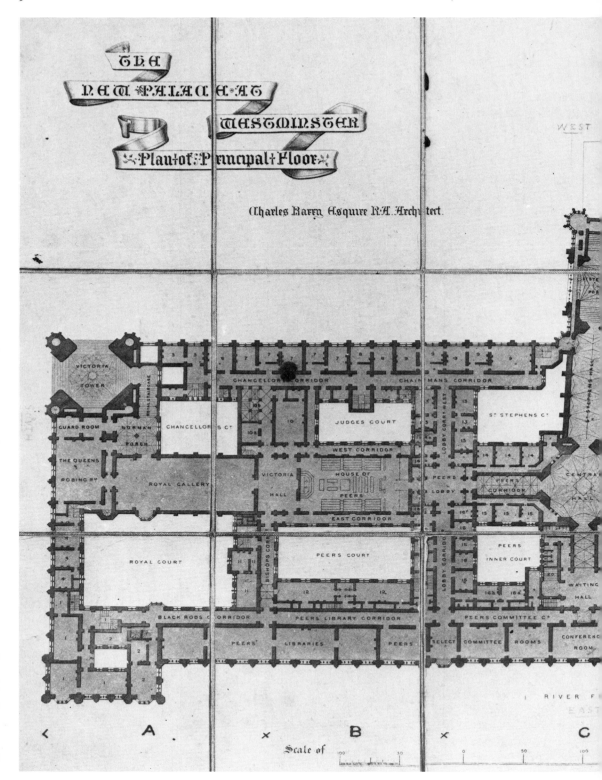

THE NEW PALACE AT WESTMINSTER
Plan of Principal Floor

Charles Barry Esquire R.A. Architect.

VICTORIA TOWER

GUARD ROOM

THE QUEENS

ROBING R.T

ROYAL STAIRCASE

NORMAN PORCH

CHANCELLORS C.T

ROYAL GALLERY

VICTORIA HALL

CHANCELLORS CORRIDOR

JUDGES COURT

WEST CORRIDOR

HOUSE OF PEERS

EAST CORRIDOR

PEERS LOBBY

CHAIRMANS CORRIDOR

LOBBY COURT WEST

S.T STEPHENS C.T

PEERS CORRIDOR

CENTRAL HALL

ROYAL COURT

BISHOPS CORR.

PEERS COURT

LOBBY CORRIDOR

PEERS INNER COURT

WAITING HALL

BLACK RODS CORRIDOR

PEERS LIBRARY CORRIDOR

PEERS COMMITTEE C.T

PEERS LIBRARIES

PEERS

SELECT COMMITTEE ROOMS

CONFERENCE ROOM

WEST

RIVER F

EAST

A

B

C

Scale of

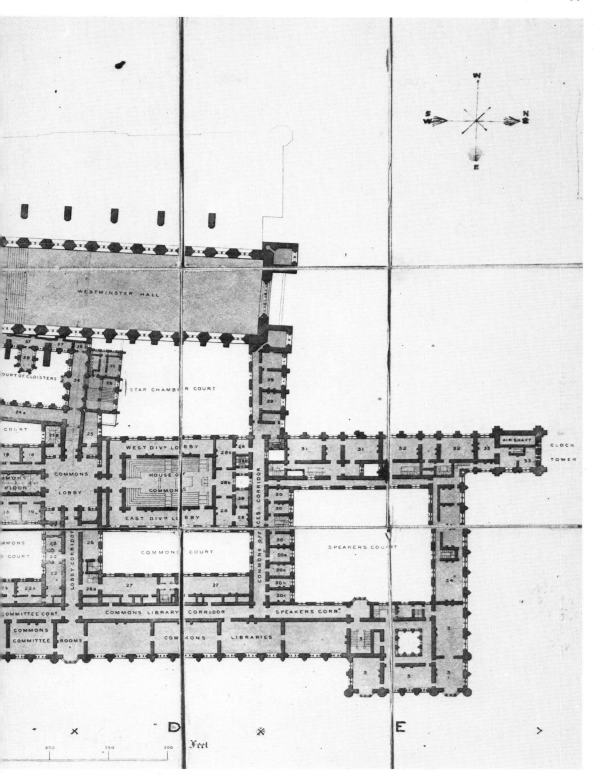

WESTMINSTER HALL

COURT OF CLOISTERS

STAR CHAMBER COURT

COURT

WEST DIVN LOBBY

HOUSE OF COMMONS

EAST DIVN LOBBY

COMMONS LOBBY

COMMONS COURT

LOBBY CORRIDOR

COMMONS OFFICES CORRIDOR

SPEAKERS COURT

AIR SHAFT

CLOCK TOWER

COMMITTEE CORR

COMMONS COMMITTEE ROOMS

COMMONS LIBRARY CORRIDOR

COMMONS LIBRARIES

SPEAKERS CORR

D   E

Feet

200   150   100

in Barry's specifications: 'The concrete forming the foundation is to consist of six measures of gravel and sand to one measure of ground stone limed mixed dry and then well worked together with water and in this state teemed and thrown into the trench from a height of at least ten feet from the present surface of the ground and the top to be levelled.' Other builders were rather doubtful about Barry's techniques, but they have stood the test of time and the dangers of the quicksands which lie under an alarmingly large part of the Westminster site.

As the building plans got under way the stone from which it all had to be constructed had, of course, to be chosen. British stone, it was felt, would be the best. Caen stone from France had been used in the old St Stephen's Chapel and the old Palace, and it was to be used again in the interior of the new Palace, but everyone agreed the stone should be British for the British Parliament. Barry, with three other experts, went off on a tour to find it. It was an enjoyable time for touring the countryside – June 1838 – so they took six weeks and ran up a bill for £1,300 expenses – an amount which, in today's terms, would cause a public scandal. Barry was accompanied by Sir Walter de la Beche, of the Geological Society; Dr William Smith, a geologist and engineer; and Charles Harriott Smith, the master mason who had carved the pillars and portico of the new National Gallery, and so presumably knew a good bit of stone when he saw it. They looked at old buildings and tried to decide what stone they had been built of and sent barge-loads of samples to London; and in the end they decided on stone from the Duke of Leed's quarry at Anston. Their decision was wrong. At the time, however, it seemed ideal since they were able to buy blocks up to four feet thick, and it was cheap. Unfortunately, because the stone was often wrongly handled and cut, and because of the effect of the London atmosphere, it has, over the years, proved a costly and troublesome decision.

'Present State of the Houses' The New Palace of Westminster, with over 1,000 rooms and two miles of corridors, was the biggest single building ever undertaken in Great Britain. Barry stole part of the bed of the Thames to build the great granite terrace in front of the Palace, and then work began on the massive super-structure.
The scaffolding used to build the Palace was itself a technical triumph and was designed by the tough Derbyshire foreman, George Allen, whose slave-driving methods and foul language caused a stone masons' strike that lasted for months

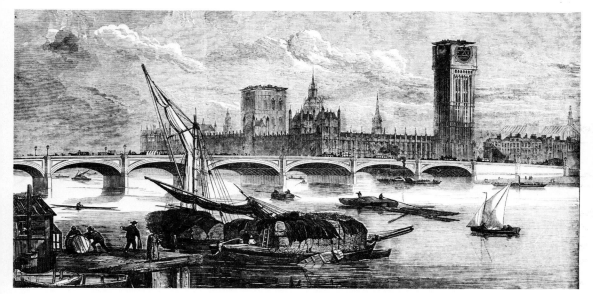

Each of the three great towers of Westminster – the Victoria Tower, the Central Tower and the Clock Tower – was built from the inside outwards, without exterior scaffolding. The foreman, George Allen, designed revolving platforms inside the towers, with steam engines to haul up the iron and stone. Anston stone from Yorkshire was chosen because it was cheap and easily worked, but it was badly quarried and prone to damage by the London air. It had to be repaired before the Palace was even finished, and has caused endless trouble ever since

The three hundred kings and queens and saints – all of them British, of course – who were scattered over the facades of the Palace in the early designs, constantly have to be renewed by carvers in government workshops, and the gargoyles and decorations have, all too often, to be protected by scaffolding from falling on the heads of passers-by. Yet, in the end, 775,000 cubic feet of stone – not, of course, all of it from Anston – were used to build a Palace that consists of 1,180 rooms, 126 staircases, more than two miles of corridors, fifteen miles of steam pipes with 1,200 stopcocks, plus some forty lifts which have been installed in recent years. There is also now one escalator; it leads up from the Members' underground car park, which was built between 1972 and 1974 (not in the place where Barry wanted his underground park for horses and carriages) at a cost of £2,500,000 – that is, roughly the cost of the entire Palace a hundred years before.

On 27 April, 1840, Mrs Sarah Barry, the architect's wife, laid the foundation stone at a point near the Speaker's House and its abutment with the river. No one else, it seems, was very keen on performing the ceremony, for by then, five years after they had accepted his plans, politicians were becoming more and more concerned about Barry's activities. They were alarmed at the frequency with which he changed his original plans, and they suspected that the costs were beginning to get out of hand.

Barry, though, still had all the confidence in the world. The tenders went out for building the river frontage and, although they were an hour beyond the allotted time for getting in their bid, the great contracting firm of Grissell and Peto won. The firm was an old hand at massive public building works; Samuel Moreton Peto was a tremendous railway builder who eventually became an MP and a baronet, and made a considerable part of his fortune out of Barry's work. Thomas Grissell was the man who directed most of the work on the building of the

Palace. He was a man of formidable organisational abilities and even *The Times*, which kept a decidedly wary eye on what was going on with the new buildings, was later to comment that 'the regularity and precision which prevails in every department' under Grissell's control was commendable.

One of Grissell's principal aids to efficiency was his foreman, a tough Derbyshire man, George Allen. Allen, however, was a tartar. He was supremely capable, hardworking and inventive – among other things, he invented a special kind of highly efficient scaffolding at Westminster – and he expected the men working under him to be as dedicated as he was. His methods, though, were counter-productive. They brought about a strike of masons working on the river frontage of the Palace that lasted for nearly 18 months – from September 1841, to May 1843. Allen was said to be of a 'proud and overbearing disposition'. He swore at his men; sacked them for no reason at all; would not let them have beer while they were working; and treated them like an army to be disciplined. When some of the masons tried to stop their colleagues from working at Allen's demanding pace, he responded with a threat of a hundred sackings, and so the strike followed. Allen said he was being persecuted by the unions; Grissell's workers, who were building Nelson's Column in Trafalgar Square, came out as a sign of solidarity; and money flowed in from sympathisers. Grissell tried bringing in blackleg labour and advertised all over the country for '150 good hard-stone masons'. The strikers claimed he was really employing butchers and shoemakers and anyone else he could get hold of at 3s. 6d. a day, when a skilled man got 5s. a day. In the end, of course, the strike petered out, and the money left in the fund was given to the few men who could not find fresh work. The strike committee had its final meeting, and by May 1843, the men were back at work and Allen was, reputedly, a rather wiser and less foul-mouthed supervisor.

As the Palace rose beside the Thames, so Barry continued with his endless changes, both major and minor. The ceremonial Royal staircase, winding round the King's Tower (the Victoria Tower), had been altered into its present scheme of a single flight of stairs leading first into the Royal Robing Room, then into the Royal Gallery, then into the Princes' Chamber (not in the original plan), and finally into the House of Lords. He completely re-aligned the two Houses so that they ran parallel to the river frontage; re-arranged and reshaped the courtyards and planned the octagonal Central Lobby. When these fresh plans were published in 1843, the newspapers said that 'the original bears the signature of the architect; and we are assured that no deviation will be made from this arrangement'.

Both the newspapers, and certainly Barry, had, however, reckoned without Dr David Boswell Reid. Dr Reid was the Great Ventilator; a phoney Scottish scientist who was imposed on Barry by Parliament as the official ventilator of the New Palace. He managed to fool the House of Lords some of the time and the House of Commons most of the time with his irrational theories about ventilating and heating and cooling their Chambers. The Great Ventilator was a thorn in the side of Barry's flesh for over a decade, and by the time Reid was finally sacked from his job, he had taken up something like a third of the entire space of the Palace with his cranky schemes and theories, and had managed to turn the building, which Barry had designed to be as fireproof as possible, into a very real fire hazard. It was Reid who insisted on taking up the space where Peers and MPs had hoped to park their horses and carriages; Reid who insisted that Barry should add a third tower – as an outlet for his unworkable primitive air-conditioning system.

As if Reid was not enough, Barry had, of course, both Houses of Parliament to contend with. As the work went on, the money poured out, and costs rose in each year's annual estimates. At one time money was cut because of defence spending requirements, and Barry constantly had to appear before more and more committees of both Houses to explain what he was doing. He had to justify the changes he was making, often without having secured official approval to explain why the costs were not keeping to his original estimates; and why it was all taking so very much longer than anyone had expected. The main reason for all these problems, of course, was that no one had ever built anything remotely like the New Palace before in England; nor had anyone working on a major project had to contend with so many masters and self-appointed experts. Each House had its own Select Committees before which Barry had to appear; they, in turn, set up Royal Commissions and Special Committees and delved and interfered with Barry's work and generally got in his way. At one time, when Lords and Commons had both been more than usually difficult, it seemed as though Barry might resign; he also felt particularly bitter about the authorities' refusal to pay him what he considered the proper fees for his work. Feelings ran high on both sides; there were suggestions that Barry was putting his expensive changes into the plans so that his fees would be increased. Somehow, he coped with the endless working hours and countless problems and, from 1844, with the mercurial Pugin, shouting and laughing and capering about at his side, the two men climbed together over the scaffolding that surrounded Barry's Great Work and persevered with the construction.

Then there was Royal interference in Barry's work. In 1841 a Fine Arts Commission was set up under the chairmanship of the Prince Consort, Prince Albert, to oversee the decoration of the Palace. Neither Barry nor, when he came to Westminster, Pugin, was invited to be a member, but they did their best to work with Prince Albert and his colleagues. 'Wherever I imagine it may be the wish of the Commissioners to decorate the walls of the building with paintings', wrote Barry, 'I am making such provision as will allow of a ground for such paintings of any kind that may be thought most favourable to the species

of painting that may be adopted.' The Queen herself came to Westminster Hall in 1843 to see an exhibition of 140 paintings which the Commission thought might be suitable to beautify the Palace (two of them now hang on the wall in a staff canteen just off Westminster Hall, only yards away from the place where they were first exhibited) and suitably classical subjects – 'Caracticus Led in Triumph Through the Streets of Rome' – were given prizes. William Dyce went off to the Sistine Chapel in Rome to study frescoes before re-introducing the art to England with his work in the House of Lords – 'The Baptism of Ethelbert' – and his paintings of the King Arthur legend in the Royal Robing Room. Plasterers, builders and the Prince Consort were very much in evidence, and while Dyce said he was greatly honoured to have Prince Albert holding his sketches while engaging in the difficult art of fresco painting, having such an illustrious attendant was, he found, rather distracting.

Albert also intervened personally when the artist Daniel Maclise was having problems with some of his work. He persuaded Maclise to paint what he called 'the grand historical works' in the Royal Gallery: two massive pictures, each 45 feet long and 12 feet high. One shows the Death of Nelson at Trafalgar; the other the Meeting of Wellington and Blucher at Waterloo. They took Maclise five years to complete using a system of waterglass paint, and he was paid a rather grudging fee of £3,500 for each work.

One piece of artistic improvement that fortunately did not come to fruition in the Palace was Barry's own idea of turning Westminster Hall into what he called an 'English Valhallah'. Barry's plan was to raise the great roof of the Hall – he was absolutely sure he could do it without harming it in any way – and then paint the walls with frescoes and murals representing great moments in British history. Banners and flags would hang from the rafters – there were, at least, mediaeval precedents for these ideas — and an avenue of statues would be set up to commemorate great British statesmen. Empty spaces would be left for great British statesmen still to come. Happily, the idea was dropped, but it finds an unhappy echo in the mistakes that were later made in Barry's splendid St Stephen's Hall, where a series of larger-than-life marble politicians was put up along each side, badly out of keeping with his original and effective handling of the entrance to the Palace.

As the arguments and changes and haggling over money continued, the timetable for completing the Great Work fell badly behind-hand. Barry simply ignored promises he had made to get the Lords into their new House some time in 1844 — he blamed, with good reason, the impossible Dr Reid and his ventilating schemes for the delay — but eventually, with the decorations by no means finished, the Peers moved out of their cramped temporary quarters and into their splendid new Chamber in April 1847. It was indeed — or it would be when the decorations were finished — 'a hall worthy of this advanced age and this opulent Empire', said *The Builder* magazine. Only one of the murals and the stained glass windows were in place, but there were plans to illuminate the stained glass from the outside with gas flares once it was all inserted — a scheme which never really worked. Pugin had run riot with carvings of countless heraldic devices, kings' heads and Royal beasts. James Ballentine made the stained glass which Pugin designed, and around the massive gilded throne, the centrepiece of the entire Palace, ran the brass railing that his friend and fellow Catholic, John Hardman of Birmingham, made for him after a great many hitches and changes of plan. The throne itself had only been installed after several changes of design. Pugin had wanted it to look highly ecclesiastical, a throne fit for a great cardinal or the Pope himself. Protestant Barry wanted it to look royal and temporal, and it was Barry's plan that Pugin carried out so splendidly. The high wooden ceiling was decorated with the scarlet and green emblems of England, Scotland and Ireland and of their kings, and in the niches round the walls stood the eighteen bronze statues of the barons who had forced King John to sign Magna Carta.

Members of the House of Commons naturally kept a jealous eye on the development of the Lords. The Commons rather liked its temporary House — it was a good deal bigger than the one destroyed in the fire, and Dr Reid's ventilating experiments seemed to have worked well — but it felt that it ought now to moving into the Chamber which Barry had, for so long, been building. Barry tried to hurry things up a little by using machines to make some of the thousands upon thousands of parts and pieces that he needed. Extensive workshops were established nearby for producing wood work from patent carving machines, and some three hundred men turned out the doors and furniture and fittings needed for the Palace. Iron for the roof came from the Regent's Canal Iron Works — the man who ran the Iron Works happened to be the contractor Grissell's nephew — and the iron sheets, three-sixteenths of an inch thick, which still roof the Palace of Westminster, were put in hand. There was trouble with the pollution from the acrid London air, and its damaging effect on the iron roof but, 'at last', wrote Barry's architect son, Edward, 'after a great many trials of different paints and other compositions, one by Mr Szerelmy, a Hungarian gentleman . . . appeared to promise a great success.' So it was smeared over the outside of the roof.

However important it was to protect the roof from the London atmosphere, the main work of getting the new Palace finished and in full operation was taking a terrifyingly long time to complete. In 1848, yet another Royal Commission was set up to try to bring the protracted and vastly expensive undertaking to a swift and efficient end. Lord de Grey, the President of the Institute of British Architects, who must have been relieved that he refused to be one of the original group of commissioners who chose Barry in 1835, sat with Mr Thomas Greene, MP, a former Commons Chairman of Committees, under the chairmanship of Sir John Fox Burgoyne, the Inspector General of Fortifications. They were to superintend the completion of the new Palace; determine its design and decorations, fittings and furnishings; and settle all relevant problems – subject, of course, to the financial control of the Treasury. The last duty was certainly a pious hope, in view of the way the money had been drained away in recent years; Barry estimated that well over another million pounds was needed, in addition to the £1,400,000 already spent. The Palace, which it had been estimated would take six years to build, had already been under construction for eight years since the foundation

Below left: *'Interior of the House of Lords'* The House of Lords – the Parliament House – was completed in 1847. The design and decoration of the Throne were a perfect example of the close co-operation between Barry and Pugin, and the Chamber itself a triumphant realisation of Pugin's Gothic dreams

Below: *'The new House of Commons, from the Bar'* The Commons moved into their new Chamber in 1850 – and promptly moved out again. They insisted that Barry should drastically alter the design of the roof. They finally took possession in 1852, but Barry would never enter the Chamber again unless he was forced to do so

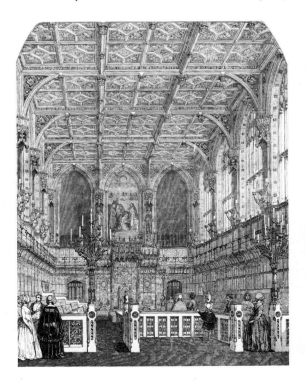

stone was first laid and was very far indeed from being finished. It had already cost more than twice as much as the original estimate and massive sums still needed to be raised. No wonder one MP fumed, 'Mr Barry should be put under curb and bridle, for he has had his way too long.'

Eventually, in 1850, the Commons was able to move into its new Chamber. It promptly moved out again. It was, it agreed, a thoroughly unsatisfactory place, in spite of the fact that Barry had only carried out their original instructions. 'Any schoolboy would be flogged for designing such a place', snapped Joseph Hume, the Radical MP who had been a loud and bitter critic of Barry's from the very beginning. Barry had designed the place for 462 MPs, plus various galleries, but the Members said they did not like the 192 seats in a gallery behind the Speaker's chair, so it had to go. They said they could not hear each other; that the Division Lobbies were too small; that, one way and another, almost everything was wrong with the House. It was, they noticed, perhaps with some envy, much less grand than the Lords, but it was intended to be both rich and practical in style. The Gothic windows which surrounded it could, like the ones in the Lords, be lit up by gas jets outside at night; carved beasts glowered from the ends of benches; green leather covered the seats, and brass fittings glittered in the patent lamps installed by the indefatigable Dr Reid. Ladies were allowed to watch the scene from behind brass grilles installed in front of their own gallery, at the back of the press seats above the Speaker's chair. The Commons, though, had become used to its old, if temporary, home where it had now sat for fifteen years, and it insisted that its new home should be changed. There was the inevitable Select Committee, and Barry, to his deep and bitter anger, was forced to lower the high, squared and carved ceiling, so that it chopped the high Gothic windows he had installed in half, and completely changed the style and character of the Chamber he had designed. The Division Lobbies had to be changed, and the side galleries enlarged. These alterations cost £15,000, and the Commons blamed Barry, and not the requirements it had imposed on him, for the extra expenditure. The Commons Chamber, said a Tory MP, was 'a complete, decided and undeniable failure'. Disraeli told the House – he was, presumably, joking – that if the government should hang the architect it would stop such blunders in future; and Barry, bitter and deeply hurt by his treatment, refused to go into the Commons Chamber again unless he was forced to do so. Perhaps, though, the government felt it had gone a little far in its attacks on Barry. In 1852 when, for the first time, both Houses sat in their new Chambers, and when Queen Victoria entered her New Palace for the State Opening of Parliament, Barry was knighted, Sir Charles Barry, architect.

CHAPTER SIX

Towers of Trouble

The towers of Westminster are the most instantly recognisable, most famous and most successful part of Charles Barry's design for the Houses of Parliament. At the north end of the Palace stands the Clock Tower, the most famous building of its kind in the world; at the south end, the massive square outline of the Victoria Tower; halfway along the great range of buildings that runs between the two extremes, the Central Tower rises like a church steeple above the complicated roofscape of the Palace. Each one of these towers caused Barry a great deal of trouble and was designed and built with ingenuity and skill; yet each caused much acrimony and argument among politicians and Barry's rival experts.

The plans for the Clock Tower were the most difficult Barry undertook. He found it impossible to complete them satisfactorily, and in the end had to rely more heavily than he later admitted on his designer, Augustus Pugin. The Victoria Tower was, technologically, well in advance of its time and, years after Barry's death, had to be massively reconstructed to save it from collapse. The Central Tower, the most graceful and elegant of the three, was not included in Barry's original design for the Palace at all, but was forced on him by the eccentric plans of the ventilator, Dr Reid. It turned out to be completely useless, although it remains one of Barry's most successful buildings at Westminster.

The Central Hall – at some stage in its history it changed its name to the Central Lobby – was planned as the focal point around which the whole life of the Palace would revolve. It was conceived of as a large and splendid place in which endless processions of constituents might come to exercise their right to see their MPs. It was to be the crossroads of the Palace through which everyone bustled, whether they were coming or going from the Lords or the Commons. It was meant to impress the awed visitor to the Palace, and it still does – but not in the way that Barry had planned. Barry originally wanted the roof of his octagonal Central Hall to be lofty, spacious and to soar high above the heads of the people waiting in the Hall below, but Dr Reid, with his impractical and unworkable ventilating schemes, had other ideas. At the time, the Ventilator also had the ear of Members of both Houses, and he persuaded them to make Barry change his designs to accommodate one of his wilder plans for getting rid of what he called 'vitiated air'. Barry was obliged to build a great chimney above the Central Hall, through which the smoke from some four hundred furnaces and fires around the Palace would be expelled, together with the vitiated air which the heat of the fires would draw up and thrust out over the rooftops of

Westminster. This is the chimney which Barry turned into the Central Tower.

The extra cost of Dr Reid's demands for a tower above the Central Hall came to over £32,000, and the Commons began to worry whether his scheme would really work. However, they agreed it should go ahead, and additional work had to be approved to construct supports for the tower. To this day, beneath the floor of the Central Lobby, there is a series of massive cast-iron pillars which were added to support the hundreds of tons of masonry needed for the extra spire. The people who work in the maintenance areas beneath the Palace have always called the structure the Bandstand, because that is what the pillars look like – they are also the focal point for the infinity of meandering passages which run far below the great building.

Nearly seven and a half feet of concrete were laid down to form the foundations and support a spire that eventually rose over 260 feet above the floor of the Central Hall. Wrought iron and cast-iron, all of it tested to breaking point, was used to hold the construction of brick and stone together. The materials were sent up to the masons and craftsmen who worked on a specially designed revolving scaffold, which two men winched round and round as the tower rose towards the skyline. It was the first of the three towers to be completed, and duly contained the useless ventilating outlets that Dr Reid had insisted upon installing at the top of the building.

Since the day the spire was completed, it has been obsolete. The only thing inside it is an electric hoist which is used to raise and lower the three-ton brass chandelier that hangs in the Central Lobby below. Yet the people who bustle through the Central Lobby miss one of the splendours of Westminster which is hidden from sight above their heads; an enormous brick funnel with, near its apex, an octagon of windows, each with eight divisions, which pour light down onto a dusty dome above the Central Lobby ceiling. This spire has about it the dramatic quality of the west end of a great cathedral, and remains hidden and unknown.

Barry's original ideas for the Central Hall also included much bigger windows than he was able to put in. To lighten it, he commissioned an Italian, Salviati, to create the mosaics for its ceiling to 'give a general cheerfulness and lightness to the place'. He acted without anyone's authority, but he thought the results were very fine, although he much regretted his failure to set marble columns round the walls. Among the mosaics, Barry had the artist include the symbols of England, Ireland and Scotland. As the guides tell their flocks when they steer them through the Central Lobby today, there is no Welsh symbol among all that carving and elaborate gilding. We do not, intone the guides, want leaks in our roof!

Work began next on the Clock Tower which, like so much else in the Palace, precipitated its own series of arguments and accusations of bad faith. There had been a clock tower at Westminster since 1365 when, so tradition said, Sir Ralph Heigham, the Lord Chief Justice of the King's Bench, (which sat in Westminster Hall nearby), had manipulated the law to help a poor man who was in trouble, and the King had fined his judge 800 marks as a sign of Royal disapproval at such mercy. The money had been used to build a clock tower – the builder was Henry Yevele, the man who built Westminster Hall – and there the clock tower stood until Sir Christopher Wren pulled it down in 1698. He did so with great reluctance, for he thought that he could repair it for £1,500, and that the result would be well worth the money. Wren wrote as much to the Lords of the Treasury, who were then responsible for it, asking them to 'yet pardon your Surveyor if out of duty he modestly aske whether it be better to pull down a public building upon so small a consideration, or to repaire it with advantage to the Beauty of the Towne, which wou'd most certainly be done in any of our neighbouring countries who are more sensible than wee, that to adorne their Towns is a lasting benefit to the poor . . .' But down it had to come.

The great bell in the Clock Tower, which had been cast by Master John Belleyetere in 1367, weighed just over four tons. For over three centuries it had tolled the hours for the judges in the Westminster Hall law courts, and once saved the neck of a young sentry who, in William II's reign, was accused of being asleep while on duty at Windsor Castle. No, said the sentry at his court-martial, he had not been asleep because he had heard the bell at Westminster strike thirteen at midnight that night. That, it turned out, is precisely what Great Tom, so many miles away at Westminster, had done, so the sentry was given a free pardon by His Majesty.

After the Clock Tower was pulled down, Great Tom was given to the Westminster Vestry, who sold it for £385.17s.6d. to St Paul's Cathedral. It fell off its carriage and was smashed on reaching Temple Bar on its way to the City, but it was recast and, in 1716, hoisted into position in St Paul's, where it remains to this day. On the rare occasions when Big Ben is silent, Great Tom takes over as the nation's timekeeper.

These were the traditions that Barry had to follow when he came to designing his Clock Tower for the New Palace. His tower had to be big enough to take the world's largest clock; it had to be an enormous chimney; in addition, the tower was to be the world's most famous, but least known, prison. In its time the Clock Tower became all three; and it is still, in theory, a prison.

By 1844, ten years after the old Palace had been burnt down, the whole site at Westminster was an enormous mass of scaffolding, which was in itself a great attraction for the crowds of tourists who flocked to see what was happening. The work was hidden behind high fences and heavy gates through which wide-wheeled carts, drawn by teams of horses, continually disappeared with their loads of stone and bricks and wood and iron. Then, mysteriously, as the years went by, above the corner of the fences by Westminster Bridge, and immediately across the road from the house in which Barry was born, there began to appear the bottom part of the new Clock Tower. Like the rest of the Palace, it was seated on many feet of poured concrete, and its design had given Barry endless problems. He worked over plan after plan and scrapped them one by one. The great clock somehow had to blend in with the proportions of the whole design, without appearing top-heavy. There had to be room for all the clock's mechanisms and bells; there also had to be space for a chimney, or air-shaft, as part of Dr Reid's endless demands for his ventilating system. There had to be room for a prison cell, which was actually a moderately comfortable room complete with yellow flock wallpaper, for anyone the Commons might decide to detain during its pleasure. Finally, Barry had to make the galling admission to himself – even if he was careful not to share it with anyone else – that he owed a great deal of the project's success to the young and eccentric Augustus Pugin.

The crowds who watched the work going on knew nothing of all this. What they saw was that, somehow, an enormous tower was being built at Westminster without, it seemed, any scaffolding at all; for the Clock Tower was being built entirely from the inside outwards. Masons and bricklayers worked from a platform inside the Tower, and the platform was designed to travel upwards as the Tower itself grew. It was a brilliant piece of Victorian ingenuity. Iron rails were laid on wooden beams, and a travelling crane moved slowly round on those rails, bringing the building materials up from far below. A steam engine chugged away, and the whole thing could be raised up, little by little, on six giant screws. The platform cost £700 to put together, but it proved to be so efficient that it took twice as many men as usual on the ground below to prepare stone for the man above.

Building the New Palace
Work on the building of the New Palace became one of the great sights of London. No estimates were asked for or given with Barry's plans, but it was expected to cost about £800,000 and take six years to build. It eventually cost over £2,000,000 and took about 25 years to build

By October 1858, the Tower was almost completed, and the great bell, Big Ben itself, was very, very slowly hoisted up through the central shaft and into position. From its base at river level to the very top of its gilded finial, the Tower had grown to be 316 feet high and about 40 feet square. In the elaborate Gothic traceries and gilded decorations which Pugin designed for the tower he carved the inscriptions, under each clockface: '*Domine salvam fac reginam Victorian primam*'. This was a phrase Pugin used again and again in decorating the New Palace, and is a prayer for the Queen from the Catholic Latin mass. Perhaps the obsessively Catholic Pugin was making a wry joke by quoting, so prominently, the Roman mass in the Palace which was the heart of the Protestant establishment.

Dr Reid had, on this rare occasion, been of some accidental use to Barry, for the shaft that he had insisted on installing in the Clock Tower proved to be a useful means of transporting material and equipment for the clock. The shaft was, of course, all part of Reid's extraordinary ventilating system for the Palace – a system which, in small part, was still in use until the First World War. A large furnace was always kept burning at the base of the Clock Tower; used air was funnelled into the Clock Tower from other parts of the Palace and it was then drawn up, by the hot air from the furnace, high over the rooftops of London.

That hot air would have wafted up past the prison cell in the lower part of the Tower (a prison room had been included in the very earliest plans for the Palace, but not in the same place) on the night of 21 May, 1880, when Charles Bradlaugh was its last occupant. In 1846, when the paint on the walls could scarcely have been dry, a Mr Smith O'Brien, who had refused to sit on the English Railway Committee, was locked up there, but Bradlaugh was the Tower's most famous prisoner. He was an atheist who, when he was eventually returned as an MP, refused to take the oath of allegience to Queen Victoria because, he said, the words in it were 'idle and meaningless'. Tremendous arguments followed in the Commons when Bradlaugh tried to take his own form of oath, and he was eventually commanded by Mr Speaker Bouverie Brand, to be placed in the custody of the Serjeant-at-Arms. Bradlaugh spent one reasonably comfortable night in the Clock Tower, where his friends dropped in to visit him, and then he was released the next day. In due course, he was allowed to affirm instead of swearing on the Bible, and so took his place in the Commons.

Once the Clock Tower had finally been built, and the clock was in good working order, it was decided that it could be used as a signal tower to inform London – or, at any rate, part of London – that Parliament was at work. In 1885, Thomas Ayrton, the first Commissioner of Works, installed a high-powered gas lamp at the top of the Tower and every night, whenever either House was sitting, a man had to toil up the 335 spiralling steps to the belfry, and then up a ladder to light it. At first it could be seen only from West London where, it was

In Durance Vile Charles
Bradlaugh in the Prison
Room in the Clock Tower.
Bradlaugh was put there,
after great disturbances in
the Commons when he
refused to take the oath, for
one night in 1880. The
prison room was
elaborately decorated with
yellow and silver flock
wallpaper designed by
Pugin. The prison room is
now used as a staff rest
room

assumed, all the people who had any connection with Parliament lived. MPs with less splendid addresses protested, and so the Ayrton light was changed to shine out for 360 degrees over the nation's – and then the world's – capital.

The Clock Tower was not completely finished when Barry died in 1860 and work on it, and on the greatest of the three Westminster towers, the Victoria Tower, was taken over by his son, Edward. Of the three, the Victoria Tower was to prove the least successful as a technical achievement, although its design and construction were well ahead of their day.

Originally, it was to be called the King's Tower – William IV was still on the throne when the plans were first drawn up – and Barry always saw it as the great ceremonial entrance for a Royal palace. The Palace of Westminster was to be a legislative castle, and the King's Tower its keep. It was the biggest and tallest tower in the world when it was built – it was taller than the early American skyscrapers – and everything about it was, and remains, on the grandest possible scale. Planning its construction caused Barry endless trouble, and Dr Reid inevitably wanted room for his ventilation schemes; windows and turrets and decorations were arranged and rearranged until the final designs were drawn up.

At the base of the Victoria Tower, Barry designed the Royal Entrance, with Gothic vaulting rising to 60 feet to form a triumphal entrance for the monarch at the State Opening of Parliament. Above the vaulted roof of the Royal Entrance, Barry placed a framework of four cast-iron girders, each weighing twelve tons, bedded into walls six feet thick. On those girders rested the base of cast-iron columns, tapering from fourteen inches in diameter at the bottom to eight inches at the top, and it was around these girders that the whole tremendous structure was built. The roof alone, made of cast-iron girders with cast-iron tiles, weighs 276 tons. The height from the ground to the top of the 120 foot wrought iron flagpole is 395 feet. The gilded iron crown on top of the flagpole is forty-two inches across. Nearly 30,000 tons of stone, bricks and iron were used to build it; as little wood as possible was used to try to make it fireproof. This great weight almost certainly began to slip before the Tower was finished, for it was built partly on the quicksand of Thorney Island, and even a 10 foot thick bed of concrete was not sufficient to support it properly.

As well as being designed as a Royal Entrance, the Victoria Tower was also earmarked as a place to store state documents. A good deal of time and money was wasted while politicians and officials argued about what papers should be stored there, and an extra 50 feet had to be added to the original plans in an attempt to meet their wishes. In the end, a spiral staircase, made of wrought iron and mahogany, curved up 416 lattice-work steps through the eight floors, giving access to each of the eight rooms on every floor. In an effort to make the place as fireproof as possible, the rooms each had iron doors set in iron frames, and every one had a little Judas-hole to peer through, making the doors look like prison cells. Today, only 80 feet of that remarkable spiral staircase remains, and the little cell-like rooms have been changed into a depository of the most modern and efficient kind.

To build such a daring edifice in the middle of the nineteenth century took all the ingenuity of Barry and his team. The foreman George Allen was, as even his brow-beaten workmen had to admit, something of a genius when it came to inventing scaffolding to build at such entirely new scales of construction. A climbing scaffold was designed, weighing forty tons, which could be screwed up in six-foot stages, by gangs of men straining at cranks. On it was perched a 'Gough's Patent' steam engine, and there it chugged away, burning three hundredweight of coal in its five-hour day, hauling up four tons of stone or bricks or iron at a time. The engine cost £1,800 to fix on the scaffolding, but in the end everything worked with quite extraordinary efficiency and safety.

Ingenious scaffolding, though, was obviously not enough to ensure that the basic design of the Victoria Tower was safe, and although it stood for nearly a century without apparent danger, by 1936 a great bandage of large wooden beans had been tied round it to strengthen the stonework. During the Second World War it provided extra support against the wartime air raids, although the top part caught fire and burnt furiously during the air raid of 10 May, 1941, which destroyed the Chamber of the House of Commons.

Some years before these wartime dangers threatened, the Victoria Tower had been abandoned to become steadily more and more unkempt and derelict. The unique collection of invaluable state documents that was kept there, was stuffed into the iron-doored rooms, and then left largely to look after itself, unchecked and often unlisted and unrecorded. The Victoria Tower became, it was officially said, 'exceedingly damp and unbelievably filthy', and both the documents and the Tower into which they were piled were gradually falling to pieces. After the war work began to put the Tower to rights. Over 400 tons of material was taken out of the structure, and steel girders were inserted to bear the massive weight of the roof. On 15 October, 1959, sixteen 20-ton jacks very gently lifted the roof-load onto the steel girders, and this great Victorian monument settled back to begin life anew.

That new life was to be as a thoroughly up-to-date archive of some three million priceless parliamentary documents. The documents go back to the first surviving Act of Parliament of 1497 – which deals with apprenticeships in the worsted industry in Norfolk – and they include perhaps the archive's most precious possession: the death warrant of Charles I. Amongst the collection, there is also an eighteenth century taxing act which is nearly a quarter of a mile long. The documents are all stored in over five miles of steel shelves on twelve floors, carefully air-conditioned and humidified. A far cry from the pre-war days when one man kept a vague record in one small notebook.

Today the Victoria Tower, visualised by Barry as the keep of a great castle, still fulfils one of the purposes of a keep – that is, as a look-out post. On every state opening, soldiers from the Royal Corps of Signals are stationed in one of the turrets overlooking Whitehall and Parliament Square, and as the Royal procession comes trotting into view far below, they signal to the Royal Horse Artillery, a couple of miles away in Hyde Park, to fire the Royal Salute precisely on time, as the Irish State Coach swings under Barry's ceremonial arch at the foot of the Tower. Above them, the Union flag, one of three sizes flown from the flag mast according to the strength of the wind (the largest is 36 feet by 18 feet) is lowered, and the Royal Standard is raised in its place. The flags are kept, skilfully folded, in a lofty room just beneath the cast-iron roof of the Tower, and they are flown from 10 a.m. until dusk (from 9 a.m. on Fridays) on days when either House is sitting. Since neither House normally sits until 2.30 p.m., the fact that a Union flag is flying from the Victoria Tower means simply that they intend to sit that day, not necessarily that they are actually sitting.

When Barry was buried in Westminster Abbey, just across the road from the Palace, the Union flag flew at half-mast from the temporary flagstaff that had been rigged up, because the greatest work of his Great Work had not yet been finished. Barry's statue was erected by grudging politicians inside the Palace that he had built for them; on his knee Barry held the plans for the keep of his great castle – the plans for the Victoria Tower.

CHAPTER SEVEN

Who Built It?

Work went on at Westminster long after the Commons was completed in 1852; long after the death of Pugin in the same year; long after the death of Barry, aged 65, in 1860. Barry's son, Edward, took over from his father, and was responsible for designing one of the most famous features of the Palace – the elegant arcade of arches in New Palace Yard. By 1870, however, both Houses had had enough, and they decided that their Palace was finished, twenty-five years after it had been started with an estimated building time of six years. Edward Barry was sacked in a letter from the Assistant Secretary of the Office of Works, which, said an MP, 'no gentleman would send to his butler'.

Edward Barry The son of Sir Charles Barry, who took over from his father as architect of the Palace of Westminster. He was responsible for the famous arcade in New Palace Yard. He was eventually sacked for the delays and expense of his work

Perhaps both Houses had, by that time, become thoroughly tired of the Barrys' and the public feuding which had broken out between Sir Charles's heirs and the family of his designer, Augustus Welby Pugin.

The families of both men were hardly worthy of their brilliant fathers. The quarrel which broke out between them was principally the result of vituperative public accusations by Pugin's son Edward, a highly self-opinionated pamphleteer of unstable and irascible temper who once, it is said, silenced the Duke of Cambridge in a swearing match before resigning his commission from a yeomanry regiment. The Reverend Alfred Barry, D.D., Principal of Cheltenham College, by contrast, was a careful, rather self-important and devious man, and one of Sir Charles's five sons. Edward Pugin and the Reverend Alfred Barry settled down, in the fine Victorian tradition, to squabble over their dead parents' reputations.

The back-biting and bitterness began in 1867, fifteen years after Pugin's death and seven years after Barry's when, as a result of criticism of the 'lamentable gables' on part of the New Palace, the younger Pugin went into print. He wrote a pamphlet called: *Who was the Art Architect of the Houses of Parliament? A Statement of Facts, founded on the letters of Sir Charles Barry and the Diaries of Augustus Welby Pugin. London: 1867.* The document carried on for 60 pages, claiming that the elder Pugin had 'actually originated and designed the whole of the elevations of the Palace, that he made the sections and working drawings for every portion of the building, and that, generally, every detail, both externally and internally, was his work.'

Without, apparently, pausing to wonder what on earth an 'art architect' could be, the Reverend Alfred Barry, who was his father's biographer, rushed to his defence with his own pamphlet. It was called *Sir Charles Barry and Mr Pugin. The Architect of the New Palace; reply to the Statements of Mr E. Pugin. By Alfred Barry, D.D.* This sufficiently interested the public to run into two editions, and brought the inevitable reply from Edward Pugin: *Notes on the Reply of the Rev. Alfred Barry, D.D., Principal of Cheltenham College, to the 'Infatuated Statements' made by E. W. Pugin, on the Houses of Parliament. By E. Welby Pugin. Second Edition, Revised and enlarged. London: 1868.*

When he brought out his biography of his father, Alfred Barry wrote an addendum, claiming that the relations between Barry and Pugin had never been broken by any dispute or estrangement. Alfred had, however, gone to considerable lengths in the book itself to point out that his father 'knew of the almost inevitable risk which he incurred of being supposed to wear other men's laurels, of having all that was good or spirited in the details attributed to Mr Pugin, and of finding it difficult or impossible to control an enthusiasm, which might work in what seemed to him undesirable methods'.

Both families settled down to raking over all the tittle-tattle they could find. There was much peering at diary entries made by Pugin about work he had done for Barry, and of payments he had received. There was the obviously fictitious claim by Alfred Barry that the initials 'A.W.P.', which Edward had found on a drawing of the Royal Robing Room, did not refer to Augustus Welby Pugin but to 'Albertus Walliae Princeps'. Both sides thus scored points against the other.

For instance, in Barry's favour there was the irrefutable fact that Pugin senior had said himself that he did not create the Houses of Parliament. 'Barry's grand plan', said Pugin, 'was immeasurably superior to any that I could at any time have produced, and had it been otherwise, the commissioners would have killed me in a twelve-month. No, sir, Barry after all is "the right man in the right place;" what more could we wish?' There was, too, the tricky problem for the pro-Pugin faction that, at the time when Barry won the competition to build the New Palace in 1835, the only thing that Pugin had actually built was his quite extraordinary house at Salisbury, and he had had absolutely no other practical architectural experience, whereas Barry already ran an extensive and prospering architectural practice.

There was, however, the problem of the letters – those that mysteriously disappeared and those that somehow survived. There was also the problem of Sir Charles's attitude towards the Barry family. When Barry was asked for particulars of Pugin's work for the New Palace he snapped: 'My dear fellow, there are no particulars; what particulars could there be?' This about a man who had done thousands of drawings for Barry as he built the Palace! Then, just before Pugin died, it was proposed to pay him an official pension, and it was suggested that Barry should become one of its trustees, since Pugin was now hopelessly mad and mentally incapable of looking after his own affairs. Barry, however, called on Mrs Pugin, who was then at Hammersmith, nursing her sick husband, to ask her not to draw him into the arrangements. A family friend, the Reverend J. M. Glennie, who saw Barry because Mrs

Pugin was out, wrote years later: 'My impression of the interview was one of great disgust, both at the want of feeling shown and the reserved and politic way in which he seemed to be acting; and accordingly I advised Mrs Pugin, whatever she might do, on no account to communicate with him as a friend, and I believe she never did so.'

The Reverend Glennie was mistaken. Mrs Pugin did not take his advice, for after her husband's death she told Barry that she had found a number of letters her late husband had written to Sir Charles in 1835–36 – the years when Barry was working flat out on his first plan for the New Palace. 'Good heavens', said Barry. 'I thought he had destroyed all my letters.' Barry thereupon asked the young Edward Pugin, then aged twenty-three, to dinner and to bring with him the letters so that they could read through them together. The eminent architect and the young man talked amiably over dinner, and when Barry casually asked if Edward had the letters, his guest took them out of his greatcoat pocket and handed them over. 'It is too late to read through them now', said Barry. 'Leave them to me and I'll look through them later.' Edward Pugin took him at his word, and left the sixty-seven letters from his father to Barry behind. They have never been seen since.

Barry, a much more methodical man than Pugin, had carefully kept all his letters, and the Reverend Alfred did not hesitate to use them in his father's cause. In one of them, dated October 1844, when Barry and Pugin were working together again after a seven-year break, Pugin

Below left: *'House of Peers'* Pugin produced an endless flow of drawings for the immensely grand and elaborate decorations of the House of Lords which both he and Barry saw as the climax for their designs for the Palace. The design of carved heads of Kings is repeated dozens of times in the Chamber

Below: *'Side elevation of throne'* Pugin's immensely detailed drawings for the throne in the Lords. He dashed off drawings of this kind at high speed, sometimes going out in storms in his boat in the Channel, and sketching under the shelter of an immense cloak

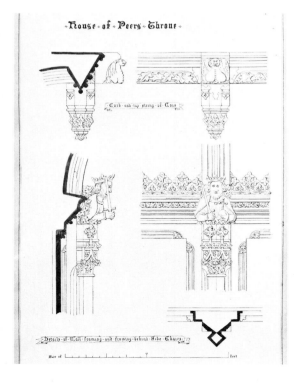

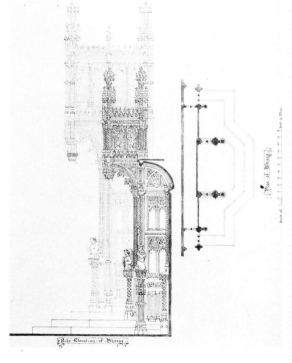

wrote to Barry: 'I am sure I can never do you real service except in absolute detail; you should fully make up your mind as to every arrangement and then turn the small work over to me.' Alfred claimed later that Pugin – 'no man was more original' than he was – 'for the sake of his art was willing to accept a distinctly subordinate position, and to work under the superintendence and control of another. His acceptance of the post (drawing details of Barry's plans), and the spirit with which he discharged his duties, showed the generosity and unselfishness which were his well-known characteristics. Nor, on the other hand, could Mr Barry be unaware of the danger of calling in a too powerful coadjutator.'

So Pugin – 'my comet', Barry called him – rushed around the growing Palace, shouting with laughter and never still or without some great scheme in his head. His and Barry's sons, Edward and Alfred, later managed to quote a variety of people who supported their respective causes, and did precious little good to the reputations of their fathers in the process.

Ironically, however, the most famous part of the entire, vast, eight acre Palace, turned out to be a perfect example of Barry–Pugin co-operation – even if Barry did not admit it. All over the world the Houses of Parliament, London, Great Britain itself, are symbolised by the Clock Tower; Big Ben as it is invariably, but wrongly, called. Compared with Barry's many problems in building the New Palace, the Clock Tower proved to be one of the trickiest, for he could not get its proportions right, or work out the way to handle such an enormous clock in such a high tower.

Barry's son, Alfred, explained: 'The clock tower was the one feature of the building which gave the greatest trouble, and for which design after design was made and rejected. It was to be what its name implies: the clock was to be the one prominent feature, not a mere accessory – treated as an architectural ornament. For practical purposes it was to be raised on the highest story (sic), and made of immense size; the ornamental character of the whole front required that the lower part of the tower should be faced with delicate panelling, and yet a 'top-heavy' effect must be carefully avoided. It was at once decided that the lower part should be solid with but slight openings. To make the clock-story duly prominent all sorts of devices were thought of, till at last an example was remembered in which the whole clock-story was made to project beyond the body of the tower. The example was eagerly caught at; the example quoted differed in almost every respect from the character to be designed, and endless modifications were needed; but the general principle is preserved, and the result is one of the most striking features of the building. Still the termination remained; designs and models tried over and over again; some forms appeared deficient in lightness, others were rejected as too ecclesiastical; till at last the form was devised which we now see.'

What the Reverend Alfred Barry omitted to mention in this description of the designing of the Clock Tower was that the remembered example that was 'so eagerly caught at' was, inevitably, a design by Pugin. In 1836 the latter had begun to work for a strange, but very rich, Catholic gentleman, Charles Scarisbrick, of Scarisbrick Hall in Lancashire. The following year, Pugin submitted rough sketches for a clock tower as part of a drastic rebuilding plan for the Hall, and he made detailed drawings two years later. The Clock Tower at Westminster was not begun until 1853, and Barry told Pugin he was still worried about the working drawings in 1852. It is quite certain that Pugin's Scarisbrick clock tower design did bear an immediate affinity to the one at Westminster, although in size, in relation to the rest of the building and the way the 'termination' was handled, it was very different. Pugin's great achievement at Scarisbrick was to project the clock face and its surround beyond the walls of the tower. It is precisely this same feature which makes the Clock Tower at Westminster so successful. Perhaps it was Pugin who had the original inspiration, and Barry who adapted it skillfully to its surroundings. In other words, the perfect partnership.

All that really matters now, 150 years later, is that two men of genius came together at exactly the right time and built, by whatever standards, the greatest single undertaking the British nation had yet attempted. Both men made their gifted, personal contribution to a work which has deeply influenced, and deeply impressed, the world ever since. Trollope, in *The Warden*, called the New Palace 'Mr Barry's halls of eloquence'. Not quite. They were Mr Pugin's, too.

CHAPTER EIGHT

Smells, Bells and the Great Ventilators

Londoners called it the Great Stink. Never was there a more appropriate name. The River Thames stank to high heaven. It curled its way through the greatest city the world had ever seen – and took with it the foul refuse from all the millions who lived and worked there. It was infested with pestilence; an open sewer that sloshed around the walls of great palaces and filthy slums, that spread disease and stench round the nation's capital.

Politicians at Westminster had complained for generations about the smell and judges sitting in solemn conclave in Westminster Hall sometimes had to adjourn their courts because the stink was so unsupportable – and that in an age where susceptibilities were a good deal less delicate than they are today. When the tide went out, the banks of the river – unrestricted by today's great stone walls – revealed acres of filthy black mud into which trickled the outfall of dozens of sewers from the houses and factories along the river's edge. Along that same edge Parliament decided to build its new Palace.

Nearly four hundred sewers spewed into the Thames between Putney and Blackwall; the Palace of Westminster added one more. Sewage simply spilled, untreated, from the Palace into the Thames through gutters that were washed out by the high tides. Riverboat owners complained that trippers would not use their boats because the smell was so bad. One MP told the House that when he had recently travelled on an omnibus over Westminster Bridge everyone on board had had to hold their handkerchiefs over their faces and 'one lady who had brought a smelling-bottle with her had it rudely snatched from her'. Slaughter-houses, tanners' yards, knackers' yards, bone and skin boilers, glue

Curing the 'Great Stink'
Vast public works were undertaken in the middle of the nineteenth century – like this pumping station for the London drainage system at Abbey Milles – to install a workable system of sanitation throughout the capital. Something had to be done about MPs' constant complaints of the stench from the Thames that flowed past Westminster

FARADAY GIVING HIS CARD TO FATHER THAMES;

And we hope the Dirty Fellow will consult the learned Professor.

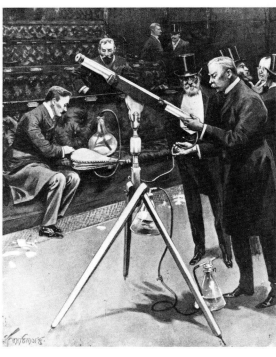

factories, soap-works and breweries all poured their refuse straight into the river, where it was carried backwards and forwards with the tides, beneath the very Terrace walls which the Commons and Lords had had built for themselves. On hot summer days the stench penetrated through Mr Barry's new Gothic windows and, it sometimes seemed, through the very walls themselves. The committee rooms along the river frontage of the New Palace sometimes became unbearable to work in and sheets of canvas, soaked in chloride of lime, were hung against them to try to keep out the strench. Nothing really worked. To make matters worse, in the winter, when the stench was not nearly so bad, everyone shivered. The Members eventually decided that the New Palace must be made more bearable in the heat of summer and the cold of winter. In the days before electricity became available this was far more easily said than done; so both Peers and Commons allowed themselves to be taken in by two Victorian charlatans of the most spectacular kind; they were Dr David Boswell Reid and Sir Goldsworthy Gurney, the Great Ventilators. Dr Reid reduced the Palace to a hole-ridden fire trap; Sir Goldsworthy Gurney came within an ace of blowing the whole structure sky-high.

Dr Reid was an Edinburgh chemistry teacher, who had apparently managed to impress a party of MPs when they visited his lecture rooms during the summer meeting in Scotland of the British Association for the Advancement of Science in 1834 – only a few months before the Palace was destroyed by fire. With vivid memories of the miseries they had suffered from heat and cold in the old House of Commons, MPs decided that their new palace should be as well ventilated as modern science would allow, so Dr Reid was selected, from among other

Above left: *The Great Stink* Endless scientific experiments went on in an attempt to make the Thames, which was a running sewer through the centre of London, more wholesome and less of a health risk. The smell became so bad that pleasure boat captains complained that day-trippers refused any longer to go for outings on the river

Above: *'The Breath of Parliament'* 'Analysing the atmosphere at Westminster. Our sketch shows the scene as an analysis was being made during the dinner hour at the House. The instrument upon the tripod is for the detection of microbes; the other is for determining the proportion of carbonic'

candidates, to do the job. No one, of course, told Barry, the architect of the Palace, who found Reid foisted on him whether he wanted him or not; and Barry most certainly did not want him. Reid was a small-minded, short-tempered querulous liar, and such a combination, which clashed badly with Barry's heavy-handed pomposity and resentment, was certain to lead to trouble. It did. 'No architect in his senses is likely to refuse advice', wrote Barry's son, years later 'in the many and various questions which must meet him in his work, from those who have made such special questions their peculiar study. But to divide power is to paralyse responsibility.' Reid was appointed to heat and ventilate the Palace in January 1840, at £500 a year.

Reid's one basic working principle was simply that hot air rises, and on this principle he based his extraordinary scheme to heat and ventilate the biggest building in the kingdom. Barry built the Palace round a series of courtyards to provide light and air, and, wherever possible, he had used stone and iron to make it fireproof. Reid now insisted on shafts being inserted behind walls and under floor cavities, an innovation which would send flames roaring through the Palace from end to end. Nevertheless the Commons were impressed. Reid had already constructed an engine to heat and ventilate their temporary House, which had been set up in the old Court of Requests after the 1834 fire and, in that restricted place, his plans had worked. The great chimney he had built for his furnace reared up over the scaffolding as the rest of the New Palace went up. To prove his theory, Reid had marched a troop of Guardsmen into the Chamber and puffed gunpowder smoke, ether and the smell of oranges at them through the new system – and they had survived. Why should the MPs not enjoy such comforts?

Reid's plans were stunningly simple. Fresh air was to be drawn in from the top of the Clock Tower and the Victoria Tower, circulated through the Palace by means of great fires that would be kept constantly burning, and then expelled through the spire which he insisted on Barry constructing above the Central Lobby. The roof was criss-crossed by galvanised iron pipes, with portholes every few yards to allow them to be swept, which led the smoke and the 'vitiated air' – a favourite phrase with the ventilators – from the rooms and Chambers to the Central Lobby spire. In the Chambers themselves, air was to circulate through grilles under the floor, heated by steam pipes in the winter and cooled over cold pipes in the summer, and then it would, naturally, rise through gratings in the ceilings and wend its way out over the roofs of the Palace.

That was the theory. Although Barry had no better ideas to put forward himself, he was quite right in claiming to committee after committee that the scheme simply would not work. Barry complained that Reid refused to produce any drawings of his plans and that 'for want of detailed drawings, such as are usually furnished by ventilators, an extraordinary number of flues has been introduced into the building, whereby it had been rendered less solid'. The haggling between the two men went on, amidst pressure from the Lords to get their new Chamber completed. Reid proposed eight different schemes, and Barry accused him of being the main cause of the delay. In the end, Barry got Reid banned from the works for a time: 'I have to request that the visits of yourself and your assistants to the works, may for the future be discontinued', Barry wrote to Reid in 1846. 'I have given orders to close the doorway by which you have lately been in the habit of obtaining access to them.'

Naturally, Barry made sure that Reid's plans cost a great deal more than his own; Reid's estimate for ventilating and warming the entire building was £62,000; Barry's was £39,000. Both were careful to hide their plans – and Barry much doubted if Reid had any worth seeing. Reid alleged that Barry had deliberately bricked up his ventilation shafts to make sure the system would not work.

The stalemate was broken by the most unworkable and illogical arrangement possible. Barry was given charge of heating and ventilating in the House of Lords – their Lordships had got more than a little tired of the difficult Dr Reid; but the Commons kept Reid on as their ventilator. Inevitably Barry immediately changed Reid's system round, with the air coming into the Lords' end of the Palace not only from the Victoria Tower, but also from ground floor level, and the two systems were separated from each other by a series of screens under the Central Lobby. Barry explained to yet another committee that his system used steam and hot water, 'and the motive power for the supply and discharge of air, independent of gravity caused by difference in temperature, consist of a powerful fan worked by a steam engine, local rarefactions, and steam jets'.

The Commons, though, stuck with Reid, in spite of the fact that Barry had told a committee that there was 'nothing whatever that is new' in the ventilator's theories. 'The only novelty', said Barry, 'and a startling one it is, consists in the mode of applying it to such a vast and important pile of building as the new Palace of Westminster.' Still, the MPs let Reid carry on until they finally moved into their new Chamber in 1852. At this point they at last realised the man was a charlatan; his system simply did not work, and they sat there, in great discomfort, to prove it. They could smell cooking from the Speaker's kitchen; they could smell horses left outside the entrance to the Ladies' Gallery – which is why, until very recently, cars could still not be parked alongside the wall by that entrance – they were cold in winter, hot in summer – *and* it was draughty. 'I am of the opinion', said one MP, 'that until some of the more robust Members who now occupy the Treasury benches are ventilated into another place . . . we shall have no remedy for the crying evils to which we are now subject.' Some Members complained of a burning sensation round the head; a swelling in the temples; and some 'of a terrible sensation, resembling that which distinguishes a fit of apoplexy'. All this meant, of course, that Reid would have to go. In

September 1852, Dr David Boswell Reid, was sacked as Ventilator to the House of Commons.

It was time to invite Goldsworthy Gurney, a Cornish inventor and one of Reid's rivals, to have a go. This Gurney did with such gusto that he very nearly took the place of poor, mad, deluded, tortured Guy Fawkes as the man who came nearest to blowing up Parliament. Gurney apparently had a predilection for gunpowder; he set off 60 pounds of it in the House of Lords to test their air supply – 'by flashing small portions in rapid succession . . . I watched the first appearance of the smoke in various parts, its apparent quantity, and noted the time it took in coming and going out'.

Naturally, Gurney turned the whole system round, and instead of drawing in air through the Clock Tower and the Victoria Tower, he drew it in from ground level, and expelled it through the Towers. Both Towers had large furnaces at the bottom to provide the up–draught, and small turrets that had three fish-tail gas jets burning inside to help the upward flow of air. The scheme did not do much good; the Commons was still uncomfortable – Sir Henry Verney kept a pair of worsted stockings and gaiters in the House to try to keep his feet warm – and, above all, the Thames still stank.

One earnest seeker after pure air suggested that fountains of fresh water should play in all the corridors and rooms of the Palace, on the peculiar assumption that the water would absorb the smells. Not surprisingly, no one took up the idea. Gurney suggested dredging deep channels parallel to both shores of the Thames into which the sewage was supposed to drift, but MPs doubted if it would work, and insisted that the old remedy should be continued – pouring ton after ton of lime into the water to try to purify it. Gurney busied himself being scientific; he hung pieces of paper soaked in acetate of lead in the Chambers of the Lords and Commons, in their Libraries, in the corridors and on the Terrace. They proved that there was sulphurated hydrogen in the air, which probably impressed the committee no end as they sat in their room behind curtains soaked in disinfectant. Yet somehow the smell had to be kept in check. Goldsworthy Gurney had an idea.

Gurney believed that vitiated air could be burnt off in flares, rather on the lines of a modern North Sea gas flare. He wanted to close off all the open sewers in London, and erect a series of flares to get rid of the gases. So why not have one on top of the Clock Tower at Westminster? MPs were willing to give almost anything a try at this stage and Gurney went ahead. He arranged for the main Victoria Sewer to be connected to the flues in the Clock Tower which carried the vitiated air from the Palace, on the theory that the gases could then be flared off from high above the building. Unfortunately the flares would not light. Next, Gurney put a coal fire at the base of the Clock Tower and tried again; this time, the gases burned. One day, though, when Mr Joseph Bazalgette, the Chief Engineer of the Metropolitan Board of Works, was examining the pipe that led from the main sewer to the Clock Tower, he discovered that there was a leak from a fractured coal-gas pipe into the sewer, and only a trap-door in the sewer was stopping the coal-gas from reaching the furnace at the bottom of the Clock Tower. There had already been one small explosion, although no one was hurt and no damage done. If the full blast of coal-gas and sewer gas had reached the furnace, then the chances are that the Clock Tower would have taken off for the moon, and the rest of the Palace would have been destroyed with it.

Gurney, who so nearly blew up the Palace of Westminster, died knighted and respected in his bed. Guy Fawkes, a bumbling plotter of ludicrous incompetence, died in excruciating agony on the scaffold not far away, in Old Palace Yard. The furnace that Goldsworthy Gurney built remained there for many years, and the Tower itself retained its function as the world's most famous, if most unknown, chimney.

Guy Fawkes and the Gunpowder plotters Fawkes is in the centre, surrounded by his colleagues, all of whom were hanged, drawn and quartered

The Palace of Westminster still stank. Lord Randolph Churchill once moved, and achieved, the adjournment of the House half-way through a debate because of the foulness of the atmosphere, and experts continued to poke about the enormous Palace – as they do today – trying to find a way to keep the place warm and free of vitiated air. William J. Prim, one of a long line of resident engineers – literally resident, for he and his successors live within the Palace – seemed to have some sort of success in the early years of this century with a system that existed, roughly in the same form, until the House was destroyed during the Second World War. Under this system, thirty-five openings were constructed along the Terrace frontage of the Palace, through which air was drawn and passed through jets of water. In hot weather it then pushed through a dozen or more blocks of ice, each weighing a couple of hundredweight, and was finally blown into the Chambers by steam-driven fans. In cold weather, the air drawn in from the river frontage was passed over steam pipes and then drawn into the Chambers. Once inside either House, it passed through grilles in the floor, and then up through the elaborately gilded louvres near the roof, all carved, over and over again, with the 'Victoria Regina' inscription. When a real pea-souper London fog came down – and the Palace alone burnt eighty tons of coal a week as its contribution to that fog – the air was driven by fans through pads of cotton wool, three inches thick. 'This interesting process', a contemporary account recalls, 'simple, yet effective, practically keeps the fog at bay. Proof of its efficiency is to be found in the fact that the wool became perfectly black after a heavy fog.'

Below the old House of Commons and the House of Lords were 'equalising chambers' of much the same size as the Houses themselves where, in the gloom, attendants opened and closed doors and traps to send up hot or cold air into the rooms above their heads, according to the heat of the day or the heat of the debate.

'With the means at his command', said an enthusiastic journalist, 'the attendant on duty is enabled to maintain an equable temperature throughout the whole area of the House. To such a nicety is the system regulated that it has been known that the spot occupied by a Member in delicate health has had special attention bestowed upon it. The air in its upward course passes through the floor of the House, composed of perforated plates of cast-iron covered with a coarse netting of whipcord and the vitiated air finds an exit through the ceiling of the chamber.

As for lighting the Palace, Barry, Reid and Gurney all tried out their various theories, and all, more or less, failed to do so successfully. Candles were used in the old Houses before the fire, and Barry brought great gas lights into the Lords to glitter among all the paintings and gilded carvings. Their Lordships complained, not surprisingly, of the heat, and so the gas lamps were raised on pullies to make the atmosphere less oppressive. Many years later this resulted in a drama which might very easily have proved fatal. In July 1980 one of the elaborately carved bosses in the wooden ceiling came unglued and crashed down onto the benches below, missing Lord Shinwell by inches. Their Lordships hastily moved out of the House into the Royal Gallery while a survey of their roof was undertaken. This showed that the heat of the gas lamps over the forty or so years that they had burned, had so charred the roof that it had gradually, with the added wear of the years, begun to turn into dust. So an elaborate, costly and lengthy restoration – in fact, rebuilding – of their Lordships' roof had to begin.

This was rather an unkind fate for the Lords since they had, in the matter of electricity as in so much else, shown themselves to be a good deal more open to modern ideas and modern sciences than the Commons. The Lords had had electric lighting installed in 1883, but the Commons did not get round to doing so until nearly thirty years later in 1912. The Commons had allowed both Dr Reid and Gurney to have a go at lighting their Chamber, with varying degrees of success. Gurney had invented a light which, he claimed, was 'a new era in the science of illumination'. Barry also lit the Commons, but they then switched to Reid and finally, when he still could not get it right, to Gurney. None of the schemes really worked, in spite of the fact that in 1866 the gas supplied by the Chartered Gas Company from their works in Horseferry Road was costing £3,505, and was being pumped through thirty-eight meters in various parts of the Palace. Nowadays, a man comes from the Electricity Board once a month to read the sole meter in the basement of the Palace. The electricity bill is about £400 a week.

High above these thirty-eight gas meters burned the fish-tail gas jets behind the four opaline glass faces of the Great Clock of Westminster, and high above the clockfaces burned the sixty-eight gas jets that made up the Ayrton light and told the city that the Houses were still sitting. Three times a week two men struggled up the stairs to wind the clock mechanism, and as they worked away, hour after hour, they would indeed have had time – if not the energy – to reflect on the extraordinary story of the Great Clock and its bells, and the man who had created it all.

Edmund Beckett Denison, QC, was a thoroughly nasty piece of work. In an age of pomposity and self-righteous priggishness, he was more pompous, more self-righteous and certainly more litigious than most. Denison was an amateur horologist of very considerable ability, but he was utterly impossible to work with or to reason with. The Reverend Alfred Barry wrote miserably after his father's death: 'No one can question Mr Denison's ability, the attention he has devoted to the clock and bells, or his desire to do good public service. On the other hand, many besides Sir C. Barry have found serious difficulties in working with him, unless prepared to yield up their opinions entirely to his, or to submit to injurious imputations in the public press, or even in official correspondence. In the course of the work upon the great clock, Sir C. Barry was unfortunate enough to incur Mr Denison's hostility, and was assailed accordingly in no measured terms.' Those terms included a letter from Denison to *The Times* in which he wrote of the 'stupidity of Sir C. Barry and his crew of hand-makers and certificate writers'. Whatever he meant by 'hand-makers', it certainly was not intended to be a compliment, and it is not surprising that *The Times* finally refused to print any more of his letters. The Astronomer Royal, Professor George Airy, who worked with Denison on the clock designs, eventually could not stand him any longer, and resigned. But the fact is that, with all his many and unpleasant faults, Denison *did* know about clocks and bells.

Not that everyone agreed that a clock was necessary for the New Palace. *The Athenaeum* magazine said, loftily, in 1844, that it doubted its use when 'almost every mechanic carries a watch in his pocket'. Politicians, though, wanted the finest clock that money could buy, and the Office of Works planned 'a noble clock, indeed a king of clocks'. Yet even before it began to tick or its bells to ring, *The Times* complained that: 'The series of blunders and misconceptions, and misunderstandings, and squabbles respecting this clock are a disgrace to all concerned in it, and to the Government which permits them to go on.' Another journalist wrote rather grandly, 'The personalities that were freely exchanged between the contending parties are reminiscent rather of Eatanswill than of Westminster; the moods in which the contesting parties are shown are characteristic more of the boudoir than of the workshop or of the Senate House.' Which perhaps says something about that journalist's own private life, in view of the activities of the contesting parties.

Everyone had expected the Royal clockmaker, Benjamin Lewis Vulliamy, to be given the job of making the great clock. Eventually, however, it was agreed that there would be a limited competition between Vulliamy, Edward Dent, and Whitehurst of Derby. Vulliamy flounced out in a huff when the Astronomer Royal called his design 'a village clock of very superior quality', and Dent won the contract, with a very low price of £1,800, to build the clock to Denison's designs.

Right: *Big Ben* The bell that strikes the hour in the Great Clock of Westminster. It weighs $13\frac{1}{2}$ tons, and is cracked

Left: *Beneath the Palace of Westminster* Some fifteen miles of pipes were installed in the palace when it was built

Right: *Parliamentary cartoons by James Gillray* From a series of cartoons in the Whips' Office at No. 12, Downing Street. Each is based on a Parliamentary phrase. 1. *Majority* 2. *Calling to Order* 3. *Tellers* 4. *The Standing Order*

Left: *Edmund Beckett Denison* Denison, a lawyer and amateur horologist, designed the great clock

Far left: *The clock mechanism* The large metal sails act as brakes to control the fall of the weights when the bell strikes

Left: *The clock face* The four dials are each 23 ft across and the roman numerals two feet long

Right: *A ticket for the Coronation Banquet of George IV, 1821*

Previous pages, right: *The House of Commons*

Left: *The House of Lords* Before the Throne is the Woolsack on which the Lord Chancellor sits

Far left: *The House of Commons* The opposition benches to the left of the Speaker's chair. Above is the press gallery

Left: *The Speaker's Chair*

Below: *The House of Commons* The government benches are on the Speaker's right; the opposition to his left. The red lines are just two sword-widths apart

Right: *The Serjeant-at-Arms with the Mace* The Serjeant-at-arms, Major Victor Le Fanu, instructs a new deputy, Major Philip Wright, in the Mace ceremonial

Far right: *The Mace on the Table* The Mace rests on the Table by the Despatch Boxes. It was probably made in 1660, but it has no hallmark or makers' mark of any kind

Right: *The Mace on the Table of the Commons* The Mace, the symbol of Royal authority, must always be present when the House is sitting. Without it, the House is totally powerless. When the Mace is on the Table, the House is in full session

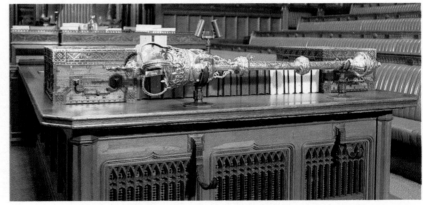

Right: *The Mace below the Table* When the Mace is below the Table, the House is in a committee of the whole House

Left: *The Serjeant-at-Arms*
The Serjeant-at-Arms, Major Victor Le Fanu, in his seat in the Commons Chamber. He is the only person in the Chamber allowed to wear a sword

Below: *The red lines*
Members may not cross the red lines when they are speaking

Above: *The Bar of the House* Only Members are allowed to cross the Bar of the House. Prisoners can be brought to the Bar and charged with a breach of privilege; the barrier is then pulled across. Normally, the barrier is open and only the white strip in the carpet marks the Bar

Right: *The door to the Commons* Members go from the Members' Lobby, beneath the bomb-damaged Churchill Arch, and into the Chamber. The Principal Doorkeeper stands by his chair

Left: *The Door of the Chamber* The damaged panel in the door on which Black Rod knocks to demand admittance at State Openings

Right: *A doorkeeper's badge* All the doorkeepers wear evening dress with silver-gilt badges. The badges have the royal coat of arms and Mercury, the messenger of the Gods. Some of the badges date to the early eighteenth century

Far right: *The Division Bell*

Right: *The Principal Doorkeeper* In the arm rest of his chair beneath the Churchill Arch, the lever which sets the division bells ringing throughout the Palace when a vote is called

Left: *The House of Commons snuff box* It is kept by the Principal Doorkeeper. Any Member may ask for a pinch of snuff before going into the Chamber

Left: *Doors behind the Speaker's Chair* The doors at the north end of the Chamber which lead to the ministerial offices

Right and below: *The Despatch Boxes* Normally they are used for Ministers and Shadow Ministers to rest their papers on. Inside them are kept the authorised and Douai versions of the Bible, and the Old Testament, and the copies of the oath which MPs have to swear before taking their seats

Below right: *The Clerk of the Commons* The Clerk sits, with two deputies to his left, in front of the Speaker's chair

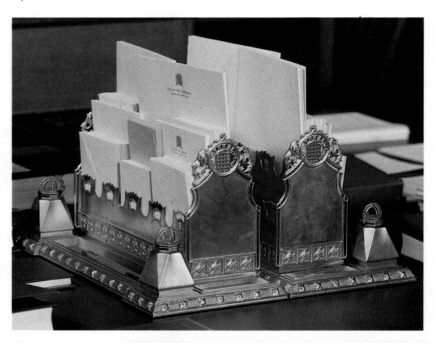

Left: *Letter racks on the Table of the House of Commons* The gilded racks were given to the rebuilt Commons after the last war by Southern Rhodesia

Right: *The House of Commons opera hat* The collapsible top hat which Members must wear if they want to raise a point of order during a division

Below: *The Member's oath* Every Member has to swear or affirm allegiance to the Queen

The Forty-eighth Parliament of the United Kingdom of Great Britain and Northern Ireland.

The Oath

I swear by Almighty God that I will be faithful and bear true Allegiance to Her Majesty Queen Elizabeth, Her Heirs and Successors according to Law

So help me God.

The Affirmation or Declaration

In lieu of the Oath required by Law I do solemnly, sincerely and truly declare and affirm that I will be faithful and bear true Allegiance to Her Majesty Queen Elizabeth, Her Heirs and Successors according to Law.

Date	Subscription of Members	Places for which returned
10/5/79	George Thomas	Cardiff West.

Above right: *Broadcasting Parliament* The commentary position which is technically outside the Chamber

Right: *The Airey Neave Memorial* His family crest was placed over the main door of the Commons Chamber after his assassination in New Palace Yard in 1979. Crests of Members killed in the two world wars are around the walls of the chamber

144

Left: *Prayer cards* Members can claim a place in the Chamber by putting a card behind the seat and being there for prayers at the beginning of the day's sitting

Below: *The Victorian Chamber* The introduction of a new Member. The Chamber was destroyed by bombs in 1941

Dent and Denison found, inevitably, that the space Barry had left in the tower for the clock was too small for Denison's specifications. Denison immediately criticised Barry, instead of blaming himself for not bothering to find out the exact measurements. Then Dent died, and there was a fine legal tussle before it was decided that his step-son, Frederick, could take over the contract. The clock was ready by 1855, at which time the bells still had not been cast, and so in 1856 Barry roofed in the tower and everything had to be hauled up on the inside – which was to produce a major problem when the bells finally did get put up.

There were, of course, furious rows about the design of the clock long before it was pulled into place. The masters, wardens, and court of assistants of the Clockmakers' Company of the City of London wanted the whole thing scrapped and started again – a suggestion which aroused Denison's most splenetic fury against 'a certain set of clock makers', and drew down accusations of underhand dealings by Barry and others. Matters became so strained between Denison and the Astonomer Royal who, between them, were supposed to be designing and organising the building of the new clock, that Airy resigned. Events, wrote Airy, had 'confirmed his opinion of (Denison's) mechanical ingenuity and horological knowledge', but events had also shown that 'their ideas of the mode of conducting public business were very different and had at last forced on him (Airy) the conviction that they could not with advantage profess to act in concert'.

Dent eventually completed the clock in 1855, and was paid £1,600 for his work – £200 less than he had expected. It was a fine achievement, whatever the atmosphere in which it had been made. The clock had to meet fifteen conditions, including the most stringent one that the first stroke of each hour must be accurate to one second, and that this must be checked twice daily by telegraph to the Greenwich Observatory; a condition that no longer applies as the clock is now checked electronically.

Then, of course, came the bells – and more furious rows. Barry wanted them to be made by George Mears at his Whitechapel Foundry but, as always, Denison knew better, and organised the contract for the great hour bell to go to Warner's, of Norton, near Stockton-on-Tees. There, the bell, weighing sixteen tons and the biggest ever attempted in the country, was cast on 6 August 1856. From Norton it was taken by train to West Hartlepool, and had its first mishap. It was dropped on the deck of the schooner that was to bring it down the coast to London; and on the way, it was nearly lost in a great storm. Still, it arrived, more or less safely in the Port of London, and was pulled, in triumph, on a great dray by a team of sixteen horses across Westminster Bridge and into New Palace Yard. The bell was the wonder of London. People turned out in their thousands to line the streets as it went by, and they were allowed behind the high fences and into the Yard to look at it. It was hoisted onto a great gallows to be tested, with its massive hammer

beating away regularly on the outside; for the bells of Westminster, unlike church bells, are fixed and then struck from outside instead of swinging and being tolled by clappers inside. There for nearly a year the bell hung, driving local residents to drink – not that most of them needed driving to it in the wretched slums and thieves' kitchens of Westminster – by the daily test ringings. Finally the inevitable happened; in October 1857, a four foot long crack appeared in the bell. It was generally agreed that the hammer had been too heavy; Denison, naturally, blamed everyone but himself.

So the bell had to be recast, this time by Mears at the Whitechapel Foundry on 10 April, 1858, and it was also slimmed down by three tons. It was tested again, and yet another snag arose. The mouth of the bell was bigger than the shaft up which it had to be hoisted. 'Some difficulty occurred in consequence', wrote Barry's son later, 'of which much has been made.' But after the general panic that ensued when the measurements were made, someone had the bright idea of turning the bell sideways, and so hoisting it to the belfry. Teams of men turned a winch for a total of thirty hours to raise it into place. Once up it was suspended from massive iron girders, and there it remains. By now all the other bells were in place, and in July 1859, it began to toll the hours. MPs immediately complained that it deafened them, and in September that year it cracked again. Denison broke out into fresh fury, accusing Mears, the founders, of bad casting and hiding the defects with colour wash. The minute hands stopped and Denison blamed Barry while Barry blamed Denison. Denison rushed out furious letters to *The Times*; Mears sued him for libel and *The Times* refused to print any more of Denison's letters because he was 'pouring out peals of jarring abuse'. In the end, the bell was turned a quarter turn; one part was cut out to tune it correctly; and the weight of the hammer was reduced from $6\frac{1}{2}$ hundredweight to 4 hundredweight. There it hangs to this day, still

'Arrival of the new Bell "Victoria"' The name Victoria for the great bell was soon dropped in favour of Big Ben. Perhaps it was named after the First Commissioner of Works, a large gentleman named Sir Benjamin Hall. More probably it was nicknamed after the great Ben Caunt, the 17-stone champion prize-fighter of his day

'The Great Bell' The recast Big Ben was found to be too big for the shaft that had been left in the Clock Tower to raise it. It had to be turned sideways, and then winched up the shaft by eight men working for 36 hours. In 1859 it cracked again, but was given a quarter turn and the cracked bell rings the hours still

cracked, but tolling the hours high above the heads of politicians and Londoners and tourists. Everyone now knows.it as Big Ben. But why?

One theory – a rather drab and worthy theory – is that it is called after Sir Benjamin Hall, a large and voluble Welshman, who was First Commissioner of Public Works from 1855 to 1858, the time when the clock and bells were being made. The bell, it was decided, should, like all bells, have a name, and then the matter was being discussed in the Commons a backbencher shouted out: 'Let's call it Big Ben'. Or so the story goes. *The Times* had been referring to Big Ben of Westminster since 1856. A much more attractive tale of how the bell got its name concerns the great heavyweight bare-knuckle champion, Ben Caunt. He was landlord of the Coach and Horses, in nearby St Martin's Lane, and a massive man of seventeen stone nicknamed, Big Ben. His most famous fight was against a man called Bendigo, in 1845:

> *And near to Newport Pagnell,*
> *Those men did strip so fine,*
> *Ben Caunt stood six foot two and an half,*
> *And Bendigo five foot nine,*
> *Ben Caunt a giant did appear,*
> *And made the claret flow,*
> *And he seemed fully determined*
> *Soon to conquer Bendigo.*

Big Ben Benjamin Caunt, Champion of England, 1841. The bell that tolls the hours in the Great Clock of Westminster was probably named after the champion prize-fighter, although no one is certain how it got its name

It went to 93 rounds, and in the end Big Ben lost on a highly dubious decision; but he remained a hero and in 1857, when he was 42, went to 60 rounds. It seems much more likely that the great British public – especially the raffish part of it that lived within earshot of the Westminster clock – should name the bell after such a man, instead of after a portly politician.

No one nowadays, of course, knows or cares very much who the great bell was named after, and they almost always use the name for the clock and its tower instead of the hour bell itself. The total cost of making the clock and bells and putting them all into place was, by 1859, some £22,000, and for that the nation got a clock of almost perfect accuracy. Even today it varies only by fractions of a second, and pennies – old, pre-decimal pennies – are added or subtracted from the weight to make up these fractions of a second. The chimes of the bell are supposed to be based on a phrase from 'I know that my Redeemer liveth' in Handel's *Messiah*, and on a board in the clock room, where the great wheels turn slowly and the huge windbreak fans whirl and clatter to control the fall of the weights as the bells strike above them, is the prayer that goes with the bell's notes:

> *Lord through this hour,*
> *Be thou my guide,*
> *That by thy power,*
> *No foot shall slide.*

Above the five tons of the clock mechanism, iron spindles disappear through each wall to join with the centre of the massive clockfaces which look out over the capital. Everything about it is monumental; the great faces are twenty-three feet in diameter, with galleries behind them through which one can stroll, listening to the ticking of the clock. On the wall behind each face, twenty-eight neon tubes light the face at night, or in dull or foggy weather. The figures are two feet long; the minute spaces are each one foot square. The minute hands are of hollow copper; weigh two hundredweight each and are fourteen feet long; the hour hands are of gun metal; weigh six hundredweight and are nine feet long. The pendulum, which beats every two seconds, is thirteen feet long, with its bob weighing some four hundredweight. The weights themselves amount to about two and a half tons. Only two of the faces of the clock are heated to protect them from the bitter cold high above London – the East and the North faces which are turned in the direction from which the worst weather comes. Ordinary domestic fan heaters have been added to the point where the spindles from the clock pass through the face to the hands, as an added precaution against their freezing up and getting clogged by snow.

Of course, there have been famous occasions when the great clock *has* stopped – for example when a flock of starlings settled on the hands. The most famous occasion of all was in August 1976, when metal fatigue produced a spectacular fault that threw massive chunks of the mechanism across the clock room, and fractured the main frame. The mechanism was extensively repaired, and the hour bell, Big Ben, was chiming out to London, and to the world through the BBC World Service microphones in the roof high above it, within a few weeks. It is a sound that says London and Great Britain the world over.

The Great Clock of Westminster The Great Clock was designed by a brilliant, but irascible amateur horologist, Edmund Beckett Denison, QC. The four dials of the clock are 23 ft in diameter; the figures are two ft long; the minute hands, made of copper, are 14 ft long and weigh 2 cwt; the hour hands, of gun-metal, are 9 ft long and weigh 6 cwt; the north and east faces are heated in the winter to keep the hands from freezing up, but the south and west faces are left unheated. The clock's mechanism weighs five tons and the $2\frac{1}{2}$ ton weights of the clock are wound by electric motor

CHAPTER NINE

Banquets and Bombs

Master Richard of Crundale, the King's plumber, was furious. He and his men had slaved for weeks to mend all the taps and basins in the lavatories and wash rooms beside the King's Great Hall at Westminster, and now look what had happened. Those drunken louts, who had swigged gallon after gallon of the wine that flowed freely from a fountain in the Hall, had destroyed their handiwork. Master Richard and his men had certainly encountered problems trying to finish the work in time. The Hall plumbing was a couple of hundred years old and very battered indeed; King John, a hundred years earlier, had even given some of the plumbing away when the canons of Waltham received 'the tin lavatory which was erected in our house at Westminster in the time of our father and which was afterwards removed'. Master Richard's crew, though, worked hard and well. They 'subtly wrought' marble columns with water coming out of the mouths of five grinning faces made out of gilded copper. Five statues of gilded tin decorated the wash-place, and they had also supplied tin cups to drink from. Now those wretched guests at the young King's coronation banquet had smashed everything to pieces.

Edward II had been determined to do things in style for his coronation banquet in his Great Hall. The grimly restraining hand of his dour father had now gone, and at twenty-three he was ready for a royally good time. His Hall, therefore, had to be made ready, and he had a new young wife, Isabella of France, to bring home for the ceremony in the Abbey on 25 February, 1308, and the celebrations in the Hall. Much of the Palace itself was in a disgraceful state, but the Hall was in reasonable repair, and vast sums of money were spent in making it fit for a King's and a Queen's celebrations. The King had the precedent of his father's coronation banquet, thirty years before, to go by. In 1274 Edward I had ordered the countryside to be ransacked for weeks to supply the provisions for his banquet. Four hundred and forty oxen and cows, 430 sheep, 450 pigs, 16 fat boars and 22,640 capons, beside other poultry, were slaughtered to feed his guests. In February 1308, not to be outdone, and with his tough and ambitious teenage wife to egg him on, his son Edward II made even grander plans. The sheriff of Wiltshire was commanded to gather together twenty-four live porkers and thirty very fat bacon hogs, and animals were driven to Westminster from all over the south of England. So many men were assembled to get the Hall and the Palace into good repair that they had to be summoned from the area round about by a great horn, and they worked far into the evening by candlelight. A massive timber hall was added to the Hall itself, specially strengthened to withstand the pressure of the people eager to see the King's enthronement ceremony. Inside the temporary hall, the throne was duly placed, smartly repaired and repainted, and fourteen other temporary rooms and shelters were built for the enormous crowds that arrived for the ceremonies. There were tables and trestles everywhere, and forty ovens were built to cope with the mountains of food that were needed to feed the King's guests. In the middle of the Great Hall itself stood the chief wonder of all the wonderous celebrations – a fountain, painted and gilded and glorious, that flowed, day and night, with red and white wine and a spiced drink called pimento. It was regulated by a system of 'divers sorts of lead pipes and other apparatus arranged beneath the ground'. When it was all over came the cold and sober reckoning; the King's plumber had to repair the smashed taps; the trampled gardens round the Palace had to be relaid; the temporary halls and buildings were taken down and the wood sent down the river to the Tower, where the young King thought it time to show the barons, who had eaten and drunk with relish at his coronation, that he meant to defend himself if they tried to depose him.

Edward III was equally lavish with the wine at his coronation – a thousand pipes of wine were ordered from Bordeaux, and the celebrations were so costly (at over £1,056) that he was saddled with the debt for years. Yet even more stunning were the celebrations held for the boy King, Richard II, in 1377. So exhausted was the young King after the coronation ceremonies in the Abbey that he fainted as he walked up the red and striped carpet in the Hall. It had been a long day. 'In the morning the King arose, and having heard mass, he was clothed in the purest vestments, and wore slippers or buskins only on his feet; he quitted his room and descended into the Great Hall with a full attendance of Princes and Nobles. There came to meet him the Archbishop of Canterbury and other prelates in pontifical habits, and the clergy of the realm in silken copes, with a great concourse of people at the high table in the Hall.' They walked, in procession, to the Abbey for the coronation, and then the King 'descended into the Great Hall, and having washed his hands, sat down in the Royal seat at the high table, where sat with him many on either hand. On the right side of the Hall the Barons of the Cinque Ports occupied the first table, the Clerks of the Chancery the second; and at the inferior tables on that side were the King's Judges, the Barons of the Exchequer, and others. On the left side of the Hall were tables for the Sheriffs, Recorder, Aldermen and many of the citizens of London. In the middle were tables filled by distinguished men of the Commons of the Kingdom.' It must have been a fairly unbuttoned occasion, for 'during the continuance of the entertainment the Lord Steward, the Constable and the Earl Marshal, with certain knights deputed by them, rode about the Hall on noble coursers to preserve peace and order among the people. All that time the Earl of Derby stood at the King's right hand, holding the principal sword, drawn from its scabbard. The Earl of Strafford performed the office of chief carver. Dinner being finished, the King rose and went to his chamber with the prelates, great men, and nobles before mentioned. Then the great men, knights, and lords passed the remainder of the day until supper time in shews, dances, and solo minstrelsy; and having supped, the King and others retired to rest, fatigued with their exertions in this magnificent festival.'

It was in that same Hall, twenty-two years later, after he had rebuilt it to become one of England's greatest glories, that Richard was to be deposed. On 30 September, 1399, with Richard a prisoner in the Tower, the freshly built walls were 'hung and trimmed sumptuously', and there had been set up 'a Royall chaire, neare to which the prelates sat, and on the other side sat the Lords, and after, the Commons in order'. Richard's renunciation of the throne was read out, and his successor stepped forward, made the sign of the cross, and proclaimed: 'In the name of the Father, Son and Holy Ghost, I, Henry of Lancaster, challenge this realm of England and the crown, with all the members and appurtenances; as that I am descended by right line of the blood coming from the good Lord King Henry III; and through the right that God, of His grace, hath sent me, with the help of my kin and my friends, to recover it; the which realm was in point to be undone for default of governance and undoing of the good laws.' Henry knelt for a few minutes in silent prayer and was then placed in the King's seat by the Archbishops of Canterbury and York. Henry IV was King of England.

Two weeks later came the coronation. Henry went to confession 'as he had good need to', remarks a contemporary writer, and then after the ceremonies in the Abbey, he and his train returned to the new Hall. The fountains, as ever, ran with wine, and for the King and his guests, as they sat beneath that mighty new roof with the arms of the deposed Richard all around them, there were boars' heads 'enarmed' with elaborate decorations; pheasants, cygnets, herons, a Lombardy pasty, sturgeon and fattened capons. Next came venison in frumenty, wheat boiled in spiced milk, jellies, stuffed sucking pig, peacocks, cranes, bitterns, rashers of ham, brawn and tarts. Finally, there came quinces in confit, partridges, pigeons, quails and other birds, tomatoes, eggs in aspic, fritters and young eagles. Between courses, subtleties of pastry, made in the form of the King's patron saints, were served.

When the young Queen Katherine, wife of Henry V, held her coronation banquet in the Hall in 1421, the court was observing the Lenten fast, so all they managed, according to a chronicler of the time, to get through for the first course was: 'a sotyltie called a pellycan, syttyng on her nest with her Byrdes and an image of St Katheryne holdyng a book and dysputynge with the doctours'. In the next two courses, they fasted on carp, turbot, tench and perch, roast porpoise and fried minnows. Finally came 'a marchpayne garnysshed with dievers fygures of angellys, amonge the whiche was set an image of Seynt Katheryne.'

Henry VIII, held his coronation banquet at Westminster in tremendous style. Although he was later to abandon the increasingly battered and dilapidated Westminster Palace for his new Palace at Whitehall, the great Hall was definitely his style and all was dignified splendour. His Queen, Katherine of Aragon, arrived on a litter borne by two white palfreys; she was 'apparelled in white satyn embroidered, her heeire hanging downe to her back of very great length, bewtefull to behold, and on her head a coronate set with many rich orient stones'. As the King and Queen walked on the traditionally blue carpet that was laid between the Hall and the Abbey, the crowd rushed up behind them, and tore the carpet to pieces to carry off for their own homes – an ancient public perk which, at an earlier coronation, had led to an outbreak of rioting with people being seriously injured and even trampled to death in the frantic rush.

Once back in the Hall, the newly crowned King and Queen sat down to the banquet, the Queen on the King's left. Trumpets brayed, and the first course was ushered in by the Duke of Buckingham and the Lord Steward, both on horseback. It was 'sumptuous with many subtelties, strange devices, with several posies and many dainty dishes'. After the 'clean handling and breaking of meats', and the 'ordering of dishes with plentiful abundance', the Lord Mayor, who had been knighted just before the banquet, offered wine and wafers to the Royal couple. Then the King and Queen moved to 'a fair house covered with tapestry and hanged with rich cloths of arras' in Palace Yard, to watch tilting and sports in their honour. There was a fountain of wine: 'a curious fountain and over it a castle, on the top thereof a great crown imperial, all the embattling being with roses and pomegranates gilded . . . And out of several places of the same castle on the several days of the coronation jousts, and tourneys, out of the mouths of certain beasts or gargels did run red, white and claret wine.'

Away with Katherine; next came Anne Boleyn 'somewhat big with child' to her coronation at the end of May 1533. The Hall was hung with cloth of arras and was newly glazed; a group of ten dishes was brought before her, and the Lord Mayor served the wine and hypocras. The King, together with a group of ambassadors, watched the ceremonies from a little closet newly built 'out of the Clozotes of St Stephen's' chapel. 'When all things were ready and ordered, the Queen under her canapie came into the hall and washed, and sate down in the middest of the table under her clothe of estate; on the right hande side of her chaire stood the countesse of Oxford, widdow, and on her left hande stoode the countesse of Worcester all the dinner season, which divers times in the dinner did hold a fine clothe before the Queene's face when she list to spit, or doe otherwise at her pleasure; and at the table's end sate the archbishop of Canterburie; on the right hande of the Queene, and in the midst betweene the archbishop and the countesse of Oxford, stoode the earle of Oxford with a white staffe all dinner time.'

Much good did all the pomp do Anne, or her successors, as Henry's queens; but her daughter, Elizabeth, went through the usual ceremonies in 1558 with aplomb and considerable relish – even though the Hall did have a rather damp air about it from fairly recent flooding.

So, with each successive monarch, the banquets and ceremonies continued in Westminster Hall. Charles II was obviously keen to make a suitable impression when he celebrated the restored monarchy in 1661, and he spent £1,558 on organising the affair properly. Queen Anne spent over £4,600 on her coronation, and she walked down the Hall plump and splendid in a dress of gold tissue set with jewels and her 'head was well dressed with diamonds, mixed in the hair which at the least motion brilled and flamed'.

Rather oddly, the more ancient the tradition of coronation banquets in Westminster Hall became, the more incompetent became their organisation. George II had invited so many guests to his banquet that when they all turned up it was virtually impossible to fit them in – perhaps too much space had been taken up by the great triumphal arch, with its figures of Fame, Neptune and Britannia which William Kent had built over the north entrance. George III also commissioned a triumphal arch for his coronation banquet, but most of the arrange-

A PROSPECT of the INSIDE of WESTMINSTER HALL Shewing how the KING and QUEEN with the NOBILITY and Others did sit at DINNER on the Day of the *Coronation*. Also the manner of the *Champions* performing the Ceremony of *Challenge* whilst the KING &c. were at Dinner'

ments degenerated into very considerable muddle. The procession to the Abbey was a shambles; the Abbey ceremonies were not correctly rehearsed; and the famished guests in the Hall were kept waiting for six hours before the King and Queen arrived. The whole place was in a state of 'confusion, irregularity and disorder' – not to mention deep gloom, for the chandeliers were not lit until the Royal couple arrived. Once they were lit, however, the Hall, according to Horace Walpole, 'was the most glorious. The blaze of lights, the richness and variety of habits, the ceremonial, the benches of peers and peeresses, frequent and full, was as awful as a pagant can be – and yet for the Kingdom's sake – and my own I never wish to see another.' Walpole gossiped to his crony: 'My Lady Harrington, covered with all the diamonds she could borrow, hire or tease, and with the air of Roxana, was the finest figure at a distance . . . Don't imagine there were not figures as excellent on the other side; old Exeter, who told the King he was the handsomest young man she ever saw, old Effingham, and a Lady Say and Seal with her hair powdered and her tresses black, were an excellent contrast to the handsome Lord. Bolingbroke put rouge on his wife and the Duchess of Bedford in the Painted Chamber; the Duchess of Queensbury told me of the latter, that she looked like an orange-peach, half red and half yellow.' These poor ladies, so cattily dissected by Walpole, had dangers other than his waspish tongue to contend with. In order to get the chandeliers lit as quickly as possible after the King entered the Hall, trains of flax had been laid from candle to candle, and once this had been lit, all three thousand wicks were alight within half a minute. The trouble was that pieces of flaring flax fell from the chandeliers down onto the heads of the people below, and especially onto the ladies sitting in the high galleries that had been built round the sides of the Hall. What was more, the ladies in their galleries were ravenously hungry, and they had to look on as their lords and masters tucked into the Royal banquet. It was too much; they shouted down to their husbands to help, and then made ropes of their handkerchiefs and ribbons. These they let down, and then hauled back again, with bits of chicken and bottles of wine tied on to the end; the King watched, astonished, as the great ladies of the land set about their improvised picnic. They did rather better than the Knights of the Bath who found that, in the atmosphere of confusion, no places had been provided for them at the banquet. 'An airy apology, however, was served up to them instead of a substantial dinner', it was said. Still, everyone agreed that the specially provided sanitary facilities, in the galleries and around the walls, worked remarkably well.

The last coronation banquet of all, to celebrate the accession of George IV, was in 1821. It was an utter and complete shambles and it is hardly surprising that no monarch has since been willing to risk embarking on such a costly and ridiculous exercise. George, after waiting so long for the throne, and given his extravagant tastes, naturally wanted to put on a large show, and he spent nearly six times the

cost of the previous coronation on his own ceremonies. Sir John Soane, the great architect who had charge of the arrangements, said he felt he would sink under the frightful responsibility of it all, but he and his staff set about them with a will. Tiers of scarlet-covered galleries rose on each side of the Hall, supported by iron pillars with Gothic capitals. A great triumphal arch was built over the north door, with turrets on each side 30 feet high, while above it there stood a platform on which trumpeters played and kettle drums thundered. A platform, 1,500 feet long and 24 feet wide, was built from the Hall to the Abbey, covered once again with blue carpet. In the gardens between the Hall and the river, twenty-three temporary kitchens were built of wood and of brick. The wretched Queen Caroline failed in her attempts to be allowed to share in any of this glory, but the King tottered through it all, growing more and more exhausted by the length of the ceremonies and the weighty splendour of the robes he had inflicted upon himself. 'Precisely at ten o'clock', recalled a spectator later, 'the King entered the Hall from the door behind the throne, habited in robes of enormous size and richness, wearing a black hat with a monstrous plume of ostrich feathers, out of the midst of which rose a black heron's plume. His Majesty seemed much oppressed by the weight of his robes. The train was of enormous length and breadth; it was of crimson velvet adorned with large golden stars and a broad golden border. His Majesty frequently wiped his face while he remained seated. In descending the steps of the platform he seemed very feeble, and requested the aid of an officer who was near him. Instead of standing under the canopy, His Majesty, perhaps afraid of the awkwardness of the barons, preceded it. The canopy was, therefore, always borne after him. When he got a little way down the Hall, he turned to the train bearers and requested them to bear his train farther from him, apparently with a view to release himself from the weight.' Off the King went to the Abbey, following the Royal Herb Women who scattered flowers on the blue carpet before him, and passing the specially built, and carefully tested, galleries with seats that cost spectators between two and twenty guineas.

The sight that met his eyes when he returned to Westminster Hall was a spectacular one indeed. From the roof hung twenty-eight chandeliers each with sixty candles. At the south end of the Hall stood a throne nineteen feet high and seven feet wide – big enough even for the portly George – covered in crimson Genoa velvet, with the royal arms elaborately embroidered on the back. The King's guests dined at six tables, each 60 feet long, which had been set, loaded with Royal china, glass and cutlery, down the length of the Hall. Prize fighters were at the doors to keep out gatecrashers, and after the problem of the King finding he had no cutlery with which to eat his own banquet had been sorted out, everyone attacked the food.

Those temporary kitchens were most certainly needed because, between them, King and guests consumed a gargantuan amount of food and drink. The cooks and the maidservants and the butlers and the waiters and the carvers and servers provided: 160 tureens of soup: 80 of turtle, 40 of rice, and 40 of vermicelli; 160 dishes of fish: 80 of turbot, 40 of trout, 40 of salmon; 160 hot joints: 80 of venison, 40 of roast beef, with three barons, 40 of mutton and veal; 160 dishes of vegetables, including potatoes, peas and cauliflowers; 480 sauce boats, 120 of lobsters, 120 butter, 120 mint. Cold dishes: 80 dishes of braised ham; 80 savoury pies; 80 dishes of daubed geese, two in each; 80 dishes of savoury cakes; 80 pieces of beef, braised; 80 dishes of capons, braised, two in each; 1,190 side dishes of various sorts; 320 dishes of mounted pastry; 320 dishes of small pastry; 400 dishes of jellies and creams; 160 dishes of shellfish, 80 of lobster and 80 of crayfish; 160 dishes of cold roast fowls; 80 dishes of cold house lamb. Total quantities: 7,742 pounds of beef; 7,133 pounds of veal; 2,474 pounds of mutton; 20 quarters of house lamb; 5 saddles of lamb; 55 quarters of grass lamb; 160 lamb sweetbreads; 389 cow heels; 400 calves' feet; 250 pounds of suet; 160 geese; 720 pullets and capons; 1,610 chickens; 520 fowls for stock; 1,730 pounds of bacon; 550 pounds of lard; 912 pounds of butter; and 8,400 eggs. It all, of course, had to be washed down with suitable quantities of drink: 100 dozen of champagne, 20 of burgundy, 200 of claret, 50 of hock, 50 of Mosel, 50 of Madeira and 350 of port and sherry. Added to this were 100 gallons of iced punch and 100 barrels of ale and porter. All that food was served on 6,794 plates, 1,406 sou-plates and 1,499 dessert plates. Not surprisingly, the King's coronation costs, not including the robes and other bits and pieces, amounted to £243,390 6s. 2d.

The 100 gallons of iced punch must have been in great demand for the heat from the hundreds of candles made the Hall overpoweringly stuffy. By the end of the banquet, the King was sweating profusely, and the ladies were fainting, and being subjected to great blobs of melted candlegrease falling down on them and ruining their expensive clothes. 'If a lovely female dared to raise her look to discover from what quarter the unwelcome visitation came, she was certain of receiving an additional patch upon her cheeks, which, in order to disencumber herself of, obliged her to wipe away also the roseate hue which had been imparted to her countenance at her toilet.' As for the clothes, they had had to be thrown together only two days before the banquet, for at that time the guests had suddenly been informed they had to wear full court dress; so men and women had to rush off to their tailors and dress-makers and not only pay off their outstanding bills in order to get new orders accepted but also pay extortionate rates for new clothes to wear at the banquet. The King, of course, had no such trouble with his splendid, if thoroughly uncomfortable, array. 'Something rustles', wrote the painter Haydon, of the scene in the Hall, 'and a being buried in satin, feathers and diamonds rolls gracefully to his seat. The room rises with a sort of feathered, silken thunder. Plumes wave, eyes sparkle, glasses are out, mouths smile and one man becomes the prime object of attraction to thousands. The way in which the King bowed was really royal. As he looked towards the peeresses and foreign ambassadors, he showed like some gorgeous bird of the East.'

Eventually, after much drinking of toasts and much braying of trumpets and rattling of drums, the gorgeous bird of the East heaved himself out of his scarlet chair, and tottered off home to Carlton House. It was the signal for mayhem. Even the prize fighters could not knock any sense or decorum into the heads of the great as they deliberately began to ransack and loot the Hall. 'For a few seconds delicacy or a disinclination to be the first to commence the scene of plunder, suspended the projected attack', wrote a witness of the scene, 'but at last a rude hand having been thrust through the first ranks, and a golden fork having been seized, this operated as a signal to all, and was followed by a general snatch. In a short time all the small portable articles had been transferred to the pockets of the multitude.

'The Lord Great Chamberlain, being alarmed by the confusion, returned to the Hall, and by the greatest personal exertions succeeded in preventing the extension of the supposed "licensed plunder" to the more costly part of the Coronation plate. With great difficulty all the remaining part of the plate was removed to Cotton Garden, and all the apprehension on this score having subsided, the marauders were left to the undisturbed possession of their coronation privileges in the body of the Hall, and thither they turned their attentions.'

So the looting went on: 'A raging thirst was the first want to be satisfied, and in a very few minutes every bottle on the board was emptied of its contents; a fresh supply was, however, soon obtained from the cellerers, and all reasonable calls of this sort were complied with. While some were thus occupied, others still pursued the work of plunder. Arms were everywhere being stretched for breaking and destroying the table ornaments, which were of themselves too cumbrous to remove, for the purpose of obtaining some trophy commemorative of the occasion; thus baskets, flower-pots, and figures were everywhere disappearing, and these were followed by glasses, knives and forks, saltspoons, and finally the plate and dishes. These last were of pewter, and engraved with the Royal arms and the letters "Geo. IV." and were, therefore, greatly coveted. The dirty state of these articles, however, added to the inconsistency of their appearance with full Court dresses, deterred many from appropriating them to their own use, although some, laying aside all delicacies of this sort, did not fail to take out their handkerchiefs and, amidst their folds, to conceal their much-prized spoils.'

Finally, when they were exhausted with drink and when they had stolen or smashed everything they could lay their hands on, the King's fine guests, the greatest and grandest and proudest ladies and gentlemen in all the land, passed out and lay in stupefied unconsciousness where they fell. 'Peers and peeresses, judges and privy councillors, knights of all orders, and commoners of all degree, lay promiscuous, some on sofas, some on chairs, and a still greater number on the matted floors of the rooms and passages in which they happen to have sought refuge.' So 'many were overtaken with sleep, and scenes were presented extremely at variance with the splendid and dignified spectacle which had been but a few hours before exhibited in the presence of the Sovereign'. Several ladies, it was reported, were 'so completely worn out that it became necessary to carry them to their carriages', but eventually, in the small hours of the morning, the place was cleared of its drunken, thieving, grandly respectable guests. They were driven to their fine homes in their fine carriages, through the mob of hungry, poor and miserable wretches who infested the stinking slums that crawled right up to the walls of the King's Palace of Westminster. A company of soldiers was brought up to drive the crowd away in case they should try to emulate their betters and carry off what little bits and pieces the ladies and gentlemen had left behind in the wrecked and ruined Hall. No wonder the banquet of 1821 was the last coronation banquet ever to be held in Westminster Hall.

One final touch of farce had been added to fat George's coronation banquet with the arrival of the King's Champion to carry out his ancient task of challenging anyone who doubted the monarch's rightful succession to the throne. On this occasion the Champion — it's an hereditary office that still exists and belongs to the same Lincolnshire family of Dymock — was an earnest young Henry Dymock, only twenty years old, who had been asked to deputise for his father, a country parson who thought that appearing in shining armour on horseback would not become his calling. Young Dymock, an enterprising youth, hired a piebald horse from Astley's circus at Drury Lane Theatre and when, during the elaborate ceremonial in which the King's Champion became involved, the guests burst into applause, the horse imagined it was in the ring instead of at a Royal banquet, and promptly began to go through its circus tricks. Young Dymock, however, had his wits about him, and got himself and the horse outside without any damage done.

Dymock was the last of his line to perform this duty at the coronation banquet – although the post still exists and so does the ancient Dymock family which holds it. They have held it for well over 600 years, perhaps since the Conquest itself, when the title came to the family through the champion of the Dukes of Normandy. The Dymocks seemed to be mildly accident-prone in carrying out the ceremonies. At the coronation of Richard II in 1377, Sir John Dymock went to the wrong place. 'Equipping himself with the best suit of armour, save one', recorded Walsingham, 'and the best steed save one, from the King's armoury and stable, he proceeded on horseback, with two attendants (the one carrying his spear, and the other his shield) to the Abbey gates, there to wait the ending of the mass. But the Lord Marshal, the Lord Seneschal, and the Lord Constable, with Sir Thomas Percy, being all mounted on their great horses, went to the Knight and told him that he should not have come so soon, but when the King was at dinner; wherefore, he had better retire, and, laying aside his weight armour, rest himself until the proper time.' Which, presumably, he thankfully did.

The duty of the Champion was to ride into the Hall during the coronation banquet and challenge anyone who doubted the King's rightful succession by throwing down the gauntlet; anyone who picked it up would then, of course, have to fight the Champion to the death. Not surprisingly, no one ever did pick it up, although, down the years, there were at least two rumoured attempts to call the Champion to fight. One was said to be at the coronation banquet of William and Mary in 1689, when an old woman on crutches hobbled forward and picked up the glove, dropped a piece of paper in its place, and then, with astonishing agility for an ancient crone on crutches, and before anyone had quite realised what was happening, slipped out of the Hall. The piece of paper was found to contain a challenge to the Champion to fight in Hyde Park the next day, and the old crone turned out to be a famous Jacobite swordsman in disguise. The circumspect Dymock pretended not to notice.

Only a few years earlier, another Champion, Sir Charles Dymock, had come something of a public cropper when, at the coronation feast of James II, he slipped and fell as he bowed to kiss the King's hand. His armour was so heavy that he could not get up again, and flunkies rushed to haul him to his feet. A bad omen, said the wiseacres; and the wiseacres were right.

The Jacobites continued to give the Champions trouble at the Coronation of George II in 1764. When the current Dymock flung down the gauntlet in the traditional challenge, a white lady's kid glove fluttered down from one of the specially built galleries to land beside it. Everyone pretended not to notice – after all, it might have been an accident – but it was rumoured that the Young Pretender had got into the Hall disguised as a woman. The *Gentleman's Magazine* noted that 'it was publically said that the Young Pretender himself came from Flanders to see the Coronation; that he was in Westminster Hall during the ceremony, and in London two or three days before and after it, under the name of Mr Brown.'

Perhaps Mr Brown – presumably he was then disguised as Miss Brown – joined in the laughter that greeted the Champion and his supporters as they went through their elaborate ceremonies. The cause of this 'terrible indecorum' was that Lord Talbot, one of the Champion's supporters, had decided that it was not proper for his horse to turn its rump on the King to walk out when the ceremony was over, so he trained it to walk out backwards. The horse, unfortunately, got the whole thing badly muddled and walked in backwards, so that the King had a good view of its rump as it walked, in stately procession, the full length of the Hall towards him.

The arrangements for the Champion at the spectacular coronation of George IV were very grand indeed. They threw contemporary journalists into a lather of purple prose. The young Dymock was ushered into the Hall by the Duke of Wellington on the right and Lord Howard of Effingham on the left. His armour was polished; his high feather plumes bobbed and the scarlet trappings looked splendid on his piebald circus horse. 'An esquire in half armour was on each side, the one bearing his lance, and the other his shield or target: the three horsemen were followed by grooms and pages.'

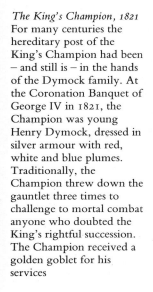

The King's Champion, 1821 For many centuries the hereditary post of the King's Champion had been – and still is – in the hands of the Dymock family. At the Coronation Banquet of George IV in 1821, the Champion was young Henry Dymock, dressed in silver armour with red, white and blue plumes. Traditionally, the Champion threw down the gauntlet three times to challenge to mortal combat anyone who doubted the King's rightful succession. The Champion received a golden goblet for his services

Three times, as trumpets sounded, the Champion's Herald read out the challenge: If any person, of what degree soever, high or low, shall deny or gainsay our Soveriegn Lord King George the Fourth of the United Kingdom of Great Britain and Ireland, Defender of the Faith, son and next heir to our Sovereign Lord King George III, the last King deceased, to be right heir to the Imperial Crown of this United Kingdom or that he ought not to enjoy the same, here is his Champion, who saith that he lieth, and is a false traitor; being ready in person to combat with him, and in this quarrel will adventure his life against him on what day soever he shall be appointed.'

Three times the Champion threw down his gauntlet, and picked it up again to great shouts of 'Long Live the King'. 'The knightly appearance and gallant deportment of the Champion obviously gave considerable pleasure to His Majesty, who taking the goblet that was presented to him by the cup-bearer, drank to the bold challenger with a corresponding air of gaiety.' The young challenger himself then proposed the King's health and, like his predecessors, was rewarded with the very valuable golden-covered cup in which the toasts had been drunk.

'It would be impossible', says the *Annual Register*, 'for us to do justice to the scene that followed; it was the most animated, the most cheering, and indeed the most sublime that was ever witnessed. A loud and involuntary cry of "God bless the King!" escaped at that moment from the Hall; the acclamation was long and loud. Women, the lovliest and fairest that ever Heaven formed, full of health and beauty, yet bending under the brilliant burden of rich but unnecessary ornaments – it was from this numerous and noble assembly that a burst of applause issued, which seemed as if it would rend the roof of this ancient and magnificent Hall. A thousand plumes waved glorious pride; a thousand voices swelled the loud acclamation; joy lighted up the countenance of beauty; and the gaze of ardent loyalty beamed around the throne of a Monarch who at that moment had much reason to feel happy . . .'

The dashing young Dymock beamed at the pretty Miss Fellowes, the King's Herb Woman, and her six attendants dressed, according to a contemporary journalist, with careful use of quotation marks, in 'virgin' white, wheeled his horse and pranced out of the Hall.

On that occasion, the cheering echoed, the trumpets brayed and the kettle-drums roared. Yet on four occasions a roar of a different kind has filled the ancient Hall; the roar of exploding bombs, three times set by extremists, once dropped during the lunacy of war. The first time – and perhaps distance makes it slightly less abhorrent than the later events – was in 1736, when a group of desperate Thames watermen left a parcel of gunpowder in the Hall. They had watched in helpless despair as the Westminster grandees decided to build a bridge across the Thames, and so swept away the living which they and their ancestors had enjoyed since the very mists of time, ferrying people and goods across the river. The bridge was built among considerable muddle – a lottery held to finance it was less than well-run – and much committee forming and meeting, but after a whole mass of Acts of Parliament, the bridge was duly built. The watermen's parcel of gunpowder exploded in the Hall, and managed to cause a great deal of excitement but not much damage. A few winters later the Thames froze solid, which made the sufferings of the watermen even worse, and caused the traders in the Hall to swear as fly-by-nighters set up their stalls on the ice and took away trade from the Hall. Showers of ancient dust fell down on them when, in 1750, the Hall and Palace were shaken by two earthquakes that rocked Westminster; but it was a shock of a very different kind that rocked Westminster, and the nation, later in the next century.

In 1883 and 1884 the country had been appalled at outrages committed by Fenian dynamiters who had ruthlessly caused damage in a number of public buildings. Then, on Saturday 24 January, 1885, they struck again, at three of the most important and significant places in the very heart of the British Empire. They exploded bombs, more or less simultaneously, in the Tower of London; in the Chamber of the House of Commons; and in Westminster Hall.

Mr Green, his wife and her sister, Miss Davis, from Cork, were among the tourists going round the Palace of Westminster that day. While they were in the Crypt Chapel beside the Hall, Miss Davis noticed 'a rough looking woman with a bulky skirt, without trimmings, passing them. This person, who looked like a man in woman's dress, was accompanied by a girl with flaxen hair, cut short, about thirteen years of age.' Shortly afterwards they saw a black bag, wrapped in a woman's dress, on the steps leading from the Hall down to the Crypt. 'Dynamite', yelled Mr Green, and he and the ladies rushed up into the Hall and shouted a warning to Police Constable Cole. Cole darted down the Crypt stairs, grabbed the bag, and ran back with it into the Hall. As he reached the platform halfway up the steps at the south end of the Hall, the bag got so hot he had to drop it. There was a tremendous explosion and he, and another constable, Cox, were blown into a hole in the stone paving, six feet wide by two feet deep. Both were badly injured, although both, astonishingly, survived. Miss Davis reported that she and her sister 'lost our bonnet muffs and bags, and I had a skirt torn from my waist. My sister and I were covered with dirt and my sealskin tippet was blown to pieces.'

Hardly had the roar from the dynamite in the Hall died down – it did relatively little damage, although it blew out the great south window – when there came another explosion, this time from within the Commons itself. Dynamite had been placed just inside the Chamber near the 'Aye' lobby, and it virtually wrecked the place. Almost all the government benches, including the front bench, were destroyed; the Speaker's chair, at the other end of the room, was damaged by flying wreckage; the Peers' Gallery was destroyed, and the Members' Lobby, including the post office, badly damaged. Sightseers had rushed out of the Chamber to discover the cause of the first blast, otherwise many more might have been hurt. Two people found stunned still inside the Chamber were hauled off to the police station for questioning; they had to be protected from a mob that tried to lynch them, but in the end were found to be utterly harmless.

At the Tower, a bomb went off in the banqueting room of the White Tower, injuring several visitors. The chief of the London Fire Brigade, the redoutable Captain Shaw, rushed from one incident to the other; the Home Secretary, Sir William Harcourt, followed him, and descriptions were put out for a man shaved of chin, rather pug-nosed, with a billycock hat, and a woman in a sealskin (or imitation) jacket. No one was caught.

America was much blamed for harbouring the dynamiters, but the Senate passed a resolution condemning the outrage. The world, however, tended to think Britain had brought it on itself. The *Moscow Gazette* was especially bitter: 'England has, at last, lived to see the day of retribution. Explosion after explosion has taken place in the Capital, until they have now shaken down the very walls of her Parliament House. At last she is herself experiencing the evil which she has always maintained for others with her sacred right of asylum.'

The cost of the damage was estimated at about £15,000 at Westminster. It certainly cost a young man named Roberts his livelihood. Roberts was an itinerant seller of lamp glasses 'in very poor circumstances'. He was passing Westminster Hall, he told the Magistrates at Westminster Police Court, at the very moment of the explosion. The blast lifted his barrow and tilted it to one side, and down went six dozen lamp glasses to smash on the cobbles. Please could he have compensation? No, said the Magistrates, he could not.

In due course, when it was repaired, the brave Cole and Cox (by now both promoted to sergeants) hobbled into the Hall, to receive the Albert Medal for bravery and cash awards from the Home Secretary, in the presence of Mr and Mrs Gladstone. 'Cole, in a voice trembling with weakness and emotion, asked the Home Secretary to thank the Queen for the honour and his friends for their kindness.' The presentation was carried out on the exact spot where the bomb had exploded.

Ninety years on, and the Irish extremists tried again. On the morning of 17 June, 1974, Westminster Hall was once more rocked by an explosion, this time from a bomb placed in a doorway just off the north-west corner of the Hall. A coded message had been phoned to the Press Association in Fleet Street a few minutes before, but there was no time to raise the alarm properly. The bomb – about twelve pounds of explosives – went off at a spot between a staff canteen and a range of Victorian offices built on the outside wall of the Hall. Eleven people were hurt, and fire engines rushed from all over London once again to save the Hall. Smoke poured out of the windows and over New Palace Yard. Three turn-tables were used to pour water down onto the great roof; firemen

Right: *Fenian Dynamiters, House of Commons, 1885* Irish terrorists, who had been carrying out a bombing campaign throughout Britain, struck simultaneously at both the House of Commons and Westminster Hall on 24 January 1885. The bomb in the Commons wrecked the Chamber – including the Prime Minister's, Mr Gladstone's seat – and did serious damage in the Members' Lobby. No one was hurt. In Westminster Hall, two policemen were injured when a bomb they had carried up from the Crypt Chapel, exploded

Above right: *Churchill in the ruins of the House of Commons* German bombers totally destroyed the Chamber of the House of Commons during the blitz on London on the night of 10 May 1941. Churchill came next day to stand among the ruins of the House that he now totally dominated. Much other damage was done in the Palace, but Westminster Hall was once again saved. The Commons moved into the House of Lords and sat there until their rebuilt Chamber was ready in 1952. On Churchill's insistence, it was much the same style – and exactly the same size – as the old bombed Chamber

in breathing apparatus fought the fire that started from a fractured gas main inside the Hall. Once again, the Hall was saved. All that remains of that piece of lunacy is a crack in the wall and a rebuilt staff canteen, which replaced the Victorian offices and which is by far the most pleasant of the many snack-bars in the Palace. On the spot where, for centuries, 'Hell' stood, and where once debtors languished and then clerks downed their ale, secretaries sip their coffee in air-conditioned, subtly-lit comfort.

Yet the most terrible danger of all came out of the skies on the night of 10 May 1941. Hitler's blitz on London was at its height and that night bombs fell in terrifying torrents on Westminster. The massive scaffolding that had been put up round the Victoria Tower caught alight, and incendiaries caused several other fires in the Palace; a turret was hit by a bomb, and the two policemen within were killed. Colonel Walter Elliot, MP, in his scarlet tabbed uniform as head of public relations at the War Office, hurried over from his house in Lord North Street nearby. He could already see that the great roof of the Hall was on fire; flames were shooting from the lantern in the centre of the roof, and once again, just as it had done in the fire of 1834, melted lead was running down from the gutters and starting more fires. Colonel Elliot was not the man to watch as the Hall burnt. He realised that it would be impossible to fight it from the St Stephen's end so, accompanied by a group of firemen, he rushed round to New Palace Yard. 'There', recalled his widow, Baroness Elliot, forty years later, 'the door was being guarded by a policeman, who stood as though nothing was happening at all. Walter said to him "Do you realise that Westminster Hall is on fire?"

and he said "No, Sir." So Walter took a huge axe from a fire officer, and smashed the door open; pushed everybody through; rushed the water in and soaked the beams the whole way down, right down to the bottom. He told me that when he left Westminster Hall four or five hours later he was up to his knees in water. That was how the Hall was saved, because the fire stopped because the beams were wet.'

Next day, Lady Elliot stood with her husband in the total wreckage of the Commons Chamber which the firemen had not been able to save. The choice had been between saving the Chamber and the Hall, and there could be no doubt, even in the ghastly tumult of that night, that the Hall, above all else, must survive. 'Next day', said Lady Elliot, 'we went together to Westminster in the morning, and I stood in what is now the MPs' Lobby, and you could see right to the sky. Everything was open. They had the Fire Brigade there pouring water on the fires, and there was a huge sort of hissing noise; steam and smoke coming up, even though it was next morning. I remember seeing – it's curious how one remembers these things – one of those barrage balloons hanging in the sky. There was nothing between where I was standing on the floor of the House of Commons and the sky.' Her husband had saved the Hall.

Below left: *Wartime defiance* The sword of Richard Coeur de Lion damaged but unbroken after the German air raid which wrecked the Houses of Parliament in 1941. The great South Window of Westminster Hall which was blown out in the raid was later restored as a memorial to people who had died in the two world wars

Below: *The Aye lobby* The Aye voting lobby of the House of Commons, destroyed in the German air raid in 1941

CHAPTER TEN

Honourable Members

According to an eighteenth century savant, Sir Edward Coke, every Member of Parliament should, in three respects at least, resemble an elephant: 'first, that he hath no gall; secondly, that he is inflexible and cannot bow; thirdly, that he is of a most ripe and perfect memory'. Things have changed over the last two hundred years. Most Members nowadays would certainly agree that a little gall, a little flexibility, the occasional tactful lapse of memory, can do wonders for their careers.

There are four ways of becoming a Member of Parliament: by birth; by consecration as a Bishop of the Church of England; by appointment and by election. The simplest method is, of course, the first; if you are the heir to an hereditary peerage you will in due time, upon the Peer's death, inherit his seat in the House of Lords. The second method is slightly more difficult; it is appointment to a life peerage, perhaps after a worthy and eminent life in one of the arts or sciences, or in a profession or trade union, or after a long and blameless career in the House of Commons. It is a system that has existed since July 1958. Entering Parliament as a bishop can only be done under strict rules; twenty-six bishops of the Church of England sit in the House of Lords by right. They are the Archbishops of Canterbury and York, plus the bishops of London, Durham and Winchester; the other twenty-one bishops take their seats in order of seniority. They can, like any other Member in either House, in theory be appointed government Ministers. The last bishop to hold Ministerial office was the Bishop of Bristol, who was Lord Privy Seal in 1711 – the last in a long line of archbishops and bishops who, for centuries, held massive temporal sway, with the King, in running the country.

By far the most difficult way of becoming a Member of Parliament is by election. Members of the House of Lords cannot be elected; Members of the House of Commons must be elected and can enter the Commons by no other route. Members of both Houses can, however, claim to be Members of Parliament. It is only by tradition that the 1,200 members of the House of Lords leave the use of the initials 'MP' to members of the Lower House.

Almost any British subject can at least try to win those letters, 'MP', after his or her name, and at each General Election at least two thousand *do* try. In the 1979 General Election there were 2,567 candidates representing 109 parties, fighting for 635 parliamentary seats. Since then, the number of seats in the Commons has been increased by 15, to 650. In order to stand as an MP the candidates have to be British by birth or naturalisation; they cannot be members of the House of Lords, ministers of the Churches of England, Scotland, Ireland or Rome, lunatics, undischarged bankrupts, members of the armed forces or the police, or holders of various judicial or public offices. They must all be at least twenty-one years of age — although that is not a qualification that has always been strictly observed.

Charles James Fox was returned for Midhurst, in Sussex, in 1768 when he was nineteen years old and made his maiden speech when he was twenty. This tradition of admitting legally 'infant' Members was an old one even then. During the reign of James I there were as many as forty Members who were under age, including several who were not more than sixteen years old. In 1667, Lord Torrington, who was eventually to become the Duke of Albermarle, spoke in a debate on the impeachment of Clarendon when he was only fourteen. When someone told the tedious seventeenth-century pedant, Falkland, that he was too young to sit in Parliament, he briskly replied that he knew of no better place to sow his wild oats than the House of Commons, since there were so many geese to pick them up.

By 1695, however, the Commons had had enough of these brash young men and passed an Act excluding those under twenty-one from taking their seats, although for some years 'infants' continued to attend, although they could not vote.

The modern scramble for the honour of representing anything from between 50,000 to 100,000 people in the Commons has developed gradually from the time when boroughs considered having an MP an affliction to be tolerated with as good a grace as possible. In the early days of Parliament, Members were looked upon as a kind of upper servant, and were sent to Westminster to do the bidding of their masters while the latter remained at home to look after their estates. Boroughs, in particular, were only too glad not to have an MP. Richard II, as a special favour to the people of Colchester for fortifying their town in the later years of the fourteenth century, absolved them for five years from the obligation of sending burgesses to Parliament. Edward III had already set a precedent by granting the same concession to the county of Northumberland because of the poverty they had suffered as a result of Scottish raids. In 1463 the then important port of Dunwich, on the East Anglian coast, bought off its Member, Sir John Strange, with 'a cade and half a barrel of herrings for his fee'.

The cost of having an MP to a town could be considerable. He had to travel backwards and forwards to Westminster once or twice a year, which could be a costly and dangerous undertaking; while he was there he had to keep himself, and so he had to be paid. The rate for an MP in the fifteenth century was about two shillings a day, although in 1444 the tight-fisted citizens of Canterbury cut their Member's pay by half — to one shilling a day. With any luck, a borough might find an ambitious man who would do the job for nothing. In the seventeenth century Sir Robert Hitcham, Judge of the County Palantine of Ely, agreed to be the

Member for King's Lynn without payment 'in consideration for which tender care for their pecuniary resources the Corporation, on the occasion of his passing through the town on his way to Ely in July 1610, entertained him handsomely and gave him a gratuity of £20'. Sometimes very ambitious men would actually pay a borough for the seat. The Wiltshire borough of Westbury cost £4 in 1571, although in the end the mayor of the town had to pay the money back when it turned out that the man who had bought the seat was an illiterate farmer. On other occasions, boroughs refused to pay their Member the money they owed him; in 1586 the Member for Grantham had to sue for his money, and although the system of boroughs paying their Members ended in 1677, the Member for Harwich was still petitioning for arrears owed to him by the town in 1681.

After the system of boroughs paying their Members was ended, MPs had to manage for a further 250 years before salaries were introduced. Having MPs without pay was, said Mr Pepys, not good enough; '. . . all concluded that the bane of Parliament hath been the leaving off the old custom of the places allowing wages to those that served them in Parliament, by which they chose men that understood their business and would attend it, and they could expect an account from, which they cannot'.

Various unsuccessful attempts were made in the nineteenth century to get Members paid, but it was not until 1912 that, in the face of substantial opposition, a motion was passed entitling Members to a salary of £400 a year. Little by little the salary has been increased, and allowances of various kinds added, with MPs in the difficult, and to some of them embarrassing, position of deciding upon their own pay. At present allowances are available for secretaries – who may, of course, be a Member's wife, if they so wish – and for researchers; for car mileage and other kinds of travel; for postage; for living in, or for not living in, London. In the Victorian ecclesiastical atmosphere of Dean's Yard, beside Westminster Abbey, the House of Commons Fees Office works out all the expenses claimed. A pair of dividers is used to check, inch by inch on a large wall map, the car mileage claimed by MPs from Westminster to their constituency; from their constituency to their home; and from their home back to London. Computers add it all up and come to the conclusion that hardly any two MPs receive the same amount of money from the public funds in any one year. On average, in 1983, backbenchers were drawing something like £30,000 each, out of which they had to pay their secretaries, researchers, possibly for two homes and the various calls that are made on them for subscriptions and help to organisations and charities. MPs are not in Parliament for the money.

Ministers in both the Lords and Commons, of course, receive higher salaries, but ordinary members of the Lords receive no salaries at all. They get, instead, a daily attendance allowance plus a travelling allowance, but they have to find the money for most secretarial help from their own pockets.

Whether or not MPs actually earn their salaries is, of course, entirely up to them. There is absolutely no obligation for a Member, once elected, ever to set foot in the Commons, although he will not get paid until he has taken the oath of allegiance to the Crown and signed the Test Roll. Once his salary begins to flow, he can do as little or as much as he wishes – although the lazy MP will soon get himself into trouble with his party's Whips, and anyone with sufficient drive and determination to get to Westminster in the first place is hardly likely to throw it all away once he has achieved his ambition.

This easy-going self-discipline by Members, however, has not always been the norm. A fourteenth century 'ordinance for the more regular attendance in Parliament' was no respecter of persons in either House: '. . . whatsoever person who shall thenceforth have such summons, be he Archbishop, Bishop, Abbott, Prior, Duke, Earl, Baron, Bennerett, Knight of County, Citizen of City, Burgess of Borough, or other singular person or commonalty whatsoever, shall be absent or shall not come at such summons, if he cannot reasonably and honestly have excuse towards the King, shall be amerced and otherwise punished'. Members were fined £20 in Elizabeth I's reign if they did not come to the House, and in the long struggle between Charles I and Parliament in the first half of the seventeenth century, repeated efforts were made to persuade Members, worried about their own safety and commitment, to attend regularly. Members went off to taverns, play-houses, dicing-houses, cockpits and bowling alleys 'rambling abroad to such places at unreasonable Hours Of the Night in antique Parliamentary robes, Vestments fitter for a Mask or Stage than the gravity of a Parliament House'.

It was therefore decided to fine any Member, who was not in his place for prayers at the beginning of each day's sitting, one shilling. 'Pay! Pay!' shouted the smug Members to late-comers, and the angry late arrivals often threw their fines on the floor for the Serjeant-at-Arms to collect. On one memorable occasion 'Sir H. Mildmay stood up and said to the Speaker (Lenthall) he did hope that hereafter he would come in time; which made the Speaker throw down the twelve pence upon the table.'

There would occasionally be a 'Call of the House' – a roll-call – to see who was present and who was absent. In the dramatic days of 1647, when Parliament was fighting Charles I, Members were fined the hefty sum of £20 if they could not answer to their names. The power to fine Members continued for centuries, although the last time that a fine for non-attendance was imposed was in 1831, when three Members were given into the custody of the Serjeant-at-Arms and were fined £8 and £10. The Lords were even tougher; during the proceedings for the degradation of Queen Caroline in 1820, they fined non-attenders £100 for absence during the first three days, and £50 for each day after that. If

'The experiences of a new MP' '1. The New MP arrives at the House, and being somewhat short-sighted, mistakes the messenger for some high functionary, possibly the Lord High Chancellor,and shakes his hand accordingly 2. Disappointment! He arrives before the writ, and has to content himself with a seat under the gallery; but some of the party come and console him 3. The introduction – enthusiastic reception – passing up the House with his two introducers amidst cheers on one side only 4. He takes the oath 5. Signs the roll 6. Shakes hands with the Speaker . . . 7. and his leader 8. He makes his maiden speech, which is listened to in breathless silence (all the Members having gone to dinner) . . . 9. and is congratulated by his supporters in the dining room, whence they have listened throughout' The procedure for swearing in a new MP after a by-election is exactly the same today as it was 100 years ago

they did not pay up they were arrested. The last time the Commons had a Call of the House was in 1836; the Lords in 1901 for the trial, before his peers, of Lord Russell.

So the ambitious MP gets himself elected, under one party label or another. He could, of course, get himself elected for several seats at once, for there is nothing to stop any candidate from standing for as many seats as he likes at any one time. If, by some extraordinary circumstance, he was returned for more than one constituency, he would be allowed to represent only one seat, and the others would have to be refought. Of course, anyone with such a curious ambition has to surmount the problem of getting ten electors in each constituency to propose him, and is faced with the prospect of losing the £150 deposit he has to put up in each case. He will lose the money unless he gets an eighth of the total vote cast in each constituency in which he stands.

There is nothing which compels an MP, once he has been elected, to support any particular party. He could, if he was prepared to risk it in the excited atmosphere of a poll declaration, immediately announce that he had switched his allegiance to another party and there would be nothing his former supporters could do about it – nothing legal, that is. Crossing the floor of the House is an ancient Parliamentary right – Churchill did it twice – and the basic principle of an MP's position in the Commons is that he represents all his constituents, whether they voted for him or not. An MP is, first and last, a member of Parliament, not a delegate from one

THE EXPERIENCES OF A NEW M.P.

group of electors in one constituency. Burke summed it up precisely in his famous address to the electors of Bristol in 1774: 'You choose a member indeed, but when you have chosen him, he is not a member of Bristol, but he is a member of *Parliament*.'

Once he is finally elected a Member, what does a new MP find at Westminster? First, he has to run the gauntlet of the policemen who guard every entrance but who, with every justification, pride themselves on getting to know the faces of every single Member within days of a new Parliament being returned. He will usually enter the Palace through the Members' Entrance in New Palace Yard, after leaving his car in the five-storey underground car park beneath the Yard; it can take 450 cars and cost nearly three million pounds to build in the early 1970s – more than the cost of the entire Palace a hundred years before. From there Members go, via an escalator, to their cloakroom, where each one has his own hook – labelled alphabetically and not by party – on which he or she can hang his or her sword. Each coat-hanger is supplied with a short loop of red tape, which is there so that Members can hang up their swords before going into the Chamber. The colour of the red tape on the hangers – much used, nowadays, for hanging umbrellas instead of putting them in the stands that Pugin designed – is exactly the same as the colour of the two red lines which stretch along the floor of the House of Commons, a few inches away from each front bench. Both the pieces

Below left: A new arrival Nervous new MPs always complain that no one tells them where to go or what to do when they arrive at Westminster.
The door-keepers, all ex-servicemen, steer them round the vast Palace

Below: Prayers Every day in both Houses begins with Prayers. No strangers are ever admitted. MPs face the seats behind them because, in the days when they wore swords, it was impossible to kneel on the floor and they turned to kneel on the benches behind them

1. THE NEW M.P. ARRIVES AT THE HOUSE, AND BEING SOMEWHAT SHORT-SIGHTED MISTAKES THE MESSENGER FOR SOME HIGH FUNCTIONARY, POSSIBLY THE LORD HIGH CHANCELLOR, AND SHAKES HANDS ACCORDINGLY

The following labels appear within the illustration:

1. GETTING HIS LETTERS
2. HURRIED LUNCH AFTER LONG MORNING ON COMMITTEE
3. PRAYERS
4. ESCORTING CONSTITUENTS TO THE STRANGERS' GALLERY
5. EACH EAGERLY STRIVING TO CATCH THE SPEAKER'S EYE
6. "LIABLE TO BE INTERRUPTED AT ANY MOMENT"
7. SINCE SUFFRAGETTE RAIDS LADIES MUST WAIT IN ST STEPHEN'S HALL FOR MEMBERS
8. CALLED TO THE TELEPHONE
9. AN INFORMAL DEPUTATION CENTRAL HALL
10. A PEEP AT THE HOUSE THROUGH THE GLASS DOORS
11. INTERVIEW WITH LABOUR MEMBERS IN THE SMOKING ROOM
12. ROUSING A SLEEPY COLLEAGUE FOR DIVISION
13. MEETING DINNER GUESTS IN CENTRAL HALL

Above: 'The Major and Minor Events of a Day at St Stephen's' The House of Commons at work, 1908

of red tape and the red stripes in the carpet are there for much the same reason – to prevent Members from attacking each other with their swords. It is, of course, absolutely forbidden for Members to take any sort of offensive weapon into the Chamber; when, some years ago, a Scottish Member appeared in full Highland dress with a dirk in his stocking-top, there were protests, but he was allowed to keep it in place.

In the eighteenth century swords were part of a gentleman's fashionable dress, but Members were obliged to leave them outside the

Chamber, hung up on the red tape provided in the cloakroom. Should, however, a Member come into the Chamber with a sword and somehow avoid Mr Speaker's notice, something had to be done to make sure he did not attempt to use his sword when debates got heated. So the idea of the red lines in the carpet was hit upon. The red lines, one in front of the Government benches and one in front of the Opposition benches, are just two sword lengths apart; so even if Members had their illegal swords with them and tempers flared, provided they stayed behind the red lines their swords would not touch and no damage would be done. It is still out of order for a Member to step across the red lines when he is speaking. Presumably another old rule still applies: that although no Members may wear their swords in the Chamber, county Members, and county Members only, may wear their spurs.

If the new MP arriving at the Commons is a woman then she will find little record of the long fight that women endured to secure a right to seats in Parliament. The only memorial to the suffragettes is a broken statue of Falkland in St Stephen's Hall, the last of a line of statues along the left-hand wall as visitors go towards the Central Lobby. Falkland was the man who was so rude about geese in the Commons, and in 1908 a suffragette chained herself to his statue. The only way to free her was to break the marble spur on Falkland's right foot, and his sword which, point down, he rests on the ground before him. The spur has never been repaired, and the sword only rather roughly stuck together. Three years after this little demonstration another suffragette, Emily Davison who, in 1913 was killed when she threw herself under the King's horse at the Derby, hid herself on a flight of steps leading to the Crypt Chapel. She was there for forty-eight hours, protesting over a census that was then being conducted. Her protest was in vain; she was counted in the census as one of the many residents in the Palace that night.

Whichever way Members enter the Palace of Westminster, sooner or later they congregate in the Members' Lobby, the crossroads, the Piccadilly Circus through which all the life of the Commons flows. It is the ante-room of the Commons; the point where, once the House is sitting, MPs are beyond the reach of the general public and where they can loiter and gossip and chatter to the Lobby journalists who are allowed to talk to them. It has been a crucial part of the process of parliamentary government ever since the Commons first had their own meeting place in 1547.

The present Lobby is a high, rather bleak place, 45 feet square, built in what has been described as 'neon-Gothic'. It has twice had to be rebuilt since Sir Charles Barry included it in his plans for Westminster after the 1834 fire; once after the bomb put in the Chamber by Irish extremists in 1885 which badly damaged the Members' Lobby as well as the Chamber; and again after the war-time German bombing of 1941, which left it in ruins. There is a souvenir of the war-time destruction in the Churchill Arch, which forms the entrance from the Lobby to the

Chamber. At Churchill's suggestion the archway was left damaged and unrepaired as a reminder of the destruction of the Chamber and as a memorial to those who fought in the war. Churchill himself now stands, a massive figure in bronze, on the left-hand side of the arch named after him, with his foot worn bright by the hands of hopeful MPs trying to borrow a little of his magic on their way into the Chamber. On the other side of the arch stands a less impressive figure of the Liberal leader, Lloyd George. A tactful readjustment of the heights of their respective plinths has recently been made, to try to make the Liberal Prime Minister look less overshadowed by the Conservative leader.

To the right and left of the Lobby are large message boards in which every Member has a small slot with his name on it. If there is a message for him, his name lights up so he or his secretary can keep a check on who wants him. As Members pass through the Lobby they can also pop into one of the two post offices that are always open at Westminster; or they can collect, from a window beside the archway, the day's parliamentary papers from the Vote Office.

'Fair Lemons and Oranges'
Orange girls used to crowd into the Members' Lobby in the eighteenth century to sell, among other things, oranges. They were run by an old madam named Mother Drybutters

The Members' Lobby is almost as heavy with tradition as the Chamber itself. When MPs first moved into the old St Stephen's Chapel in 1547, they simply turned the area beyond the great rood screen they found there into their Lobby – a place to plan and plot and gossip. They could glance through the double door in the screen to keep an eye on the Chamber, and slip quietly in and out of the House as the debates progressed. Gradually, the Lobby became part of the institution of the Commons, and the smart place for London society to be seen. The orange girls came there selling, among other things, oranges. A woman known as Mother Drybutters ran them, and she, it was said, knew more about the Members' private lives than 'all the old bawds in Christendom put together'. When eighteenth century Members should have been paying attention to the dramas of the American War, their minds, in fact, were on Mary Mullins, one of the girls who loitered in their Lobby, 'a young, plump, crummy, rosy-looking wench, with clean white silk stockings, Turkey leather shoes, pink silk *short* petticoat, to show her ankle to the young bulls and the old goats of the House'. As one sardonic poet put it:

> *Mark with what grace she offers to his hand*
> *The Tempting orange, pride of China's land,*

Mullins, they said, killed more men in the Commons with her eyes and her sighs than did many a general with cannisters and grapeshot in the American War.

It was in the Members' Lobby that real death was done on 11 May, 1812, when the Prime Minister was assassinated at the very door of the Commons. Spencer Perceval had been Prime Minister for about two years when he arrived that day to the Commons. As he walked through the Lobby a tall man in tradesman's dress stepped towards him, took out a pistol and shot him dead on the spot. In the ensuing panic, the murderer, who immediately admitted what he had done – 'I am that unfortunate man', he said – was grabbed and instantly hauled before the House. He was packed off for trial and hanged within seven days.

The assassin turned out to be John Bellingham, the son of a Huntingdon land surveyor who had died insane. John had tried his luck in Russia and subsequently had been imprisoned there for five years for debt; as a result he became obsessed with Perceval's failure to get him released. When he eventually returned to England, he went to the Commons with two loaded pistols. In the event he had to use only one of them. Perceval's last words were 'Oh! I am murdered.' When guides today tell wide-eyed school children about the gruesome scene, they invariably add: 'And those were the only true words ever spoken by a Prime Minister!' The children never know whether they are supposed to laugh or not. They are also shown a spot on the floor where the pattern in the tiles is clearly completely muddled and wrong. They are told that this marks the spot where Perceval fell – which, if it is true, shows a remarkable degree of perception on the part of the Victorian craftsmen who actually laid the tiles some forty years later!

In the Upper Waiting Hall, a part of the Palace which people on guided tours normally never see, stands a large and splendidly carved oak table which once graced the Commons and, by tradition, was designed by Sir Christopher Wren. At the time of Perceval's murder the table had been moved from the Chamber and into the Lobby, and he is said to have fallen against it and stained it with his blood as he died. These days the table is usually hidden away behind exhibition stands, and its dramatic legend forgotten.

The dramas of the contemporary Lobby are dramas of political plotting and intrigue, and as Members pass beneath the Churchill Arch on their way to the Chamber they can stop to clear their heads with a pinch of snuff from the official House of Commons snuff box. Once there was a snuff shop in the Lobby, but now the box is kept on a ledge beside the Principal Doorkeeper's deep green leather chair, immediately outside the Commons door. The box is made from oak saved from the bombed Chamber after the last war, and it contains a blend of snuff milled especially for the Commons. On top of the box there is a silver plaque which lists the names of the Principal Doorkeepers who have guarded the Chamber door.

As new Members or visitors enter the Commons Chamber their reaction is always exactly the same. How small it is! It is certainly much too small to hold all 650 Members, and this is quite deliberate. Only 346 Members – not much more than half their total – can actually sit down at any one time; all the rest have to crowd round the door and in the gangways, and around and behind the Speaker's chair, if they want to hear what is going on. The number who can be seated is exactly the same as in the pre-war House; when it came to the rebuilding after the war–

time bombing Churchill's influence saw to it that the size remained identical in the new Chamber. He felt, quite correctly, that given the style and traditions of the House, its size was just about right. Except on great occasions, there are seldom more than twenty Members present during the major part of most debates, and if the House was any bigger it would look even emptier than it often does. When those great occasions do occur, the crowds of Members bustling and pressing and jostling for space adds enormously to the drama and tension of decisions which may very well change the course of the nation's history. The old, sixteenth century MP's description of the House then as 'being framed and made like unto a theatre' is still perfectly apt, especially at those moments. Round the sides of the Chamber there are galleries for Strangers and journalists and some overspill seats for MPs (from which they may, but usually do not, attempt to speak), bringing the total number of seats in the Chamber for Members, Strangers and journalists to 935. Small indeed for a place of such great importance.

The present Chamber, designed by Sir Giles Scott, and opened in 1950, is much in the spirit of the bombed Chamber designed by Sir Charles Barry. The inevitable committee which supervised its rebuilding said that they thought the 'sense of intimacy and almost conversational form of debate encouraged by the dimensions of the old House should be maintained'. So they were. The five rows of leather benches, in the traditional green of the Commons, are still there; although now there is bright and diffused lighting from panels in the high oak ceiling. From a point above the Strangers' Gallery the lens of a periscope peers down into the Chamber so that engineers can see how full or empty the House is, and adjust the air-conditioning accordingly. A mottled brown carpet runs the length of the room, interspersed with the essential red lines, and the oak headboards above the benches hold little bronze portholes, which are loudspeakers that amplify the speeches which are picked up by the microphones hanging above the MPs' heads. At one end of the Chamber is the Bar, a white line on the carpet beyond which no one who is not an MP may venture. If anyone is brought to the Bar of the House charged with offending its privileges, two bronze railings, the gift of Jamaica, can be drawn out from oak barriers on either side of the Bar, and the offender must stand behind them to hear his fate.

At the far end of the Chamber from the Bar is the Speaker's canopied chair, still placed on top of what were once altar steps, to commemorate the lay-out of St Stephen's Chapel. In front of the Speaker, three wigged and gowned clerks sit at the Table of the House. They have before them a series of clocks which have been set running to time the lengths of debates or divisions, since time is a vital ingredient in the procedures of the Commons. On the right of the Speaker's chair is the Treasury bench – that is, the Government front bench, called the Treasury bench because the Prime Minister's principal title is First Lord of the Treasury. To the left of the Speaker are the Opposition benches, where leaders of the main opposition party sit on the front bench; the other parties who oppose the government of the day sit among the rest of the opposition MPs on the back benches. At the end of the Commons Table, which runs between the two front benches, are the Despatch Boxes.

Like almost everything else in the Chamber, the two Despatch Boxes were presented by a commonwealth country – in this case, New Zealand – for the post-war rebuilding scheme. The boxes are used as lecterns on which Ministers and Shadow Ministers place their papers when they address the House, and over the years the bronze fittings on the tops and sides of the boxes have become worn smooth as the sweating ministerial, or shadow-ministerial, hands have nervously rubbed them away. The boxes are most certainly not used for sending or containing despatches. They are used to hold Bibles.

Every Member of the Commons has either to swear or to affirm his loyalty to the Crown. Those Members, and they are the great majority, who swear, do so upon a Bible, and so these are kept ready in the Despatch Box on the Government side of the Commons. There is an Authorised Version, a Douai Version (for Catholics) and an Old Testament (for Jews), plus the forms of oath or affirmation that every Member must read out before he can take his seat. In the Despatch Box on the Opposition side, which is never opened, rests one badly charred Authorised version of the Bible, rescued from the war-time bombing.

The oath that MPs take is short and simple: 'I . . . do swear that I will be faithful and bear true allegiance to Her Majesty Queen Elizabeth, her heirs and successors, according to law. So help me God.' It was not always as easy as that. In the Reformation days when the Pope's authority in England was so hotly disputed, Elizabethan MPs had to swear that 'no foreign prince, person, prelate, State or potentate hath, or ought to have, any jurisdiction, power, sovereignty, pre-eminence or authority, ecclasiastical or spiritual, with this realm'. In the anti-Catholic atmosphere precipitated by the Popish Plot dreamed up by Titus Oates in 1678, Members had to swear they did not believe in transubstantiation, the invocation of the saints and the sacrifice of the mass; a long process that must have taken many hours when there were a number of new Members. When Catholics were finally allowed to sit in the House in 1829 they had to swear a very long oath saying, among many other things, that they did not believe that the Pope had any temporal power in the kingdom.

Jews fought a long and bitter battle before they were allowed to take an oath which would admit them to their elected seats in the Commons. Naturally enough, they objected to the phrase 'upon the true faith of a Christian' which appeared in the long parliamentary oaths, and it took Baron Lionel Nathan de Rothschild nearly twelve years of campaigning after his first election as Member for the City of London before he could actually take his seat in the Commons. Attempts by the House to change the law dealing with oaths, which would have allowed Jews to sit, were invariably thrown out by the Lords, and although another Jewish MP, Alderman Solomons, did sit for a time, he became embroiled in long legal wrangles concerning his right to do so. Baron de Rothschild himself spent endless hours sitting below the Bar of the House of Lords, an ever-present and deep reproach to their bigotry, but the Lords ignored him. Eventually, in 1860, religious barriers for Members were swept away and in 1868 the Promissory Oaths Act, which also abolished a whole mass of oaths which had to be taken by various officials outside Parliament, brought in the present form of wording.

The oath is administered to new MPs by the Clerk of the House, who then invites the Member to sign the Test Roll. At one time this was a roll of parchment, which Members had to sign to test their acceptance of the monarch as head of the Church in England; today it is a book, interleaved with sheets of pink blotting paper between each page. Once the Test Roll is signed with his name and constituency, and the correct official form from the local election returning officer has been given to the Clerk, all that is left for the new Member is to be formally presented by the Clerk to the Speaker. The Clerk calls out the name and constituency of the new arrival; there is a shaking of hands and a word of welcome, and the dazed new MP finds himself behind the Speaker's chair. With the oath taken and the Test Roll signed he can safely claim those magic initials – 'MP'.

As he gathers his wits about him after the nerve-racking strain of coming to the House for the first time – and it is much more difficult for a Member who has won a by-election, since he attracts the full attention of an often excited House as he takes the oath – he will realise that the area behind the Speaker's chair, where he is now standing, plays an important part in the life of the Commons. It is a political no-man's-land; this is the part of the Commons where apparent political enemies will chat amicably together, give private explanations that they could not make in public, or make arrangements for one side to drop some contentious piece of business providing the other side will make a similar concession. It is a vital area of parliamentary compromise which allows business to proceed smoothly.

On the high back of the Speaker's chair – which was donated by Australia and is made out of black bean wood – is a brass hook from which hangs a large green baize bag. This is the bag in which petitions to the Commons are placed and from which, in due course, they are taken to disappear into obscurity among the millions of documents in the Victoria Tower.

Petitioning Parliament is an ancient and honourable tradition, for Acts of Parliament were merely a development of petitions to the King. The first petition to Parliament was submitted in 1327, and both British citizens and foreigners living here have the same rights of petition today, if they feel they have grievances that need to be corrected. The petitions have to be worded in a suitably humble form: 'To the Honourable the

Commons of the United Kingdom of Great Britain and Northern Ireland, in Parliament assembled . . .' and end: '. . . and your petitioners, as in duty bound, will ever pray'. Petitioners can pray for pretty well anything they like within the law, but they must do so in their own handwriting; petitions must not be typed or printed; they must be in English; there must be no crossings-out or corrections. Petitioners must sign only their legal names; men have been sent to prison for impersonation on a petition. In 1887 Reginald Midmead was brought to the Bar of the House for forging nearly 1,700 names to petitions. There is, of course, no limit to the number of genuine signatures that they can contain. The most famous of all, the Chartist Petition of 1842, had three and a half million names on it. That, however, was a mere nothing compared with some other monster petitions. A petition drawn up in 1890, in favour of a Local Taxation Bill, was eight miles long, and another, to do with the licencing laws, was almost as immense. Whether they, or any of the petitions that are still solemnly presented to the House by MPs on behalf of their constituents, are worth the paper they are written on is another matter. Presumably petitions do work off local steam; but that is all. At least the system has given a handy expression to the English language. When petitions are placed safely in the huge green baize holder behind the Speaker's chair, they are well and truly 'in the bag'.

In the bag The green felt bag behind the Speaker's chair in which petitions to the House of Commons are placed – so 'in the bag'. Petitions may have just a few signatures, or several millions; the most famous petition of all, the Chartists' Petition of 1839, had nearly one and a half million signatures, but was by no means the largest. Petitions must always be handwritten; in English, and respectful in their requests

Among the many rituals of the Commons that a new Member has to work out for himself is where to sit. Tradition alone dictates that governments sit on the Speaker's right and oppositions on his left. In practice, of course, the seating arrangements are strictly formalised. The Prime Minister, or the senior Government Minister in charge of the business then going through the House, sits opposite the Government Despatch Box; his Shadow Minister sits in the same position on the Opposition front bench. Other Ministers and Shadow Ministers spread along their front benches, and on the end seat of the two front benches sit the two Chief Whips or the senior Whips present in the House. Along the end wall to the right of the Speaker's chair is the civil servants' box; technically, it is outside the Chamber, and it is here that ministry officials sit listening to the debates and sending advice and information to their Ministers.

The two long banks of green benches that run the length of the Chamber are divided, halfway along, by a gangway. By tradition, the first seats below the gangways are reserved for former Prime Ministers, and there is a rather less precise tradition that the rest of the front bench seats below the gangway are occupied by people who like to think of themselves as the active and lively consciences of their respective parties. Senior backbench Members have their favourite seats from which junior Members scurry when the great man arrives to claim it, and minor parties also claim various groups of seats as their own.

At either end of the Chamber rows of green benches run along the end walls. These are the overflows. Members cannot speak from this spot and on long, late night sittings, they tend to come in handy as places where Members can stretch out, as they say in Parliament, 'with their eyes closed!' There is, however, one way in which ordinary backbench Members can claim a seat for themselves. Behind each place along the benches is a small bronze frame in which Members can put Prayer Cards – cards on which they write their names and then put in place before prayers begin. If the Member is in that seat when prayers start, he can claim it for the rest of the day. Traditionally, Labour MPs do not use Prayer Cards; no one seems to know why.

In the days when MPs wore top hats, they could reserve their places by putting their toppers on a seat, but they had to do this with the brim upwards and crown down. They had to be genuine 'working hats' belonging to the Member himself. One smart operator apparently arrived in a four-wheeler brimming over with top hats, which he proposed to use to bag all the available Commons seats for his party in an important debate. The Serjeant-at-Arms said 'no' and made his displeasure known.

Members can, if they wish, still wear hats in the House and very occasionally do. They have to take the hats off if they want to speak, and raise them in acknowledgement if anyone refers to them. A new Member might, however, be astonished to see a top hat whizzing

around the Chamber as an important and necessary part of the Commons proceedings. It is a rule of the House that, in a division, any Member who wants to raise a point of order must do so sitting and with his head covered. The reasons for this are quite simple: when a division is taking place, several hundred Members are milling around the Chamber, so it is essential that anyone who wants to raise a point of order with the Speaker does something to draw attention to himself. He does so by breaking a series of rules. Members may not speak when they are sitting down, and they may not wear a hat when they are speaking. When a Member does both at the same time, he can hardly fail to attract the Speaker's notice. He always succeeds in doing so, mainly because of the general glee that sweeps the House when the official top hat is called for.

The House of Commons top hat is a collapsible opera hat, of exactly the same kind from which magicians extract white rabbits, and it is kept by the Serjeant-at-Arms, in an OHMS envelope, under his chair near the door of the House. When it is wanted the Serjeant produces it; it is snapped open by the strong springs inside; and after it is put on by the Member, the point of order may be raised. Amid much hooting and shouting, the hat is then collapsed and, as often as not, it is skimmed round the Chamber, like a flat stone over a pond, from Member to Member. It is not enough for a Member to try to cover his head with a paper or a handkerchief; it must be a hat. In spite of the official top hat, any hat will do; lady Members have been known to lend their millinery to a hard-pressed male Member who missed the official topper when it spun his way.

It is, as Members with a sensitivity for these sorts of things like to point out, one of those little traditions that add colour to the ancient life of the Commons. How much it does for its dignity is, of course, another matter. Perhaps an excess of dignity does not help to make good law!

CHAPTER ELEVEN
Order, Order!

The Speaker of the House of Commons does not speak. That is to say he does not make speeches to the House, and plays no part in debates or discussions in the Chamber. He is not a Minister of the Crown; he is not a member of the Cabinet; he is not a member of a political party. He is the man who speaks on behalf of the Commons to the monarch.

This function has now become largely formal and ceremonial, and the Speaker's job, in practice, is to preside over the debates of the House of Commons. It is the Speaker who selects which MPs shall be given the floor in any particular debate, although, like everything else in Parliament, the decision is governed by parliamentary traditions and rules. It is the Speaker who decides which Members will ask supplementary questions of Ministers at Question Time. It is the Speaker who has, by wit and wisdom, to control the House at moments of excitement and anger; who must memorise the name of every one of the 650 members; who must know the rules, ancient traditions and precedents of the House for instant and effective use; who must protect minorities and also ensure that majorities use their rights without abusing them; who must rule on what the House may or may not do, no matter how strong the pressures on him, and no matter which powerful factions he may offend in the process. He must be all-wise; all-patient; all-knowing; tolerant; firm and yet pliant. As one great occupant of the chair, Speaker Lowther, once said: 'The office of Speaker does not demand rare qualities. It demands common qualities in rare degree'. He is, at one and the same time, both the master of the House and its servant. No wonder that some extraordinary men have occupied Mr Speaker's chair over the centuries.

The list of men who have presided over the Commons goes back to 1258, when Peter de Montfort acted as spokesman for the House, its 'pourparlour', at the Mad Parliament that met in Oxford. The title of 'Speaker' emerged in 1376 with Sir Peter de la Mare and Sir Thomas Hungerford – Sir Thomas was the first designated Speaker. Sir Peter, however, established the right of the Commons to speak with firm honesty to the King when it thought it necessary. At that period, the Commons met in the Chapter House of Westminster Abbey, and there it fumed against demands for yet more taxes from the King, Edward III, at least partly to support his mistress, Alice Perrers. Sir Peter, steward to the Earl of March and a knight from the Welsh borders, a man of powerful and impressive character, was commissioned to speak to the King on behalf of the Commons. 'By common consent', says a contemporary account, 'because Sir Peter de la Mare was so good a speaker and summed up the views and suggestions of his colleagues so ably, expressing them in fact better than they could have done themselves, they begged him to undertake for them the task of announcing before the Lords in full Parliament what they had decided to do and say in the light of their consciences. And Sir Peter, out of duty to God and his good companions, and for the benefit of the country, undertook the duty.' In the process, Sir Peter established the right of the Commons to be heard by the Lords if it so wished. When he alone was granted access to the House of Lords, and the rest of the Commons was shut out, he held up the proceedings for two hours until the Commons was permitted to join him at the Bar of the House. 'What one of us says, all of us say and consent to', said Sir Peter, in a declaration which remains true today. Sir Peter, however, paid the price for his boldness and became one of a long list of nine Speakers who ended up in prison, or dead, because they had annoyed the King. He was sent to languish in Nottingham Castle to contemplate his outspokenness.

Two hundred years later, a man who had been both Speaker of the Commons and Lord Chancellor, Sir Thomas More, was to be imprisoned and then beheaded for his refusal to accept the dictates of a despotic King. More was Speaker for less than six months, from April to August 1523, but in that short time he defied both the King and the great Cardinal Wolsey, and established the fundamental right, jealously guarded now as it was then, of the Commons to refuse the monarch money if it thought there was good reason for doing so.

More had been appointed Speaker on the recommendation of Wolsey, and he was the first Speaker to claim from the King his indulgence for any words which might be spoken by Members during their debates – a privilege which MPs still enjoy – 'to give to all your Commons here assembled your most gracious licence and pardon freely, without doubt of your dreadful displeasure, every man to discharge his conscience . . .' More's conscience drove him to refuse Wolsey's demands for £800,000 (then a vast sum) for the French wars. Wolsey, the Lord Chancellor, made the wholly unconstitutional decision to come to the Commons himself to demand the money 'with his maces, his pillars, his poleaxes, his cross, his hat and the Great Seal, too'. The House froze into disapproving silence at the Cardinal's arrival; it was, said the tactful More, who had fallen upon his knees, 'abashed at the sight of so noble a personage, who was able to amaze the wisest and most learned men in the realm'. Then, 'with many probable arguments he (More) endeavoured to show the Cardinal that his manner of coming thither was neither expedient nor agreeable to the ancient liberties of the House, and in conclusion told him that except all the members could put their several thoughts into his head, he alone was unable in so weighty a matter to give his Grace a sufficient answer'. Wolsey swept out of the House in a towering passion. Henry VIII, equally furious, sent for an influential Member of the Commons, Edward Montague and, placing his hand upon the terrified and kneeling man's head, shouted: 'Get my

Bill passed by tomorrow, or else tomorrow this head of yours shall be off.' As far as Montague was concerned, this was an unanswerable argument, and the Bill did, indeed, go through, although in a greatly modified form. But, the House had defied the King, and established its right to do so in the future.

Not all Henry's Speakers had More's courage or principles. It was one of his successors, Sir Richard Rich, who visited More when he was imprisoned by Henry in the Tower of London, and who then falsely and treacherously reported their alleged conversation to the court which condemned the great man to death. Rich, however, was much more in keeping with the tradition of Henry's Speakers than More had been. Rich fawned upon the King, and told him that 'as the sun expells all the noxious vapours which would otherwise be hurtful to us, and by heat cherishes and brings forth those seeds, plants and fruits necessary for the support of human life, so this our most excellent prince takes away by his prudence all those enormities which may hereafter be anyway hurtful to us and our posterity, and takes care to enact such laws as will be a great defence to the good and a great terror to evil doers'. What was more, the King could be compared for 'justice and prudence to Solomon, for strength and fortitude to Samson and for beauty and comeliness to Absolam'. Henry was, in fact, fat, drunken and degenerate!

Elizabeth I had the Speakers firmly under her control. One of them, Sir Edward Coke, a very able man, could unblushingly tell her that, under her guidance, Parliament was 'that sweet commonwealth of little bees'. The Queen was, of course, the Queen Bee, and 'under your happy government we live upon honey; but where the bee sucketh honey there also the spider draweth poison. Some such venoms there be – but such drones and door bees we shall expel the hive and serve Your Majesty, and withstand any enemy that shall assault you. Our lands, our good, our lives are prostrate at your feet to be commanded.'

Speakers remained very much Kings' – and Queens' – men; they still have to be formally approved by the sovereign on being elected by the Commons. In 1629, Speaker Finch, firmly in Charles I's pay, refused to put a proposition to the Commons which he knew the King opposed. As the House became more and more insistent, so Finch became more and more distressed; until he finally burst into tears and tried to leave the chair. He was thereupon grabbed by irate Members, and held down in his seat until he had agreed to their demands.

It was another weak Speaker who, nevertheless, established the absolute independence of the Commons from the Crown. He did it almost by accident; a vascillating, place-seeking turncoat who became the greatest name in the long history of the Speakership – yet died in misery and bitter disgrace. History arranged for Speaker William Lenthall to be sitting in the Speaker's chair, in the tense, expectant House of Commons, when on 4 January, 1642, Charles I came to try to arrest five Members of Parliament. This was the first and last time that a

monarch has ever crossed the Bar of the Commons while it is sitting. It established a precedent so potent that when King George VI came to Westminster over 300 years later, to re-open the Commons chamber after the bombing of the Second World War, the ceremony was conducted in Westminster Hall and not in the Chamber itself – although the King did become the only reigning monarch since Charles I to enter the House when he, accompanied by Queen Elizabeth and Queen Mary, was shown round it the day before the official opening.

Charles I brought seven charges of treason against five Members, Pym, Hampden (the 'Village Hampden'), Holles, Haselrig and Strode. He believed that these men were the ringleaders in getting the Grand Remonstrance, criticising his rule and making demands for reform, through the Commons. He brought troops with him, although he left them outside the Commons, where they waved their swords and cocked their pistols at the MPs inside. The furious, horrified Commons watched as he walked up to Lenthall and said: 'By your leave Mr Speaker, I must borrow your chair a little.' At the Table in front of him, the Clerk, Rushworth, was furiously scribbling down everything that occurred in the Chamber.

Charles called out the names of Pym and Holles, and when he got no reply – the five had been warned in advance that the King was on his way and had left by boat down the Thames, from the Speaker's Steps just outside the Chamber – he demanded to know where they were. This was Lenthall's greatest moment. From somewhere out of his devious and doubtful character he dredged up his splendid defiance; he fell on his knees and told his King, 'May it please Your Majesty, I have neither eyes to see nor tongue to speak in this place, but as the House is pleased to direct of me, whose servant I am; and I humbly beg Your Majesty's pardon that I cannot give any other answer than this to what Your Majesty is pleased to demand of me.' Charles was staggered at hearing words of defiance coming from such a man, but he recovered his dignity, and said, after a long stare round the House, 'Well, I see the birds have flown', and promptly walked from the Chamber, his ears filled with the angry cries of 'Privilege, Privilege' from the excited Members.

So Lenthall established that great and fundamental independence of the Commons from the Crown – and Charles, by asking for Pym and Holles by name incidentally established the tradition that Members never use names in the Commons, but always refer to each other indirectly in the third person. The Commons also had a new lock put on their door, in case of a repeat visit.

Lenthall survived as Speaker for some fifteen years, and desperately tried to curry favour with the King's party when Charles II was restored on the throne. He had, however, been the Speaker who had put the motion to the Commons that they should try Charles I, and for that he could not be forgiven. He died in his bed, a forgotten and bitter man, on 3 September, 1662, lucky not to have died on the scaffold as a regicide. 'No excuse can be made for me', he said, in his final confession, 'that I proposed the bloody question for trying the King; but I hoped even that when I put the question, the very putting the question would have cleared him, because I believed there were four to one against it – Cromwell and his agents deceived me.'

Perhaps out of some sort of gratitude for his time serving, Cromwell made the Speaker the first citizen in the land – he is now the third Commoner, after the Prime Minister and the Lord President of the

Council. However, the office continued to lose power under the Commonwealth and in the early days of the Restoration, Speaker Edward Seymour, who took the chair in 1673, resurrected at least some of its importance by his tremendous dignity. On one occasion he ordered an eminent lawyer, who got in his way as he went through Westminster Hall, into the custody of the Serjeant-at-Arms for showing no respect for the Speaker's rank and office. Again, according to his contemporary, Lord Dartmouth: 'On one occasion, in passing through Charing Cross, the Speaker's carriage broke down, and he ordered the beadles to stop the gentleman's they met and bring it to him. The gentleman in it was much surprised to be turned out of his own coach, but Sir Edward told him it was more proper for him to walk in the streets than for the Speaker of the House of Commons, and left him so to do without further apology.' To this day, the Speaker has his own carriage; an ancient, springless and elaborate affair, kept for him in a London brewery and used very rarely indeed. The archways between the courtyards that separate the Speaker's official residence at one end of the Palace of Westminster from the Lord Chancellor's residence at the other end, are said to have been built just wide enough to allow the carriage to pass through when Mr Speaker wished to make an official visit to his noble neighbour!

The dignity established by Speaker Seymour was, however, very badly dented some years later by Speaker Sir John Trevor, a hard-drinking, uncouth Welsh lawyer. He had a ferocious squint in his bulbous face, and it is thanks to him that the Speaker today has to call each Member by name – the only person in the House allowed to do so, once the Charles I tradition was established. Until Trevor, Members simply had to 'catch the Speaker's eye', and they then got up and spoke. So bad was Trevor's squint that no one could be certain which Member he was looking at, and rows broke out when two Members got up at the same time and claimed he had been looking at them. To get round the problem, it was decided that, from then on, Speakers would have to announce the person they had chosen to speak by name.

Speaker Trevor's other claim to fame is that not only did he get the sack from the Commons, but he also had to sack himself. He was found guilty of taking a bribe to help get a Bill through the House for the relief of orphans, and of helping the East India Company. Both the City Corporation and the East India Company actually entered the bribes in their books, and when he was caught by the House, ironically, Sir John Trevor presided in the Speaker's chair while the debate on his wrongdoings was underway. 'That Sir John Trevor, Speaker of this House, receiving a gratuity of 1,000 guineas from the City of London, after passing of the Orphans Bill, is guilty of a high crime and misdemeanour.' The Speaker himself put the motion for his own dismissal, and it was passed almost unanimously. He rushed from the chair and next day sent a message saying that 'after rising this morning he was taken suddenly ill with a violent colic', whereupon the Commons expelled him both from the Chair and from the House. Trevor, however, was a great survivor. He kept the job, which he already held, as Master of the Rolls, and was one of eight Commoners to be elected to the first Privy Council.

A later hard-drinking Speaker, Speaker Charles Wolfran Cornwall, also temporarily instituted a rather odd change in the procedure of the House of Commons. He drunk porter by the potful, which he kept by the side of his chair – any Member who tried to do the same thing today would certainly incur the most profound displeasure of Mr Speaker. Cornwall, however, reigned in the days when MPs ate oranges, apples, pears and biscuits in the Chamber, so no one was very much surprised as he sat drinking and sniffing snuff. In those days there were no Deputy Speakers (there are three now) and even Speakers are human. The time inevitably came when Mr Speaker wanted to slip away. As he could not leave the chair, he had certain arrangements made. Curtains were put up round it; the seat could be lifted up, and a commode appeared beneath the green leather. The curtains would be drawn; the House would talk on and, in due course, the curtains would be pulled back, and the debate continue!

Before Cornwall made the Speaker's chair so eminently convenient, the status of the Speakership had been improved dramatically by one of its greatest holders, Speaker Arthur Onslow. He went to the chair when he was thirty-four, and remained there for thirty-three years from 1728 to 1761. He was the third member of his family to hold the office (the first had been an Elizabethan) and although he was authoritarian and did not suffer fools gladly, he was re-elected to office five times. Onslow was a figure of vast dignity, and Members were said to go in dread of being 'named' – that is, expelled from the House for a day or more – by him. When asked what he would do if a difficult Member refused to go, Onslow replied, 'The Lord in Heaven only knows.' When Fox later asked Speaker Fletcher Norton the same question, that Speaker replied, 'Hang me if I either know or care.'

Onslow was one of the last Speakers ever to make a speech in the House. Speakers had, by tradition, the right to make speeches when the House was sitting as a committee. On one occasion, Onslow was listening from a gallery and, in order to tempt him down onto the floor of the House, a Member suggested that the Speaker should be exempted from the tax that was being discussed. Onslow was so determined to be above suspicion that he even refused to accept any form of official salary, so this proposal brought him down hot-foot, to argue long and loudly, and successfully, against the Motion.

Onslow was endlessly patient, kind and understanding, but immensely imposing and stern when he wanted to be. It is difficult to imagine him tolerating, as Sir Edward Phelips had to in 1610, a Member who, according to the minutes of the House, 'put out his tongue, and

Speaker Arthur Onslow (right) He became Speaker at 34, and was re-elected five times. He was Speaker for a total of 35 years. In this Hogarth picture, he is talking to the first Prime Minister, Sir Robert Walpole

popped his mouth with his fingure in scorn', at him; or a Member who went up behind Speaker Lenthall and shouted 'Baugh' in his ear 'to his great terror and affrightment'.

Sir Fletcher Norton, who held the post soon after Speaker Onslow, would not have been much to his liking, either. Norton positively encouraged rowdiness and bad behaviour in the House; he also much disliked the imperious attitude of the Lords and determined to cut them down to size. In 1772, when Burke had taken a Bill to the Upper House he had been kept waiting three hours; when the Bill was returned to the Commons, Norton threw it right across the Table onto the floor beyond, and watched with approval as Members kicked it along the floor, out of the door of Chamber and into the Lobby. Norton, though, eventually went too far. He, like Onslow before him, decided to take part in a debate during a committee sitting, and the argument degenerated into a furious row with the Prime Minister, Lord North. The affair became 'pure Billingsgate', and when Norton came up for re-election some months later he was thrown out of office by a shocked House of Commons.

The last Speaker to take part in a debate also got himself effectively voted out of office. Speaker Charles Manners-Sutton, Speaker for eighteen years, was charming but biased – a Tory Speaker against Liberal members who was, nevertheless, elected by five Houses. 'A man of more conciliating, bland and gentlemanly manners never crossed the threshold of St Stephen's', a dazzled fan wrote of him, yet when the Whigs put up a rival candidate, and Manners-Sutton kept the job by only six votes, he felt it was time to go, and collect the by now inevitable peerage.

Undoubtedly, the Speakers' Speaker was Speaker Henry Bouverie Brand because, by taking a firm attitude with Irish nationalist MPs, he provided governments with a method of stopping endless debates in the Commons. In 1881, a debate on Irish matters went on and on and on for forty-one and a half hours. Until then, there was nothing anyone could do if Members were prepared to talk interminably, but Speaker Brand announced that 'a new and exceptional course is imperatively demanded' to end the nonsense and preserve the dignity of the House. So he simply stopped the debate – closed it. With that precedent, he established the Closure, now a recognised and important part of parliamentary procedure, which prevents absurdly long and deliberately delaying debates, and which thus makes the Speaker's life a good deal more tolerable.

Hospitality has always been an important part of the Speaker's duty in the Commons. He does not, by tradition, mix with Members in the bars and dining-rooms of the Commons, but he does give regular dinners and receptions in his splendid State Apartments at the Commons. These are at the north end of the Palace, in the part of the building that projects from the Clock Tower to the river; fine rooms of much gilding and carved stonework, reached by a divided staircase of the grandest proportions, with massive portraits of past Speakers lining the walls. The Speaker's office overlooks the Terrace; one reception room is furnished with chairs and sofas in oyster-coloured silk; beyond that is a room on the corner, overlooking Westminster Bridge decorated with a large portrait, and the coat of arms, of Mr Speaker George Thomas; and finally, the grandest room of all, the State Dining Room, massive, high and overwhelming, with huge portraits of former Speakers round the walls. In these apartments, the Speaker is the only Commoner entitled to have levees in Court dress – although it is many years since one was held. Splendid dinners are arranged here, around a table that can hold sixty guests at one sitting, heavy with silver, dating from 1834, and fine glass and china. These are no longer the Speaker's perks as was once the case; the Onslow family acquired large quantities of silver from their various years in office, since Speakers were given new silver services, which they kept, every time they were elected or re-elected. They also kept their Speaker's chairs – the Onslows at one time had seven. In 1833, the sum said to be allowed to the Speaker in lieu of 4,000 ounces of White Plate (that is, not gilt), was £1,400, calculated at current silver prices; in addition, the incumbent received an outfit allowance of £1,000 every time he was elected, and coals and candles for his official residence. All this grandeur was too much for William Cobbett. He declined an invitation to dine with Speaker Manners-Sutton on the grounds that he was 'not accustomed to the society of gentlemen'.

Gentlemen, in every true sense of the word, Speakers certainly have to be. They are forced to live an isolated existence in an organisation which is geared to a gregarious type of life; they cannot afford to be wrong on even the most obscure and complex matter; they must exercise both absolute fairness and absolute authority in their command of the House; they must run a large and complex department within Parliament with efficiency and economy; and they must at all times preserve the dignity of their office without pomposity. How strange that only one of their number has ever become a saint!

Speakers of the House of Lords, on the other hand, claim three saints among their predecessors. Speakers of the Lords are, of course, the Lord Chancellors, with a history going back to the ninth century Bishop of Winchester, St Swithin; the great St Thomas à Becket of Canterbury; and St Thomas More. Lord Chancellors sit on the Woolsack, which is technically outside the Chamber, and do not have to be Peers, although, with very few exceptions, they always have been.

Their history dates, give or take the rather doubtful St Swithin, back to the coming of the Conqueror. As well as being Speaker of the Lords, a job which involves little more than calling divisions, since they do not control the conduct of debates, they are also Keepers of the Great Seal, traditionally Keepers of the King's Conscience – which, until relatively recently, prevented a Lord Chancellor from being a Catholic since the

King's conscience was indisputably Protestant – and heads of the judiciary. They are also members of the Cabinet and as such make political speeches both inside and outside Parliament – something which the Speaker of the Commons never does.

The Lord Chancellor can, and does, preside over House of Lords Appeals and makes judicial appointments, down to local magistrates. He is the highest civil subject in the land, and takes precedence, after the Royal Family, before all the Queen's subjects, except the Archbishop of Canterbury. It is high treason to kill him, and neither he nor the Great Seal could leave the country. One of the charges brought against Wolsey, at the time of his downfall, was that he had taken the Great Seal to France to join Henry VIII at the Field of the Cloth of Gold.

From the introduction of the office of Lord Chancellor until the seventeenth century, the post was frequently held by an ecclesiastic, since priests were among the few people who could read and write, who busied himself at his task behind the 'cancelli', or screens of the Court. The Lord Chancellor took on the King's conscience as a sideline to his clerical duties and, in the case of St Thomas, paid with his life for so doing. The last ecclesiastic to hold the post, from 1621 to 1625, was Archbishop John Williams of York.

The Reformation brought an end to ecclesiastical claims to the Woolsack (Archbishop Williams was an exception), and Elizabeth I joined together the posts of Lord Keeper of the Great Seal and Lord Chancellor. The man she appointed was the large and portly Sir Nicholas Bacon, who was so grand that when he went to the barber's and fell asleep in the chair, no one dared wake him up. When he eventually awoke of his own accord, he was chilled to the bone. 'I durst not awake you', pleaded the wretched barber. 'By your civility I lose my life', thundered Bacon. He was right. A few days later he was dead.

Even Bacon, however, was less terrible than a predecessor of his, Lord Chancellor Wriothesley. Wriothesley served under Henry VIII and was both legally incompetent and a religious bigot. When Anne Askew was condemned to torture on a religious charge, the Lord Chancellor, with his own hands, turned the wheel of the rack on which she was tied. It was his duty to announce the death of Henry VIII to the House of Lords, and this man who could deliberately torture a woman, broke down before his fellow Lords and burst into tears as he delivered the news.

Just as terrible as Wriothesley was Baron Jeffreys, Judge Jeffreys, who came to the Woolsack over a century later. Jeffreys dropped in on King James II at Windsor after carrying out the Bloody Assize in the West Country, to report on the vengeance he had wreaked on the supporters of Monmouth's abortive rising against the King. James was delighted at the thoroughness with which his wishes had been carried out. 'Taking into account his royal consideration, the many eminent and faithful services which the Chief Justice has rendered to the Crown' he appointed Jeffreys to the Woolsack on 28 September, 1685. This was yet another of James' terrible mistakes. Jeffreys was sometimes drunk on the Woolsack, as well as being domineering and offensive. When James had to flee the country, Jeffreys hoped to follow him. He disguised himself as a sailor, and tried to find a boat to France. The opportunity of having a drink proved too much for him while he was waiting, and he dropped into the Red Cow Inn, near King Edward's Stairs at Wapping, where he was recognised by a scrivener who had been one of his victims in court. The hue and cry was raised, and the mob marched him off to the Mansion House. The Lord Mayor of London, on seeing such a formidable man as Jeffreys, fainted clean away, but was brought round sufficiently to commit the Lord Chancellor to the Tower. There, in the following April, Jeffreys died.

One Lord Chancellor who, unlike Jeffreys, was not prepared to tug a forelock to the King was Lord Thurlow, Tiger Thurlow, who came to the Woolsack a hundred years later. He was said in Cabinet to have 'opposed everything, proposed nothing and was never ready to support anything', and when he took some Acts of Parliament to King George III (with whom he was on friendly terms) for the King to sign, he read one or two through to the King and then stopped. 'It's all damned nonsense trying to make you understand this', said Thurlow, 'so you'd better consent to them at once.' The King did.

Even odder than Thurlow was the eccentric Lord Eldon, who always wore his Chancellor's full bottom wig, whether in the House or outside. He was once asked, after reading Milton's *Paradise Lost*, what he thought of Satan. 'A damned fine fellow', replied the Keeper of the King's Conscience. 'I hope he may win.'

Odder still was Lord Brougham, a bombastic bore, who was heartily disliked by almost everyone who came across him. The Duke of Wellington once snubbed him by saying that Brougham would be remembered only for the carriage named after him. The Lord Chancellor retorted that Wellington would be remembered as the inventor of a pair of boots. 'Damn the boots', said Wellington. 'I had quite forgotten them; you have the best of it.' Drink, however, tended to get the best of Brougham. As a Member of the House of Commons he had annoyed his fellow MPs by loudly sucking oranges; on the Woolsack, with no one to stop him, he supped deeply of mulled port. In 1832 he made a four-hour-long speech at the end of the debate on the Great Reform Bill imploring their Lordships not to throw the Bill out. During his speech he downed five glasses of mulled port and brandy, and finally got to the last sentence. 'I warn you, I implore you – yea, on my bended knees I supplicate you, reject not this Bill', and down he went on his knees on the Woolsack to suit action to the words. From the Woolsack he slipped gradually but inevitably to the floor and, it was recounted, 'he continued some time as if in prayer, but his friends, alarmed for him less he should be suffering from the effects of mulled port, picked him up and placed him safely on the Woolsack.'

Both those eccentric Lord Chancellors, Eldon and Brougham, treated their duties as Keeper of the Great Seal rather strangely. Lord Eldon was so concerned for the Seal's safety that he slept with it every night in his room, and once, in 1812, when his house caught fire, he rushed with it into the garden and buried it in a flower-bed. But, susceptible man, as he admits in his diary, 'so enchanted was I with the pretty sight of the maids who had turned out of their beds and were handing in buckets of water to the fire-engine in their shifts', that next day he had quite forgotten where he had buried the Great Seal. Everyone had to join the search. 'You never saw anything so ridiculous as seeing the whole family down the walks dibbling with bits of stick until we found it.'

Every bit as ridiculous was the time when Lord Brougham tried to impress the ladies with the Great Seal. While he was staying with the Dowager Duchess of Bedford in Scotland, the ladies in the party stole it from his bedroom and hid it. They then blindfolded the Lord Chancellor and made him hunt for it in the drawing-room. When he found it in a tea-chest, he then allowed the ladies to use the two silver discs as a sort of waffle iron to make pancakes. The King was furious when he heard of these goings-on. 'The peripatetic keeper of the King's conscience has not once been admitted since his return from his travels to the honour of an interview with Royalty, either at Windsor or Brighton.'

The Great Seal is a splendid piece of silver weighing eighteen pounds, from which the seals are made for attachment to proclamations by the sovereign, writs, letters patent and documents which give power to sign or ratify treaties. A new seal is made for each new monarch, although since the days of William the Conqueror the design has remained much the same – the sovereign on horseback on the obverse, and enthroned and robed on the reverse. The present one was designed in 1953 by Gilbert Ledward, RA, and makes an impression six inches across. Nowadays, sadly, the seal itself is made not with scarlet sealing-wax, but with plastic. It has proved to be easier to handle and more durable.

Edward III passed an Act which made it high treason, punishable by death, to imitate or forge the Great Seal – a fact which put Cromwell and Parliament into a considerable panic. Charles I had taken his court to York in 1642, and had carried off the Great Seal with him. Parliament wanted to have their own Great Seal made to replace the King's, but it took it a long time to pluck up the courage to order Mr Thomas Simonds, a medal maker, to 'make a new Great Seal for England, and that he shall receive £100 for his pains'. When Parliament eventually recovered the King's Great Seal it took it to the Lords and there had it broken to pieces by a blacksmith. Eventually it had its own seal made with the words, 'In the First Year of Freedom by God's Blessing Restored, 1648' around the picture of the Commons in session on one side, and a map of England, Ireland, Jersey and Guernsey on the other. Blacksmiths had a busy time destroying Great Seals as the fortunes of

James II throws the Great Seal into the Thames When James fled the country in 1688 he threw the Great Seal into the river in the belief that the country could not be governed without it. It was later recovered, accidentally, in the nets of two Thames fishermen

Parliament and Charles II ebbed and flowed. Charles II even arrived in England with one he had had made in Paris, and altogether four were ceremonially smashed to bits.

James II did not destroy the Great Seal; he deliberately threw it away. On the night of 10 December, 1688, with men flocking to the standard of William of Orange, he deserted his country. He fled in disguise to a boat on the Thames at the horseferry, where Lambeth Bridge now stands, and rowed over to Vauxhall, where horses were to meet him and his companion, Sir Edward Hales. With the boat well away from the bank, James deliberately dropped the Great Seal into the depths of the river, on the assumption that without it William and Mary would not be able to rule. He had not counted on the resourceful Thames fishermen; shortly afterwards a group of them accidentally caught the Great Seal in their nets, and handed it over to the authorities.

They were a great deal more honest than whoever stole the Great Seal – the only time it has been irrecoverably lost – from the Great Ormond Street house of Lord Chancellor Thurlow in March 1784. When he discovered the theft, Thurlow rushed to Pitt, the Prime Minister, in Downing Street, and both hurried off to the King, George III. They ordered an exact replica to be made, which was ready within thirty-six hours. There were rumours that the burglars were in the employ of the Whigs, for the day before the Great Seal was stolen Pitt had decided to call a general election; the Whigs did not want one so, it was said, they arranged for the Great Seal to disappear to prevent the sovereign dissolving Parliament.

One tradition associated with the Great Seal is that when a King dies and a new one is made, the old seal is formally defaced and is then given to the Lord Chancellor of the day. Inevitably, this has led to trouble. When William IV came to the throne a dispute arose because Lord Chancellor Lyndhurst was in office when the new seal was ordered, and Lord Chancellor Brougham when the new seal was finished and put into use. The King, with the wisdom of Solomon, divided the Great Seal up and gave half to each of his warring noblemen, tossing a coin to decide who should get which side. Queen Victoria did the same thing when a similar quarrel broke out fifty years later.

On official occasions, the Great Seal is, in theory, carried in the Purse by the Purse Bearer in front of the Lord Chancellor. In practice, the Purse is invariably empty, and the Great Seal is kept in a green, gold-embossed, leather box in a safe in the Lord Chancellor's office. The Purse itself, symbol of the Chancellor's office as Keeper of the Great Seal, is made of stiffened squares of heavily embroidered and betassled red velvet, with the Royal coat-of-arms surrounded by cherubs' heads picked out in gold thread. At one time this, like the Great Seals themselves, also became the property of the Lord Chancellor whenever the seals were changed, and one Lord Chancellor's wife acquired so many Purses that she was able to make them into a bedspread. Nowadays, however, they are far too expensive to be given away. The present Purse was made by the Royal School of Needlework shortly after the Second World War when clothes were still rationed, and the current Lord Chancellor had to find a dozen or so clothing coupons for the red velvet. On the death of George VI, in order to save money, the Royal monogram was skilfully reworked on the Purse and turned from his GR into that of his daughter, Elizabeth, ER.

When the House of Lords is sitting, the Purse, together with the Lord Chancellor's tri-corn hat and one of the two Maces of the House, is placed upon the Woolsack, facing the throne and behind the Lord Chancellor's back. The only time when the Purse actually has anything in it is during the State Opening ceremonies when the Lord Chancellor produces the Queen's Speech from its depths and hands it to her when she is seated on the throne – and then has the tricky task, dressed in his immensely heavy and long golden gown, of walking backwards down the steps of the throne to his place in the House.

The two Maces of the House of Lords are also on show during the State Opening ceremonies; two Maces because the Lord Chancellor has the dual role of Chancellor and Speaker of the House of Lords, and so has both symbols of office for his two spheres of authority.

The House of Commons, however, has only one Mace, but of all the symbols of power and high authority, it is the most potent. Without it the country cannot be run because the Commons cannot even debate, much less decide any questions unless the Mace is in place within the Chamber. If it is taken from the Chamber the House is not in session. It is only when Mr Speaker is in his chair and the Mace is on the Table that the House is permitted to open proceedings. Unlike the Speaker, the Mace is irreplaceable; a Deputy Speaker can be found, but there is no deputy Mace.

'When the Mace lies upon the table', says Hatsell, the great eighteenth century Clerk of the House and authority on procedure, 'the House is a House; when under, it is a Committee. When out of the House, no business can be done; when from the Table and upon the Serjeant's shoulder, the Speaker alone manages.' When a nineteenth century Commons went on a junket to a Spithead naval review, it came back to London in two special trains, and the official with the key to the Mace cupboard came on the second train. This arrived back in London an hour late, so the MPs who had already reached the House had to wait for him to unlock the Mace before they could start talking. During a particularly furious debate in 1626, the Serjeant-at-Arms tried to bring the row to an end by walking off with the Mace, but a fast-moving Member grabbed it from him, locked the door of the Commons and pocketed the key.

The Mace symbolises the authority of the monarch handed down to the Commons, and emphasises that the House is acting on her behalf. When it is lying on its two bronze plinths at the end of the Commons Table, near the two Despatch Boxes, with its top facing towards the Government benches, the Commons is in ordinary session. When it is placed on two large supports at the foot of the Table, the House is in committee. Precisely why it is placed below the table when the House is in committee is not certain; perhaps it is simply to underline the different procedures for a committee session; perhaps because the House originally went into committee to discuss things they did not want the monarch to know about – usually money – and so had to hide the symbol of the monarchy, although they could not constitutionally do without it.

The Mace was originally a club carried by the King's attendants to clear a way for him through the mob, but it gradually assumed a symbolic use as a representation of authority. The present Commons Mace, which dates probably from 1660, is made of silver-gilt; it is 4 feet $10\frac{1}{2}$ inches long, with a crown, topped by an orb and cross at one end, and a small knob or cop – originally the 'business end' of the Mace – at the other. It is much decorated with roses and thistles, harps and fleurs-de-lis and the arms of Charles II and the initials CR. It has no inscription, maker's name and no hallmark; nothing to identify its maker or its age.

One possibility, a romantic and rather unlikely one, is that the present Mace is the very same one that Cromwell ordered taken from the Commons in 1653; that 'bauble', as he called it. Cromwell had had the Mace, and the rest of the Royal regalia, destroyed in 1649, and a new Mace was made by Thomas Maundy for the Commons – the Mace that was to become the 'bauble'. One story claims that, after the Restoration in 1660 the 'bauble' Mace was brought out from wherever it had been placed, and re-worked to take on the Royal symbols and cypher. In fact, the Mace was replaced in the Commons in both 1670 and in 1693, and again on four other occasions. The last time it was changed was in 1819 when the Restoration Mace of 1660 was finally brought back. It is a nice thought, though, that it may – just may – be that famous 'bauble'.

Since the Mace is the symbol of the Royal authority, it is, like the Lords' Mace, superfluous when the Queen herself is present, so on ceremonial occasions it is covered. It can, however, be used to make arrests on behalf of the Commons. From the House of Commons *Journal* of 27 February, 1575. 'After sundry Reasons, Arguments, and Disputations, it is resolved, That Edward Smalleye, Servant unto Arthure Halle Esquire, shall be brought hither Tomorrow, by the Serjeant; and so set at Liberty, by Liberty by Warrant of the Mace; and not by Writ.'

The Mace is also used in the symbolic ritual of electing a new Speaker; it is placed on the brackets below the Table until the new Speaker has been selected; it is carried on the Serjeant's left arm when the House goes in procession to the Lords to inform them of their choice; it is carried on the Serjeant's right arm when they return to the Commons and the new Speaker takes his chair. At the beginning of each sitting day it is carried, by the Serjeant, before the Speaker as he walks in procession to take the chair. At the end of each day it is carried out of the Chamber by the Serjeant, to signify the end of the day's business.

As the Mace leaves the House, policemen in the Lobbies shout 'Who goes home?' along the emptying corridors of the Palace, so that parties of Members can group together to go out into the dangerous, cobbled streets of Westminster, and perhaps hire a link-boy to show them, with his flaming torch, to the safety of their homes!

The parliamentary day is over. The Commons *Journal* of 21 January, 1580: 'which ended a Motion was made, that Mr Speaker, and the Residue of the House of the better Sort of Calling, would always, at the Rising of the House, depart, and go forth, in comely and civil Sort, for the Reverence of the House; in turning about with a low courtesy like as they do make at their coming into the House; and not so unseemly and rudely to thrust and throng out, as of late Time hath been disorderly used: Which Motion was very well liked of; and allowed of all this House.'

'Who goes home?' At the end of every Parliamentary day, door-keepers and policemen shout 'Who goes home?' along the endless corridors of Westminster. It is a custom dating from the days when the streets of Westminster were dangerously full of thieves, and MPs used to gather together in groups for safety, with a link-boy to light them through the dark streets

CHAPTER TWELVE
Privilege, Ladies and Whips

'Privilege, Privilege!' shouted the angry, excited, outraged Members of Parliament as Charles I, on a bitter January day in 1642, made his fateful, and eventually fatal, attempt to arrest five MPs who had opposed his wishes. As he made the appalling tactical error of entering the House of Commons to find them, their angry shouts reiterated the rights that were already centuries old. Those rights were – and still are – that the House of Commons, and the House of Lords, must be free to debate and administer in whatever way they please, without being subjected to any outside interference or interruptions or pressures, from whatever source.

Privilege is Parliament's most ancient claim; it has sometimes been grossly abused in individual Members' interests; it has sometimes been abused by the House itself in vindictive anger against people who have emphasised the rights of the ordinary citizen; it has meant very different things at different times in Parliament's long history. It is, however, a fundamental constituent in the way that the British parliamentary system works.

These claims of privilege go back to the reign of Edward I, when the King refused a petition from the Knights Templars to distrain on the goods of Members who owed them rents. Eventually it developed into today's much wider definition that nothing must be done or said which could interfere with the workings of Parliament or its Members. Precisely what could interfere with those workings is a matter of opinion which has changed drastically over the years, and nowadays breaches of privilege are very seldom raised in either House. The privilege of freedom of speech for Members has been claimed, and granted by the Sovereign, since the days of Elizabeth I, and no one would now think of challenging it. It does, however, mean that while they are speaking in the House, Members can say whatever they like about anybody or anything, and however wrong or libellous their words, the wronged or libelled person can do absolutely nothing, in law, about it. If an aggrieved individual tried to take a Member to law, that would certainly be held to be a breach of the House's privilege, although no court would allow him to start proceedings in the first place. So it is up to each individual Member's sense of responsibility to decide what he should, or should not, say, given his protected position in the House; and he also knows that journalists, provided they report what has been said correctly and fairly, share in this privilege.

Members also have the right of freedom from arrest – although this is now very much a theoretical freedom, and does not, in any case, apply to criminal charges. A Member who once found himself in the Marshalsea for pick-pocketing was left to rot there, and Members have even been arrested in the Central Lobby itself. The theory behind the freedom is, however, that Members are so important to the well-being of the nation that the nation's justice should be suspended while they are playing their parliamentary part. In the past it was a freedom that was much abused. In 1807 a man named Mills, who was in debt to the tune of £23,000, bought a rotten borough for £1,000 and so avoided imprisonment; in 1825 a man elected for the borough of Beverley while he was in prison for debt was released on the order of the Speaker; and a couple of years later an Irishman, in prison for debt, managed to get himself elected to an Irish constituency, whereupon, once released, he fled to the Continent.

The third freedom that Members of both Houses claim at the beginning of each new Parliament is freedom of access to the sovereign. This does not mean that an MP can go off to Buckingham Palace and demand to see the monarch, but that Members have access through the Speaker of the Commons or the Lord Chancellor as Speaker of the House of Lords.

The House of Commons can, in theory – and, in the past, certainly has done in practice – imprison anyone who offends against any of these privileges for the rest of the session in which the breach occurred. The Lords can impose indefinite prison sentences; as the High Court of Parliament they had once unstoppable power. Those powers were formerly used with vicious brutality against supposed offenders. A Welsh judge, David Jenkins, was hauled before the Long Parliament for calling it a 'den of thieves' and was condemned to death, although he was later reprieved. Earlier in the seventeenth century, an MP – for MPs, like ordinary mortals can themselves be accused of breaching the privileges of their own House – was accused of insulting the daughter of James I, and was sentenced to be degraded, branded, whipped, fined £1,000 and to stand twice in the pillory, and finally to be imprisoned for life. As late as 1727 another Member, named Ward, was sentenced to stand in the pillory and be expelled from the House. That power of expulsion still exists. In 1810, Sir Francis Burdett, the Member for Westminster, defied the Commons over its decision to send a publisher of a mildly critical pamphlet to prison, and the riots that ensued from his refusal to appear to answer charges of Breaches of Privilege resulted in the Commons having to call out the Life Guards to haul him off to the Tower of London.

People appeared on their knees at the Bar of the House for the most trivial offences; for poaching Admiral Griffiths, MP's fish; for cutting down a Member's tree; for arresting a Member's tailor for debt. In 1750 a brave man named Murray, accused of fiddling an election for the City of Westminster, refused to kneel. 'Your obeisance Sir', thundered the Speaker. When Murray still refused, the stunned House passed a resolution that Murray, 'having in a most insolent, audacious manner, at the Bar of this House, absolutely refused to be upon his knees as required

. . . is guilty of a most high and dangerous contempt of the authority and privileges of this House'. They packed him off to Newgate in solitary confinement, without pen, ink or paper, and even when he became very ill they refused to let him out. At the end of the session, the Commons' order against Murray automatically lapsed, and although it tried to have him arrested again when the new session began, Murray had prudently disappeared, and was never heard of, by the Commons, again. He had, at least, won the right for anyone accused of offending the Commons to defend himself with dignity.

The House of Lords, however, managed to get itself involved in quite the silliest breach of privilege case of all. In 1827 a Stranger visiting the Lords was ordered by an attendant to leave his umbrella in the cloakroom. The umbrella disappeared, and the owner brought an action against the attendant and was awarded £1.0s.4d. damages. The Lord Chancellor, Lord Eldon, thereupon summoned the wretched Stranger to the Bar of the House of Lords and ordered him, on pain of imprisonment, to refund the money to the attendant and apologise. The overawed and terrified man scuttled off into the rain, thankful he still had his bowed and worried head on his shoulders.

Women could also be brought to the Bar of the House, for although they were not seen as bright, able, or experienced enough to serve in it, or even to watch its tremendous proceedings, they could naturally always offend the House, or be forced to beg from it, or satisfy its prurient curiosity. Ann Fitzharris, widow of a certain Edward Fitzharris, who had been executed on trumped-up political charges, came to the Bar of the Commons on 16 March, 1688, to give evidence on the plight of herself and her three children. Predictably, a committee was set up to look into the whole thing, and Mrs Fitzharris and her three children were commended to Charles II as 'an object of charity'.

The infinitely less respectable Mrs Clarke, a very good friend of the Duke of York, was called to the Bar of the Commons to give evidence concerning charges brought against the duke for the corrupt sale of commissions in the army. Mrs Clarke decided to enjoy herself, and she had the place in stitches. She appeared at the Bar of the Commons on 1 February, 1809, dressed to kill and utterly in command of the entire proceedings. 'A lovely Thais', said one besotted writer, 'she dazzled the gravest.' She made things particularly hot for the duke, who had ditched her because of her part in the disclosures of the scandal, and the grim-faced Wilberforce subsequently wrote of her appearance: 'This melancholy business will do irreparable mischief to public morals by accustoming the public to hear without emotion shameless violation of decency. The House examined Mrs Clarke for two hours, examining her in the Old Bailey way. She, elegantly dressed, consummately impudent, and very clever, got clearly the better of the tussle.' The House eventually decided to do nothing about the duke, but the duke himself had the wit to resign his command of the army before he was pushed. Mrs Clarke retired into a somewhat tarnished, but comfortable, obscurity.

Women, of course, have always played their part in politics, although they have only been allowed to play it publicly at Westminster for the last sixty years. When Parliament was still very young they turned up in considerable and effective force to protect one of their own. In 1428, according to the chronicler John Stow, 'one Mistress Stokes, with divers others stout women of London, of good account and well apparelled', went 'openly to the Upper House of Parliament and delivered letters to the Duke of Gloucester, to the Archbishops, and the other lords, because he would not deliver his wife Jaqueline out of her grievous imprisonment (she being then detained as prisoner by the Duke of Burgundy) and suffering her there to remain unkindly whilst he kept another adultress contrary to the law of God and the honourable estate of matrimony.' The Commons supported the duchess, and they tacked onto a subsidy which they granted to her husband this addendum: 'My Lady of Gloucester liveth in so grete dolour and hevyness and hath so lamentably written to our Sovereign Lord and to all the Estate of this noble Roiaume to be pourveyed for by way of tretee or in otherwise by the high wisdom of our Sovereign Lord and the habundant discretion of the Lords of his Counseill', that the Commons were constrained to ask 'that her person and the alliance between this noble Roiaume and her lands' might 'be put in salvetee and sickernesse in singular comfort of the said Commons and of all that they byn comyn for'. The duke gave in and paid up.

Ladies, of course, continued to run things discreetly from behind the scenes, but by the eighteenth century they had become brazen about the whole thing. They turned up in the very Chamber itself, and sat down beside their husbands or current admirers on the Members' benches. 'They attend', it was reported, 'in such numbers as to fill the body of the House on great political occasions', although they all scuttled off when such other thrilling diversions as the Cock Lane Ghost became the talk of the town. But eventually they over-did things. They had become so used to coming and going as they pleased at Westminster that some of the stuffier Members dared to revolt against them, with the result that they were thrown out altogether.

On 2 February, 1778, there was to be a great debate on the state of the nation, and it was *the* social event of the week. The ladies came in droves, and bagged every seat they could get. A no-nonsense naval captain MP complained that he and his companions could not find seats, so the order was given for the ladies to leave. They refused to go; they shouted and cheered and jeered, but would not budge. The Speaker commanded them; the attendants glared at them; Members argued but they would not shift. Eventually, after two hours of uproar and anger, they drifted away to find some other amusement, and a total ban on ladies entering the Chamber was promptly put into force. It was only broken by a couple of enterprising individuals, Mrs Shere and the beautiful Duchess of Gordon, turning up dressed in men's clothes.

The House of Lords had had a ladies' gallery since 1698 – the Commons had no special provision for them – so when, in 1738, the Lords decided to throw out the ladies and let MPs have their gallery instead, the Peers should have known they were asking for trouble, and they got it. Led by Lady Huntingdon and the Duchess of Queensbury, a whole crowd of aristocratic women literally laid siege to the Lords'. The door was locked in their face – and in everyone else's faces, since no one could get in – and remained locked while the ladies pounded upon it, kicked it, and shouted and yelled abuse at the Lord Chancellor inside in a most unlady-like way. Then they changed tactics; Lady Huntingdon and the duchess ordered absolute silence and the Lords were fooled into believing they had gone away. They had not. When the doors were open to let in impatient MPs, the ladies rushed past them into the Chamber, and remained there for the rest of the day, cat-calling and shouting at their Lordships' attempts to speak. The Lords learnt their lesson and let them stay.

After the fire destroyed both the old Houses in 1834, it was decided to make proper provision for ladies. The Commons set up the inevitable committee and decided that 'a portion of the Strangers' Gallery at the north end of the House, not exceeding a quarter of the whole, and capable of containing twenty-four ladies, be set apart for their accommodation, divided by a partition from the rest of the gallery, and screened in front by open trellis-work'. Everyone got themselves into a considerable lather about such a revolutionary idea. 'The feelings of the gallant old soldiers and gentlemen', it was reported, 'would be so excited and turned from political affairs, that they would not be able to do their duty to their country.' Not that the gallant old soldiers or gentlemen would have been able actually to see the ladies, because they were put behind heavy brass grilles, made by Pugin's friend Hardman, the Birmingham button manufacturer, which turned the Gallery, complained a frustrated MP, into something 'between a birdcage and a tea-caddy'. Some of the old diehards continued to believe that it was an utter outrage to admit women to the precincts of Westminster at all. 'It is', fumed the decidely eccentric Lord Brougham, 'contrary to the principle that ought to govern legislative proceeding.' 'I think', he said, 'the ladies would be better employed in almost any other way than in attending parliamentary debates.'

Still, the ladies got their gallery – for a time – and in 1841 they presented a piece of plate to Mr Grantley Berkeley, MP, who had supported their cause. By 1888, however, they had been thrown out again, because some of them had started shouting in support of the 'votes for women' campaign, and Mr Speaker Peel had their gallery shut. It was not until 1909 that it was opened again, and ladies who wished to enter had to sign an undertaking to behave themselves. In 1918 the grilles

Votes for women Visitors in the Ladies' Gallery demonstrating during the Suffragette campaigns at the beginning of the century. One woman chained herself to the brass grills through which they had to peer down onto the Chamber below. The police could not undo the chains, so they had to remove the grill and take the woman out, still attached to it

were taken away and re-erected in the windows round the Central Lobby, and ladies were allowed to sit in the ordinary Strangers' Gallery. They lost two privileges in the process, however. They were no longer permitted to stand in the Members' Lobby and peer through a little window into the Chamber – that had been stopped in 1908 when a female visitor rushed through into the House shouting 'votes for women'. By losing their own gallery they also lost the rather odd distinction of being able to enter the Chamber when no other Strangers were allowed in. Their gallery was technically outside the Chamber itself, so they could therefore not be removed during prayers – Strangers have never been allowed in the Chamber during prayers – and they could not be thrown out if the House went into private session.

Lady Members did not arrive at Westminster, of course, until 1919, although Countess Markiewicz, a Sinn Feiner, had been elected the previous year but did not take her seat. Lady Astor took her seat in 1919 – and the event is remembered now by a painting of her entering the House of Commons on that memorable occasion, which is, rather ungraciously, hanging immediately outside the door of one of the gentlemen's lavatories. The first woman to hold cabinet office was Miss Margaret Bondfield, who was Minister of Labour from 1929 to 1931.

Women took their seats in the Lords after the passing of the Life Peerages Act, in July 1958, and from 1963 hereditary Peeresses have also been able to sit in the Upper House. The first woman ever to make a speech in the Lords was Lady Elliot, the wife of Colonel Walter Elliot, whose swift actions had saved the nearby Westminster Hall in the blitz. She recalls the occasion with considerable pleasure. 'The House was very kind to me. I was about the second or third speaker in the debate. There were quite a lot of people there, but suddenly the whole House filled up because this was the first time a woman's voice had been heard in the Chamber. I was quite nervous but I had something to say, and you say it as well as you can. That is the only way to get things across.' Four other women had been made Members of the Lords at the same time, and she had been a Life Peer only about a week before she spoke. Like all Peers, she had been formally introduced into the Lords, wearing scarlet robes and, she recalls, 'a little three-cornered hat'. As they were the first women Life Peers, there was no precedent for the shape of the hat, so it was designed by Lady Cholmondeley to resemble the three-cornered hat worn by WRNS officers. Her robes were borrowed; 'I have quite a number of nephews who are members of the House of Lords', explained Lady Elliot, 'and I borrowed one of theirs.'

In sixty years in Parliament women have, of course, risen to the highest post in politics, and when she became Prime Minister Mrs Thatcher made some firm, although not particularly elaborate, changes to the Prime Minister's room in the House of Commons.

The Prime Minister's room resembles what a first-class waiting room must have looked like in the better kind of Victorian railway station. It is large, airy, light and rather forbidding. The high Gothic windows along one side overlook New Palace Yard and the traffic swirling round Parliament Square – double-glazing helps to keep out some of the noise – and it is, frankly, unimpressive as the room of the most powerful person in the land. Prime Ministers do the great majority of their work at their official residence at 10 Downing Street, and tend to use their Commons office relatively infrequently. Even so, some massively important decisions have been taken there, such as Mrs Thatcher's major decisions in the Falklands war. When such a fast-moving, dangerous and dramatic situation arises that room, which was once the dining-room of the Clerk of the Commons, becomes the focus of action and executive power.

Visitors reach the Prime Minister's room from the corridor behind the Speaker's chair in the Commons. They walk past a small conference room just beyond the Chamber, where swift and impromptu meetings between Ministers or Whips can be held, and then past the Chancellor of the Exchequer's and the Foreign Secretary's rooms, to the outer office of the inner sanctum. All is heavy, dark brown carved oak, with black and gold fingerposts on the walls pointing the way. It is remarkably like the corridors which always seem to lead to a headmaster's study or to the consulting room of an eminent surgeon. The hush and sense of awe is most certainly the same.

Spanning the middle of the room is a massive, Pugin-designed oak table which, when Mrs Thatcher arrived, was covered with green baize. 'I didn't know what was underneath', she recalled later, 'but we prowled around it, and it looked like oak, so we took the baize off and it was this beautiful oak Pugin table. It can be larger or smaller, and I keep it large because sometimes we have Cabinet meetings round here when people are all across here voting on Bills in the House. One or two very important decisions have been taken around this table.'

Mrs Thatcher had a fine silver-plated letter rack put in the middle of the table, and chose the centre seat, looking out over Parliament Square, as the place to do her work. Behind the Prime Minister's chair stands a grandfather clock, a fine eighteenth-century piece that originally came from Downing Street, and a splendid pair of Pugin-designed cabinets, one of which was formerly used to block a door into an adjoining room. That one is, officially, the Prime Minister's cabinet, and it was first brought to the room by Arthur Balfour. At each end of the room stand massive carved mirrors, with mottoes in Norman French – 'Do good and fear nothing'. 'That's terrific', said Mrs Thatcher. 'I think it has served us well throughout the year.' Forming an angle at one end of the room, is an area rather like a small drawing-room. When Mrs Thatcher moved in, this part was divided off, but she had the partition removed, and had pleasantly informal armchairs, with flower-patterned upholstery, and coffee tables put in. In one wall are stained glass windows lit from behind, and on another a portrait of one of Mrs Thatcher's heroes – the young, unscathed Horatio Nelson. In essence, the room is partly informal and relaxing, partly an office in which Prime Ministers can exercise their power.

The Prime Minister's room becomes the hub of much feverish activity regularly twice a week, when last minute preparations are in hand for Prime Minister's Questions – the Tuesday and Thursday rituals when, for about quarter of an hour, the Prime Minister has to face the crowded House of Commons and give an account of the Goverment's activities and policies. Question Time is one of the most hallowed traditions of the Commons, as Westminster MPs think that it gives them the world's most effective legislative check over the executive.

Question time happens every Monday, Tuesday, Wednesday and Thursday from about 2.30 p.m. (the daily prayers take up the first few minutes) until 3.30; there are no questions on Fridays, when the House sits at 9.30 a.m. Both sitting times are, incidentally, relatively modern. In Charles I's day, the Commons sat at 7 a.m. (sometimes after first going to a 6 a.m. service at St Margaret's church across the road) and later they sat at varying times between 8 a.m. and 3 p.m. Nor did they always sit only from Mondays to Fridays; in Stuart times both Houses sat on Sundays, even on Christmas Day. The Great Reform Bill received its Second Reading in the Commons on Sunday, 18 December, 1831.

By the time the Reform Bill was fought through both Houses, Parliamentary Questions were fairly well established. Like so many other innovations in Parliament, they began in the Lords. In 1721 Earl Cowper asked the Government about reports that Robert Knight, the Chief Cashier of the South Sea Company, had fled to Brussels. The

Prime Minister, the Earl of Sunderland replied, giving the known facts. The South Sea Bubble had burst. The Commons took up the new piece of procedure rather slowly, although questions were allowed by 1783. Fifty years later the Commons began to print questions that were due to be answered, but it was not until 1869 that they appeared, fully fledged and in their own right, on the Order Paper, and the daily ritual of Question Time dates from then. Thus one of Parliament's proudest traditions, which it confidently claims is superior to any other system in any country in the world, is not much more than a century old. Even then, it took a long time to make its mark on Parliament, for in the whole of the year 1900 only about 5,000 questions were raised, and twenty-five years later the number had merely doubled. It was not until relatively recently that the numbers of questions put down each day rocketed to the present total of well over 40,000 a year or over 300 a day, at a cost to the taxpayer of considerably more than £1,000,000.

Questions can be either oral – that is, answered by a Minister at the Despatch Box in the Commons; written – that is, answered in writing and published by a Minister and not in the Chamber; or a Private Notice Question – a special question about a recent and major event which can only be put by permission of the Speaker. Oral questions are answered by Ministers on a rota system, so that each government department, represented by its Secretary of State with his junior Ministers around him, is questioned about once a month. Normally some twenty-five questions are dealt with in the hour, and those that are not reached then receive a written answer instead. The questions themselves have to be kept within certain circumscribed limits; they must either ask for information or for a Minister to take action on a particular matter; they must not deal with anything that is currently before the courts, nor must they be offensive towards the Crown, the judiciary or Members of either House. They must deal only with matters for which the Minister answering is responsible, and they should be precisely worded and reasonably brief. Irish Members, in the days before Home Rule, took to putting down immensely long questions, and then standing up and reading them out slowly, word for word. Now, all a Member does is call out the number of his question, without reading it.

The art of the question is, of course, the supplementary. A question of the most innocuous appearance may hide a supplementary of devastating force which can leave an unprepared Minister floundering and his political enemies in a state of high euphoria. It is therefore up to the Minister and his staff to prepare for any and every eventuality and a vast amount of departmental time – and public money – goes into briefing Ministers for every possibility. Since the great majority of oral questions never, in fact, get asked, much of this expensive effort is wasted. Never was this fact more striking than in the days when questions, as a part of the parliamentary system, were still developing. In 1854 Lord Aberdeen's ministry had been accused of not supplying the figures that a

Member had requested. In due course a pile of papers weighing 1,388 pounds was placed upon the Table of the House. This 'reply' had involved the sending of 34,500 circulars and letters and cataloguing and tabulating all 34,500 replies. The House was told that if they wanted the information to be extracted from the papers, it would take a year's work and that, in the end, it would produce figures and information which the House already had. The House went on to other business.

Since the broadcasting of Parliament began, the twice-weekly Prime Minister's Question Time has become a national institution – if only because of the noise and uproar which it usually creates. This is an even newer parliamentary institution than Question Time itself. Originally, Prime Ministers answered questions on any day, once Question No. 45 was reached. Since Question 45 was hardly ever reached, this was changed to answering all questions after No. 40 on Tuesdays and Thursdays. This still did not produce the desired results, especially for the Opposition, of getting the Prime Minister regularly to the Despatch Box. To change this situation, in the late 60s, the Labour Opposition decided not to turn up for the first three dozen questions. Mr Macmillan, the Conservative Prime Minister, was forced to face the House for nearly an hour, and also forced to change to the present system of two fifteen minute sessions each week. This means that the Prime Minister faces the House for about twice as long each month as any other Minister, and it also raises the problem of what questions can be asked that fall within the complicated rules that govern the Prime Minister's area of direct Ministerial responsibility.

The answer is the open question. A favourite open question – and a couple of dozen of similarly worded questions may appear on the Order Paper on any Tuesday or Thursday – is to ask for the Prime Minister's engagements on that day. Everyone knows this is a meaningless enquiry, and everyone knows that the entire point is for the backbencher asking it to get up and to try, if he is on the Opposition benches, to become an instant hero by pole-axing the Prime Minister with a question of Machiavellian unpredictability. If he is a Government supporter, the open question will allow the Member to demonstrate his ripeness for promotion to Ministerial office by the earnest support he gives to the Government and the opportunity he carefully provides for the Prime Minister to make a major, publicity-winning, political point.

Backbenchers can, of course, help any frontbencher by putting a sympathetic, carefully timed question, and the art of the planted question is one which the Whips of both Government and Opposition constantly pursue and constantly refine. It is a sort of sub-art of the great art of Whipping itself – and Whipping is a part of the parliamentary system which is of great importance to the smooth running of both Lords and Commons. It is not much publicised by the careful wish of its practitioners; and, not surprisingly, it is fairly thoroughly misunderstood outside Westminster.

Right: *The Lords' Dining Room* A tapestry-hung room of baronial grandeur

PEERESSES
and
UNMARRIED
DAUGHTERS
OF PEERS
before taking
a place in the
PEERESSES
GALLERY
or
BELOW THE BAR
are requested to
LEAVE THEIR NAMES
with the
DOORKEEPER
HUSBANDS
OF WOMEN PEERS
are similarly requested to
LEAVE THEIR NAMES
with the
DOORKEEPER

WIVES
OF PEERS'
ELDEST SONS
and
MARRIED
DAUGHTERS
OF PEERS AND
PEERESSES
IN THEIR OWN RIGHT
before taking
a place in the
PEERS' MARRIED
DAUGHTERS' BOX
are requested to
LEAVE THEIR NAMES
with the
DOORKEEPER
AT THE BRASS GATES

PEERS
OF IRELAND
PEERS' ELDEST
SONS
and
PRIVY
COUNSELLORS
before taking a seat
on the steps of the
THRONE
are requested to
LEAVE THEIR NAMES
with the
DOORKEEPER

Above: *Members' Cloakroom, House of Commons* The pieces of red tape are for Members to hang their swords on before entering the Chamber

Left: *The Prince's Chamber, House of Lords* It takes its name from a room in the old Royal Palace

Below left: *Order of Precedence* Instructions, on a wall in the Prince's Chamber, for visitors to the galleries in the House of Lords

Above right: *The new Master of the Rolls* Sir John Donaldson is sworn in by the Lord Chancellor, Lord Hailsham, who is head of the judiciary. The Great Seal, which is in the Lord Chancellor's keeping, hanging from the official document

Right: *The Lord Chancellor's Procession* The Lord Chancellor goes in procession to the Lords at the beginning of each day's sitting. Ahead of him goes his Mace, carried by the Yeoman Usher of the Black Rod, and the Purse which, theoretically, contains the Great Seal

Far right: *Adjusting the clocks.* Two men repair and adjust over a thousand clocks at Westminster and Downing Street

Left: *The Library of the House of Lords* All the upholstery in the House of Lords area of the Palace is in red; in the House of Commons area it is in green

Below left: *The Bishops' Bench, House of Lords* The only bench in the Lords with arm rests. The side of the Lords on which the bishops sit is the spiritual side. The other side is known as the temporal side

Below: *Black Rod* The staff of office of the Gentleman Usher of the Black Rod. At its head, a golden lion with the Royal coat of arms. A 1904 gold sovereign is set in the end of the rod. The mounting of the sovereign is damaged from the rod being used to knock on the Commons door when Black Rod demands admission at the State Opening

Right: *Mr Gladstone in the Central Lobby*

Below: *The missing finger* Gladstone used to cut down trees to work off his surplus energy. He once chopped off a finger on his left hand

Right: *Grills in the Central Lobby* The brass grills used to be in the Ladies' Gallery in the House of Commons so that the sight of the ladies would not distract MPs in the Chamber below. The grills have now been moved to the Central Lobby

Far right: *'With this ring I am wedded to the realm'* Elizabeth I rejects the Commons' petition to her to marry. The picture, on the main staircase of the Palace, is by Solmon J. Solomon; he painted it in 1912, and used faces of contemporary politicians for Elizabeth's courtiers

Left: *An entrance to the Terrace from the House of Commons* On the walls are reconstructions of the paintings from St Stephen's Chapel

Above: *The corridors of power* Signs showing the way to senior Cabinet Ministers' rooms

Right: *The 'No' Voting Lobby, House of Commons* Members voting 'No' in a division pass through the lobby to the left of the Chamber; those voting 'Aye' the lobby to the right. The Lobbies are long corridors where Members can write letters and read official papers

Below: *The 'No' Lobby* During a division, clerks sit at the high desks and tick off the names of Members on a nominal roll.

Right: *Through the Voting Lobby* The doors beyond the Division Lobbies are kept open just wide enough for one Member to pass through at a time. They must bow as they pass through, and the numbers are checked by whips from each side standing just beyond the doors

Far left: *The Members' Dining Room* Strictly for Members only; no guests are allowed in their dining rooms. Political parties each have their traditional tables

Left: *The Serjeant-at-Arms' Office* A room in the cloisters of St Stephen's Chapel, and one of the most attractive rooms in the entire Palace

Above: *The Speaker's Dining Room* The table can seat sixty guests

Left: *Mr Speaker Thomas* Mr Speaker George Thomas (now Lord Tonypandy) with his wig and ceremonial gown. It is embroidered with real gold bullion

Right: *A banquet in the Speaker's Dining Room* The Prime Minister, Mrs Thatcher, is among the guests

Left: *The House of Commons Library* Only MPs are allowed in the Library

Below left: *The Smoking Room at the House of Commons*

Right: *The tea room, the House of Commons* Strong traditions dictate where various groups of MPs sit. The tea room is the centre of much Parliamentary gossip and behind-the-scenes manipulations

Right: *The Member's staircase, House of Commons* It leads from the Members' cloakroom to the Members' Lobby

Far right: *The Members' Lobby* The ante-room of the House of Commons. Members rub the foot of the Churchill statue (*to the left of the arch*) for luck as they go in to debates

Left: *Lord Falkland and a suffragette* In 1908 a Suffragette chained herself to the statue of Lord Falkland, a seventeenth-century politician, in St Stephen's Hall. The spur and the sword of the statue have remained broken ever since. It is the only memorial at Westminster to the suffragettes

Right: *The Vote Office, Members' Lobby* Members collect their Parliamentary papers here each day

Far right: *The Fees Office* The office responsible for MPs' pay. Their claims for car mileage allowances are meticulously checked on a map

Right: *The Whips' Office* Government whips at their weekly meeting at Number 12 Downing Street

Above: *The Prime Minister's Office* The table is sometimes used for urgent ministerial meetings. The grandfather clock was originally in Number 10 Downing Street

Left: *The Prime Minister in her Office* Mrs Thatcher prepares for her twice-weekly question time with her Parliamentary Private Secretary and a member of her staff. Her red ministerial despatch box is on the table beside her

Right: *Sir Robert Walpole (the first Prime Minister) addresses the Cabinet*

Not for nothing does the name derive from the hunting field where whippers-in keep the field from straying.

Disraeli said that the office of the Government Chief Whip required 'consumate knowledge of human nature, the most amiable flexibility, and complete self-control'. While the phrase about 'amiable flexibility' would certainly surprise a good many Members, Disraeli got it precisely right. The Chief Whips, both Government and Opposition, are the people who, with their assistants and deputies, organise the complex system of getting the parliamentary business done. Along with the Leader of the House and his shadow, they are known as 'The Usual Channels', a mysterious, behind-the-scenes system of parleying between two enemies. In fact, of course, there is generally an amiable relation between the two sides, who talk informally together to work out the arrangements and deals and sessions of give and take that are vitally necessary to help the business of Parliament – the majority of which is humdrum and relatively non-contentious – get through smoothly to everyone's advantage. The two Chief Whips sit in their traditional places on the front bench immediately beside the gangway and can, occasionally, be seen to wander off together for a brief chat beyond the Bar of the House; they return to their seats, pass a quick word to their leaders, and the House learns that this or that suitable agreement has been reached. Or they will go off more privately and hammer out, with much hard bargaining, some major agreement involving subtle understanding; or they will not agree at all, and fur may fly!

The job of the Chief Whips, and their subordinates, is, above everything else, to ensure that the party leadership, sometimes remote and always very busy people, know what is going on among the backbenchers. If the troops get restive, the generals certainly will not be able to march them towards the sound of parliamentary gunfire, and thus a constant system of informal soundings takes place in the Tea Room, Smoking Room, in the bars and dining-rooms, in the corridors and in the endless meetings that take up Members' time outside the Chamber. No Chief Whip worth his salt – or who hopes to keep his job – should ever be surprised by the result of a vote, and neither should his front bench. The Government Chief Whip, who also holds the ancient but obscure title of Patronage Secretary, reports regularly to Cabinet meetings (although he is not a member, he is frequently invited to attend) and to Cabinet committees; the Opposition Chief Whip attends Shadow Cabinet meetings, where his report is second on the agenda.

So important are the Whips considered to the system, that, apart from the Leader of the Opposition, the Opposition Chief Whip, his deputy and one other Whip are the only Opposition members who receive special salaries. In the Labour Opposition, the extra salary is paid to the Pairing Whip who, together with his opposite number in the Government, is responsible for organising the pairing system – that is, arranging for a Member who has good reason to be absent from a vote to be

Left: *Memory Woodfall* William Woodfall was a journalist at Westminster in the eighteenth century when Parliamentary reporting was forbidden. He had a photographic memory, and after listening to a debate would transcribe it for his newspaper without notes

cancelled out by someone on the opposite side who also has good reason to be away from Westminster. It is relatively seldom that even important votes approach the total number of MPs in Parliament, and it is inevitable that some will be ill, some away on official government business, and so on. So the pairing system is brought into play. Only on the most vital votes, on which the future of a government may hang, is pairing stopped; and the papers are then full of horror stories of gravely ill MPs being brought, half dead, by ambulance to Westminster for a vote.

All the Government Whips are Ministers, and they make up the largest group of Ministers on the Government front bench: fourteen in all. The Chief Whip, besides holding that title and that of Patronage Secretary, is also Parliamentary Secretary at the Treasury, and five others are Lords Commissioners at the Treasury. Five Assistant Whips are Treasury Ministers, and three are members of Her Majesty's Household. The last three are ancient offices and the Deputy Chief Whip invariably holds the post of Treasurer of the Household; he, along with the Controller of the Household, another Government Whip, has the ceremonial duty of travelling in the Royal procession when the Queen comes to Parliament for a State Opening. The third Whip who is a member of the Household, the Vice-Chamberlain, has other very specific duties besides his normal active parliamentary duties. At State Openings, he remains behind at Buckingham Palace and stays there until the Queen's safe return – a hostage for her safety when she goes down to a potentially rebellious Parliament. The Vice-Chamberlain is also the Queen's messenger to the Commons, so when, on formal occasions, a message has to be brought to or from the Commons, he has the duty of delivering it. He carries a wooden wand of office which used to be broken by the monarch to show that the message had been safely delivered. Queen Victoria, however, grew too frail for the task, so now it has a silver collar in the middle which can be easily unscrewed.

The other daily task of the Vice-Chamberlain is to write a private report to the Queen of the day's proceedings. This tradition began in the reign of George III who wanted to know, in the days before proper Parliamentary reporting, news of the battles between John Wilkes and the Commons. The King commanded the Leader of the Commons to keep him informed, and ever since then a nightly report has been sent to wherever in the world the monarch happens to be. Nowadays it is written by the Vice-Chamberlain instead of by the Leader of the House; in the days when Lord Randolph Churchill was Leader of the House, he accidentally enclosed a tin of tobacco in the box in which the report was sent to Queen Victoria. She was, it appears, amused.

As they whirl round the Commons, sharp-eyed and ears pricked, the Whips also have specific duties to attend to. Each ministry is watched over by a Whip so that he is always there when matters of concern to the department are being discussed in the House; or when those matters are

Above: *'Duty Versus Gallantry'* 'While members are dining, they are informed of the progress of business by an indicator, which tells what member is speaking, and also gives the signal for divisions. Even when a member is entertaining a fair guest he must rise and rush into the lobby the moment that the signal is given for a division'

Above right: *'Division Lobby of the House of Commons'* During a division, Members are divided alphabetically – A–K and L–Z they pass, one at a time, before the clerks who tick their names off a nominal roll. Every Member has to call his name, otherwise his vote is not recorded

being considered by one of the many groups of backbench MPs with special interests who meet informally outside the Chamber. MPs from various parts of the country – Wales, Scotland, North-East, North-West and so on – also have Whips, so that, little by little, the gossip they hear, the grumbles they pick up, the pleasure at this Government action, the approval of that Opposition decision, are all fed back to the party and government managers.

In the end, of course, the effectiveness of the Whips is judged by their success in getting the Members to vote according to their party's wishes. Every Member knows exactly how he is supposed to vote, because each Thursday he is sent a written agenda, also known as a whip, setting out details of the coming week's events. Under each piece of business there are either one, two or three lines in heavy print: a one, two or three-line whip. A one-line whip is a relaxed affair when there probably is not going to be a vote, and says that a Member's attendance is 'requested'. A two-line whip is considerably more important, and Members are expected to be present, for unless they are officially paired, their attendance is 'particularly requested'. A three-line whip, the strongest of all and one on which the Government's future may depend, says that a Member's attendance 'is essential'. A Member ignores a three-line whip at his peril. There is no reason, other than tradition, why the system should stop at a three-line whip – in the past there have been four and five-line whips, but these days three lines, and the tough efficiency of the Whips' Office, is thought to be quite sufficient.

The divisions themselves are lengthy, cumbersome affairs that the House periodically thinks it should change, but never does. When the

Speaker 'puts the question' – that a Bill should get a second reading, or a Motion be passed, or an Order confirmed, or whatever the business under discussion may be – the supporters shout 'Aye', the opponents 'No'. If there has been no agreement on the business, then there is a vote. Those voting 'Aye' go into the Voting Lobby – a long, wide corridor, lined with books and writing tables set into big window recesses – to the right of the Speaker's chair. Those voting 'No' go to the left of the chair. Bells ring all over the Palace and in offices beyond, and Members have eight minutes to come hurrying into the Lobbies; after eight minutes the doors are locked, and any latecomers cannot be counted. Then the Members separate into two files, A–K and L–Z, and so past two clerks sitting at high desks with nominal rolls, each Member calling out his name as he does so. Beyond that, two doors are held open just wide enough for one person to pass through at a time, and as he goes through each Member must bow. Some say that this rule originated because MPs once used to send their servants to vote for them and to stop this abuse Members had to show their faces; others say it is because, in the old chapel of St Stephen's, MPs used to pass through the low door of the rood screen to vote, and they had to duck to get through. Beyond the door and the bowing, two Whips act as tellers and call out the number of Members passing through. When they have agreed on the final numbers, Whips from both lobbies return to the Chamber and announce the result. The House knows who has won before the figures are read out, because the Whips from the winning side always stand to the Speaker's left as they move to the Table. They then step forward a pace, bow, and the senior teller from the winning side reads out the results, which are then carried by a clerk to the Speaker, who reads them out again. The whole procedure takes up to twenty minutes to get through and seems a tedious, over-elaborate ritual for a modern Parliament. Members, however, cling firmly to tradition. It's a system which can be traced back to the first recorded division in 1553, and the present arrangement of walking past the teller goes back to 1836. MPs can vote as often as they like during a sitting, according to the business under discussion – they voted 43 times in one sitting in 1907 – and if there is a dead heat, the Speaker, who normally never votes, has the casting vote. He then invariably gives that vote in such a way that the matter can be discussed again by the House, so nothing he does as an impartial Speaker can appear to have changed the law of the land. In practice, this usually means that he gives his casting vote to the Government. MPs claim that, time-consuming though the voting ritual may be, it does mean that they get together to argue and generally keep the wheels of politics turning in a way that would be impossible if they had an electronic system of voting. They usually end the discussion by claiming that you cannot trust electronics. You can trust MPs.

The House of Lords has a system of voting that is very similar, although not identical to that used in the House of Commons. There the

'The Tellers Reading the Result of a Division' The four tellers – two from each side – line up at the end of the Table in the Commons after a division. The senior teller from the winning side stands at the right-hand side of the Table to read the results

Peers vote 'Content' and 'Not Content', and the Lord Chancellor, unlike the Speaker in the Commons, normally votes, although he does not actually walk through the lobbies. The senior tellers have little ivory batons to show their authority, and any Peers who want to abstain can go behind the rails round the throne, where they are not offically in the House.

The House of Lords is, of course, considerably larger in numbers than the House of Commons. It has a potential membership of nearly 1,200 members, although relatively few attend; the average daily attendance is between 250 and 300. Cabinet Ministers, who always include the Lord Chancellor and the Leader of the House of Lords, are joined there by a dozen or more other Ministers. The Government Chief Whip in the Lords is the Captain of the Honourable Corps of the Gentlemen at Arms, and his deputy is the Captain of the Yeomen of the Guard.

The entire atmosphere in the Lords is more relaxed and amiable than in the Commons. There are invariably a few questions at the beginning of each day, although there is no formal Question Time. There are also what are always known as 'unstarred questions' on some days, which are, in fact, opportunities for short debates on matters of particular interest to individual Peers – a system which is effectively unknown in the Commons. Also unknown to the Commons is the idea of crossbenches, a series of short benches which literally go across the House instead of lengthways along the highly ornate and elaborate walls. Like all the other benches in the Chamber, they are upholstered in scarlet leather and it is here that Peers who do not want to ally themselves with one or other of the political parties sit in the House.

Although the Lords organise their daily business much along the lines of the Commons – and each House refers to othe other as 'the other place' – the Lords are expected to know how to behave themselves without having the full authority of a Speaker over them. Peers who

Lord Eldon, Lord High Chancellor 1807–1827 Lord Eldon, an eccentric and difficult Lord Chancellor, conferred legality on the illegal Press Gallery by bending down and picking up a reporter's note book that he had accidentally knocked from the journalist's hand. When asked, after reading Milton's *Paradise Lost* what he thought of Satan, Eldon, the Keeper of the King's Conscience, replied: 'A damned fine fellow. I hope he may win'

want to speak in a debate put down their names in advance; during long debates the House sometimes adjourns 'during pleasure' to give Peers time for a civilised meal in the baronial splendour of their dining-room, and they refer to each other with grave courtesy as 'My Noble Friend' or 'The Noble Lord' since, technically, they address each other and not the chair. Peers have their own edition of *Hansard* which is prepared and published quite separately from the House of Commons' version, and it is unthinkable that any sort of major interruption from the floor of the House should ever be recorded in it. Should the noble tempers become too frayed, then the Leader of the House asks the Clerk to read the standing order against asperity, which was passed in 1626 and still applies. 'To prevent misunderstanding and for avoiding of offensive speeches when matters are debating, either in the House or at Committees, it is, for honour's sake, thought fit, and so ordered, that all personal, sharp or taxing speeches be foreborne, and whosoever answereth another man's speech shall apply his answer to the matter without wrong to that person; and as nothing offensive is to be spoken, so nothing is to be ill taken if the party that speaks it shall presently make a fair exposition or clear denial of the words that might bear any ill construction; and if any offence of that kind be given, as the House will be very sensible thereof, so it will sharply censure the offender, and give the party offended fair reparation and full satisfaction.' Which, three hundred and fifty years later, sums up parliamentary courtesy, and parliamentary discipline precisely.

CHAPTER THIRTEEN

The Press Gallery

The Lord High Chancellor of England, Lord Eldon, swept through the House of Lords. At the Bar of the House stood the Speaker with a formal message from the Commons. The Lord Chancellor moved forward in his full-bottomed wig, lace at his throat, and silver-buckled black shoes on his feet. Over his court dress he wore a gown of heavy black silk. Below the Bar of the Lords, huddled round the door of the Chamber, stood a group of journalists, trying hard to look inconspicuous. Officially, they were strictly forbidden to be there but their presence was now a fact of parliamentary life and, like their brothers in the House of Commons, they had developed a well known, and generally accepted, system of bribing the doorkeepers to let them in.

The journalists respectfully stepped back as Lord Eldon moved towards the spot where they were standing. The Lord Chancellor drew his gown around him and, as he did so, the heavy silk billowed out and knocked the notebook from the hand of an appalled reporter standing nearby. The reporter and his colleagues froze in horror; the doorkeepers faced instant dismissal on the horizon for allowing them into the Chamber. The journalists saw themselves being called on their knees to the Bar of the House, as so many of their colleagues had been called before them, to receive a reprimand. Instead, Lord Eldon, the Lord Chancellor, paused, bent down, picked up the notebook, bowed to the reporter and, with a murmur of apology, returned the notebook. With this tiny gesture the Lord Chancellor himself had at last made honest men of the journalists who had, for centuries, tried to report the proceedings of Parliament and who had all too often been made to pay stiff penalties for trying to do something so outrageous.

MPs, Peers, a future Archbishop of Canterbury, a future Lord Chancellor had all tried their hands at parliamentary reporting – in spite of the fact that this was quite illegal. A king had even tried a little editing of a parliamentary report. MPs had bribed or, at any rate, tried to bribe journalists to report their speeches, while at the same time supporting laws which banned the journalists from doing any such thing. Parliamentary reports were burned by the Common Hangman in New Palace Yard; the Lord Mayor of London himself was sent to the Tower in the cause of parliamentary journalism; and the Prime Minister scarcely escaped with his life when the mob rioted in support of the Lord Mayor. Nevertheless, it is still technically illegal to report the proceedings of Parliament to this very day. Motion after motion was passed by both Houses in the eighteenth century, specifically and absolutely forbidding the reporting of debates and these motions remain in force.

All that Parliament has done since then is to say that it will not actually use the powers that it gave itself through these motions; it has not abolished them. Perhaps it is not without significance that the last man to be brought to the Bar of the Commons as a prisoner, accused of a breach of parliamentary privilege – that is, offending against the dignity of the House – was a journalist: John Junor, the editor of the *Sunday Express*, called to account in 1956. He, at least, unlike so many of his predecessors, did not have to go on his knees to beg forgiveness of the Commons.

The obsession with secrecy which has pre-occupied politicians for so many centuries arose from two reasons: firstly, because they did not want the king, with whom they were frequently at odds, to know what they were doing and what they were saying – although Charles I, at least, had a number of MPs in his pay to report back to him. With the king in ignorance of its discussions and decisions, the House of Commons was much more likely to be able to outflank him and get its own way.

The second reason for the emphasis on secrecy was the simple fact that MPs were drawn from the patrician classes of society and were not used to having their opinions questioned or their actions criticised. What they decided was good for the country, *was* good for the country, and that was that. If their discussions were reported then the people – or at any rate, those who could read – might want to have their say, and that would never do.

Yet people always wanted to know what was being done and decided in their name by those who claimed to represent them, and there have always been journalists ready and willing to tell them. One of the earliest reporters was, inevitably, an MP – and a particularly tedious and pompous one at that. He was Sir Symonds D'Ewes, a one-eyed lawyer who sat for Sudbury, in Suffolk; a devout, ambitious, conceited and snobbish bore. In the first half of the seventeenth century, D'Ewes drove his fellow MPs to distraction with his endless points of order, but he made it his duty to transcribe the *Journals* of the House, the dry-as-dust records of the proceedings of the Commons, into something a good deal more readable. There was a good deal of trouble, but D'Ewes retorted snappily, but with some truth, that, 'if you will not permit us to write, we must go to sleep, as some among us do, or go to plays, as others have done'.

D'Ewes, however, was not the only one trying to report Parliament. On 8 January, 1640, it was ordered that: 'Overton, the stationer, who falsely printed an Order of this House, without any authority of this House, and made additions of his own, be sent for by Mr Speaker's warrant . . .' Overton duly appeared next day and 'kneeling upon his knees, Mr Speaker told him that his Offence was of a high nature to presume, upon his own authority, to print any Order of this House, and not only so, but to misprint it, and to make Additions to it of your own: And, however, the House does incline to extend Mercy to you at this time in letting you pass with this sharp Reprehension only: Yet they would have you call in and suppress so many of the Copies as you can and take Care how you run into the like great Offence again.' A noble lord fared no better. In 1641 Lord Digby printed the speech which he had made during the debates on the Bill of Attainder that sent King Charles's favourite, Strafford, to be beheaded on Tower Hill. The Commons resolved that: 'No Member of the House shall either give a copy, or publish in print, anything that he shall speak here, without the leave of the House.' Digby's pamphlet, it was decided, 'deserves the brand of this House', and it was ordered that it should be burned 'publickly by the hands of the Common Hangman' in Palace Yard, Westminster, and at Cheapside and Smithfield in the City.

One of the Commons' Clerks, John Rushworth, the Clerk Assistant, was a good deal luckier than Lord Digby. Rushworth was sitting in his place at the Commons Table when, in January 1642, Charles I made his attempt to arrest five Members in the Chamber. Rushworth calmly made a note of all that went on as the King took the Speaker's chair and demanded to know the whereabouts of the five Members. Next day, the King himself sent for Rushworth's report and made one or two corrections to it. The Commons, though, decided that it had had enough of its Clerk's scribbling. They ordered him to stop taking notes, and a committee was set up to look through the ones he had already taken to see what was worth keeping. Carlyle was later to call Rushworth's 'Historical Collections' a 'rag-fair of a book; the mournfullest torpedo rubbish-heap of jewels buried under sordid wreck and dust and dead ashes, one jewel to the wagon load'. The greatest jewel, of course, was the one that recorded Charles's entrance into the Chamber.

Cromwell and the members of his Long Parliament, though, understood the advantages of firmly controlled, carefully angled publicity. They ordered broadsheets to be printed and posted in Westminster Hall, Whitehall and at the Mansion House, containing information about government actions and policy, and they also ordered that the regular publication of the Diurnal Occurrences should continue – or, as the first edition called it, the *Daily Proceedings of Both Houses in this great and happy Parliament from 3 November, 1640, to 3 November, 1641*. People who broke the reporting rules were, of course, still punished. One MP was sent to the Tower for publishing speeches, and on the very day that the House of Lords, in January 1643, ordered the Clerk of the Parliaments to 'provide a printer that shall print those things that shall be appointed by Parliament', Black Rod brought to the Bar of the Lords a number of people accused of 'printing false and scandalous pamphlets'. They were held in custody until they 'put in good security for their better behaviour for the future', says the Lords' *Journal*, and they had to promise that they 'do not hereafter print any Thing concerning the Parliament without special order under the hands of the Clerk of either Houses of Parliament'.

There was, at that time, a 'perfect Diurnall' on sale in Westminster Hall, under the very noses of Lords and Commons. It was printed by a man called Samuel Peche, and he had as a competitor a tailor named John Dillingham, who brought out the first copies of his *Parliamentary Scout* on 27 June, 1643.

With the restoration of the monarchy, in 1660, after the repressions of the Commonwealth Government, the system of sending out hand-written news-letters began to grow. Since these were not printed, they were less liable to control, but when John Dyer, a Tory and a High Churchman, began to send out his pamphlets in 1693, he soon found himself in trouble for writing 'false news'. Dyer was brought to the Bar of the Commons and there, on his knees, he was reprimanded by Mr Speaker for 'his great presumption' in trying to report the proceedings of the House. Dyer was allowed to go free, but the Commons then passed a resolution that: 'No news-letter writers do in their letters or other papers that they do disperse, presume to intermeddle with the debates or other proceedings of this House'. It was the first of a long line of resolutions forbidding 'intermeddling', each resolution more ineffectual than the last. The Commons tried to make the ban on news-letters more effective by having them banned also from the coffee houses; but in this they inevitably failed.

The more Parliament threatened, the more journalists grew determined to report its proceedings, and the news-letter soon gave way to parliamentary reporting in the newspapers. Abel Boyer, a Frenchman settled in London, began his magazine *The Political State of Great Britain* in 1711, and was so successful that Members personally sent him their speeches for publication. After his death in 1729 came the rise of his most successful imitator, Edward Cave, with his *Gentleman's Magazine*.

Cave was the son of a cobbler from Newton, near Rugby, and he eventually found work in London at the Post Office as the important official, the Clerk of the Franks. When his paper, which he ran at the same time as his official post, appeared to be receiving rather too much political news, it was alleged that he took advantage of his official position to open letters, and then shamelessly used the information he gleaned in the columns of his newspaper. It was Cave who, in March 1728, sent Robert Raikes, printer of the *Gloucester Journal*, a paragraph about the Commons proceedings. Raikes printed a piece in his Gloucester paper headed 'Westminster, 5 March', giving the results of a committee vote on the National Debt. 'The Debates on the said question, wherein Mr Pulteney and Sir Robert Walpole were chiefly engaged, one against the other, lasted till 9 at night.' That is all Raikes reported, yet it landed him on his knees at the Bar of the House, to receive a reprimand from the Speaker. Ruefully, he wrote on his own copy of the *Gloucester Journal* (it still exists), the words: 'The Woeful Paragraph', and 'This paragraph cost R. R. £40'. That was not a fine; it was the fee that Raikes had to pay to the Serjeant-at-Arms for the privilege of being arrested. The fees the Serjeant charged prisoners brought to the Bar (the Serjeant kept the money for himself), included: £5 for taking a Knight into custody and £3.6s.8d. for taking a Gentleman into custody. Every day in custody cost £1; and he charged additional sums for bringing a criminal to the Bar, 6s.8d.; and riding fees of 6d. a mile – and riding charges from London to Gloucester to arrest Raikes would have been very heavy.

Cave, of course, was at the Bar with Raikes, as he had supplied the offending piece of information. He was accused of 'having presumed to disperse written news-letters containing accounts of the proceedings of this House', and he was 'found guilty of a breach of privilege of this House'. Cave, too, had to pay his fees to the Serjeant, but he was totally unabashed and unrepentant, and he and his *Gentleman's Magazine* went from strength to atrength. He bribed his way into the Strangers' Gallery of the Commons and, when he was not steaming open MPs' letters, paid other journalists to supply him with additional news. One of these was William Gutherie, the son of a Scottish Episcopalian clergyman, who rewrote Cave's pieces for him. After a debate, Gutherie and Cave would go off to the nearest tavern, and there were plenty around Westminster to choose from, and work upon their reports.

With the success of the *Gentleman's Magazine* came the imitators. The most successful of these was the *London Magazine*. Both magazines claimed to have the best informed parliamentary reports and both claimed to have the largest circulation – and both simply lifted pieces from each other whenever they felt like it. Since the rules of the non-reporting of Parliament were still strictly enforced in the first half of the eighteenth century when the two papers flourished, they each had to use thinly-disguised devices to get round these restrictions. In the *Gentleman's Magazine* they were the reports of 'Debates in the Senate of Magna Lilliputia', and in the *London Magazine* they were 'Reports of the Roman Senate'. In the same way both publications used equally thinly disguised names for the Members. In the Senate of Lilliput Sir Robert Walpole was 'Sir Rubs Waleup'; Pelham was 'Plemham'; and Pulteney was 'Pulnib'. In the Roman Senate there were 'Julius Florus', and 'Pomponius Atticus'. What the *Gentleman's Magazine* did have which gave it the edge over the *London Magazine* was its Parliamentary Correspondent, Dr Samuel Johnson.

Dr Johnson was the first of a long line of major literary figures who tried their hands at parliamentary reporting. With splendid arrogance, he simply ignored what the politicians actually said, and made up their speeches himself – a habit, some modern politicians would claim, which has not altogether died out in Dr Johnson's successors.

Dr Johnson, however, changed many of the politicians' speeches so that they emerged a great deal better than those they could have produced on their own. Some of the Members were later proud to have Johnson's version of those speeches published among their collected

works. Johnson, though, never made the mistake of actually hearing speeches, or actually going to the Commons. 'Sir, I never was in the Gallery of the House of Commons but once'. His editor, Cave, bribed the doorkeepers to let in the *Gentleman's Magazine*'s reporters, and those reporters then brought their notes to Johnson. 'The whole was afterwards communicated to me, and I composed the speeches they now have in the Parliamentary debates, for the speeches of that period are all printed in Cave's magazine.' 'I took care', the great Doctor added, 'that the Whig dogs should not have the best of it.' One evening, at a convivial dinner, someone commented on the effectiveness of a speech made by William Pitt the elder in 1741. Johnson stirred himself. 'That speech I wrote in a garret in Exeter Street', he intoned.

For three years, from November 1740, until November 1743, Johnson reported the Senate of Lilliput. Sometimes the reporters supplied him with notes, but just as often, according to Boswell, he was only given the names of the speakers and which side they were on. Johnson could, if only he had known, have used the shorthand notes taken by the Bishop of Oxford, Dr Thomas Secker, who later became Archbishop of Canterbury, of the debates in the Lords. Secker's shorthand notes of one debate claimed the Secretary for War, the Duke of Argyle, referring to the increased number of army officers, had said 'Tradesmen from the counter were made officers, and numbers taken from school looked as if their cockades would tumble them over.' Johnson's version of the same piece goes on for at least ten times that length and says that 'we have seen the same animals today bringing behind a counter, and tomorrow swelling into a military dress, we have seen boys sent from school in despair of improvement, and entrusted with military command – fools that cannot learn this duty and children that cannot perform it.'

At full tirade Johnson was formidable, but towards the end of his life he regretted his part as a parliamentary journalist. He warned Tobias

Above left: *Edward Cave, publisher of the 'Gentleman's Magazine'* Cave was both a journalist and a senior official in the Post Office. Publishing Parliamentary reports was illegal, and he appeared at the Bar of the Commons accused of 'Having presumed to disperse written news-letters containing accounts of the proceedings of this House'

Above: *Dr Johnson* Dr Samuel Johnson was employed by Cave to write reports of Parliamentary debates although, as he said, 'I never was in the Gallery of the House of Commons but once.' Because of reporting restrictions, he had to call the Commons the Senate of Lilliput, 'I took care that the Whig dogs should not have the best of it'

Smollet, who was writing a history of England, not to rely on his reports. Boswell said that, once Johnson realised his reports were being accepted as true accounts of what had actually been said, he 'determined that he would write no more of them "for he would not be accessory to the propagation of falsehood".' Yet when Cave, the publisher of the *Gentleman's Magazine* in which these false reports had appeared, died in 1754, his hand was clasped in the hand of his greatest contributor – Dr Samuel Johnson.

A far less likely recruit to the Parliamentary Correspondents' ranks was the sensitive poet Samuel Taylor Coleridge, who made a brief attempt at reporting the Commons in 1799–1800. Like Dr Johnson, Coleridge was not too fussy about the accuracy of his reports. He worked for the *Morning Post*, and as a young man of twenty-six, he was particularly proud of his report in that paper of a speech by Pitt in February 1800, in favour of war with Napoleon. 'My report of Pitt's speech made a great noise here', wrote Coleridge to a friend – although he did not think much of the ideas in the speech itself. 'What a degraded animal man is to see anything to admire in that wretched rant.' Canning said that the report did 'more credit to the author's head than to his memory', but one must remember that Coleridge was doubtlessly exhausted before his day's work of compiling it had even begun. He had to queue up at seven o'clock in the morning, many hours before the speech was due to be made, in order to get a seat in the Strangers' Gallery, and he kept falling asleep as Pitt droned on. Nor could he take shorthand, so Canning's dismissal of Coleridge's work is hardly surprising. A much disillusioned Coleridge wrote to his fellow poet, Southey, about this time: 'I shall give up this newspaper business; it is too, too fatiguing. I have attended the debates twice, and the first time I was twenty-five hours in activity, and that of a very unpleasant kind; and the second time from ten in the morning until four o'clock in the afternoon.' Nor would money keep Coleridge in parliamentary journalism; he turned down an offer of a half share in the *Morning Post* and *The Courier*, and went off with his family to the Lake District to the far more congenial job of writing poetry.

Thirty years after Coleridge, a very different man came to the Press Gallery of Parliament. Far from finding life there 'too, too fatiguing', he found it exhilarating and exciting, and he even found time, between the long hours that he worked, to start writing the first of his great novels. Charles Dickens was a brilliant parliamentary reporter, and he was at Westminster during one of its most exciting and tempestuous times. He reported the Great Reform Bill of 1832, and the Poor Law Bill of 1834; he was a parliamentary reporter when the Palace was burnt down in 1834; and he was in the Press Galleries of the Lords and Commons when they were finally established in 1831 and 1835. Before the Galleries were provided, he had joined all the other reporters in working in great discomfort. 'I have worn my knees by writing on them on the old back row of the old Gallery of the old House of Commons', he recalled many years later, when he was a famous author. 'I have worn my feet standing to write in a preposterous pen in the old House of Lords, where we used to huddle together like so many sheep, kept in waiting until the Woolsack might want restuffing.'

Dickens had influence behind him when he first went to work in Parliament. His feckless father, John, had worked there on the *British Press* and later on the *Morning Herald*, and Charles's maternal uncle John Henry Barrow, started a paper called *The Mirror of Parliament* in 1828. Charles, however, worked first on the *True Sun* and then, in 1833, transferred to his uncle's paper. He wrote Gurney's shorthand at a formidable speed; David Copperfield was to buy a book on 'an approved scheme of the noble art and mystery of stenography' for 10s. 6d., and he then 'plunged into a sea of perplexity which brought me in weeks to the confines of distraction'.

Young Dickens, however, thrived on Gurney's perplexities, and he recalled many years later how Edward Stanley, the Chief Secretary for Ireland (the future Earl of Derby and a Prime Minister) dictated to him in his house at Carlton House Terrace the text of a major speech he had made in the Commons on the Irish question. The Irish debates, though, so affected Dickens that he was unable to write as he listened to the descriptions of poverty and violence.

Dickens rushed out his copy for his newspapers at top speed, and it was while he was working in the Press Gallery that he met his friend and biographer, John Forster. The reporters had, apparently, threatened to strike over some grievance, and their spokesman was a young man, recalled Forster, 'whose keen animation of look would have arrested attention anywhere'. It was, of course, Dickens. Dickens filled column after column in his papers reporting Palmerston and Peel, Lord John Russell and Lord Althorp, William Cobbett and Wellington, and Lord de Grey, the Prime Minister – who, incidentally, Dickens heartily disliked. 'The shape of his head (I see it now)', he wrote thirty years later, 'was misery to me and weighed down my youth.'

In 1835, Dickens switched from the *Mirror of Parliament* to the Whig *Morning Chronicle* at a salary of five guineas a week. He was now twenty-three, and brilliant. James Grant, who worked with Dickens on the *Morning Chronicle*, said of him that 'literary abilities of a high order with reporting capacity of a superior kind are seldom found in conjunction. They were so in the case of Mr Dickens in a measure which I venture to say they never were before in any other man since Parliamentary reporting was known.'

By this time Dickens was becoming successful as an author. By 1836 he had started to write *The Pickwick Papers* and he decided it was time to leave the Press Gallery.

It would have taken Dickens' pen to do full justice to scenes which had occurred in the Gallery fifty years earlier when Parliament and Press

A page of Charles Dickens' shorthand When Dickens worked as a reporter in the Press Gallery of the Commons he wrote a complicated system of shorthand known as Gurney's. The firm of Gurney's are still the official shorthand writers to the House of Commons

collided head on; when the mob nearly lynched the Prime Minister; and when the Lord Mayor of London himself ended up in the Tower of London. The instigators of these dramas were two totally different politicians: Colonel George Onslow, a quintessential military man of the old school, and the radical reforming John Wilkes. Between them came the City of London, only too happy to use the two men as an excuse to pick a fight with the House of Commons.

Colonel Onslow was 'Little Cocking George', a lieutenant colonel in the 1st Footguards, the Member for the Borough of Guildford, and the bearer of a great family name; three Onslows had been Speakers, one of them from 1728 to 1761, the longest term in the history of the office. 'I am not an enemy of the liberty of the Press', declared Colonel Onslow, in the ancient tradition of his kind. 'I think people have a right to print things against Ministers and private persons.' He then settled down to a long series of attempts in the Commons to stop people doing anything of the sort. It was while trying to enforce the various bans on reporting Parliament that Colonel Onslow engineered through the Commons that he came up against the formidable John Wilkes.

Wilkes had been a Member of Parliament first for Aylesbury and then for Middlesex, but he had been expelled from the House and subsequently outlawed for the attacks on the King's speech of 1763, which had appeared in his paper, the *North Briton*. He returned to England in 1768, and he had become a City magistrate when, in 1771, the Commons sent its messenger to the City to arrest John Webble, printer of the *Middlesex Journal* and *Chronicle of Liberty* – a tri-weekly paper supporting Wilkes – and Richard Thompson of the *Gazeteer*, for printing parliamentary reports. Not surprisingly, Wilkes promptly used his powers as a magistrate to free both Webble and Thompson. Little Cocking George was furious. He made a series of accusations against the Press, and this was followed by a great deal of earnest debate in the Commons. 'I by no means approve of the licentiousness of the Press', thundered one Member of the House.

The Commons would not give up. It sent a messenger of the Serjeant-at-Arms, a man named Whittam, to the City to make another arrest; this time the accused man was John Miller, the printer of the *London Evening Post*, which had also carried parliamentary news. It was, however, the Serjeant's messenger, Whittam, and not Miller, who found himself under arrest on a charge drummed up, largely by Wilkes, under a City charter of 1327. Whittam was brought before the Lord Mayor, Alderman Brass Crosby, MP, and Alderman Oliver, MP. The Lord Mayor was ill with gout, so Whittam was taken to his bedroom at the Mansion House and, at first, committed to prison, before being bailed out by the Deputy Serjeant-at-Arms. In the Commons the result was uproar, as the House fumed and raged at having its authority so thoroughly defied. Brass Crosby and Oliver were commanded to attend in their places in the Chamber to answer for their conduct in detaining a

messenger of the House. Crosby had to be carried into the Commons by three Members, his gout-swollen limbs swathed in bandages. He was a loud-mouthed, hard-drinking man, an attorney and a Member for Honiton in Devon; Oliver was an East India merchant and a good deal more sedate. Both, however, defied the Commons, as much in the interest of the ancient rights of the City as in the rights of a free Press.

The House strongly criticised the Lord Mayor's behaviour, and the King himself tried to intervene. 'It is highly necessary', he wrote to North, the Prime Minister, 'that this strange and lawless method of publishing debates in the papers should be put a stop to.' While the Commons were wondering what to do about such a difficult Lord Mayor, the King wrote again to North: 'The authority of the House of Commons is totally annihilated if it is not in an exemplary manner supported . . . by instantly committing the Lord Mayor and Alderman Oliver to the Tower.' The King added, 'As to Wilkes, he is below the notice of the House.'

To the Tower the Lord Mayor and Oliver duly went, amid the yelling of the mob and the whining of the by now much alarmed and frightened Little Cocking George Onslow. When the Lord Mayor, still swathed in bandages, was carried off to imprisonment, Onslow lamented, 'I had no object in view but the honour of the House. I had no private motive, so help me God. I may be mistaken; it may be the prejudice of education. If I have erred, I have erred with my ancestors. Could I have supposed that the Lord Mayor would have acted as he has done? I have frequently drunk a bottle of wine with him. If I had foreseen what has happened, I believe I should not have done it.' He would most certainly not have done it, for his actions in the Commons raised the London mob in support of the Lord Mayor and Alderman Oliver. The Lord Mayor came to the House escorted by thousands from the City; troops were ordered to stand by in readiness to repel them; the Commons sent for the Westminster magistrates to read the Riot Act, but when the magistrates tried to do so they were howled down. The constables had their staves pulled from their hands, and then they had to stand powerlessly by as the mob in Palace Yard turned on the Prime

Minister's coach, dragged him from it, and hit him over the head with the stolen batons. North escaped with his life into Westminster Hall, but his coach was reduced to matchwood, and his hat torn to pieces. 'Gentlemen, gentlemen, is this liberty?' shouted the wretched North as he made his escape. 'Do you call this liberty?' 'Yes', shouted one of his attackers, 'and great liberty, too'.

In the Chamber, North, shocked by his man-handling, was in tears, but the Commons voted to send the Lord Mayor to the Tower by 202 votes to 39. The King suggested sending him by water to avoid the mob, but the Lord Mayor eventually went by coach, which was pulled through the streets by the crowd. Brass Crosby himself had to rescue the Deputy Serjeant-at-Arms from the mob when they tried to hang the wretched official from a lamppost, and he went off to the Tower where, according to Horace Walpole, he was 'half-drunk, swore, and behaved with a jollity ill-becoming the gravity of his office and cause'. That cause – the right to print reports of Parliament – had by then long been forgotten or confused with the City's ancient claim to its own rights and privileges. The mob, however, had had a splendid time, and the Lord Mayor and Alderman Oliver, whose food was paid for by the City Corporation during their imprisonment, were set free after six weeks of comfortable captivity. They were borne off to the Mansion House in tremendous state, celebrated by a twenty-one gun salute and the ringing of church bells. When he arrived back at his Mansion House, the Lord Mayor threw a great party, and then lived for another twenty-two years, to enjoy the good things of life and curse his gout.

Watching these extraordinary events in the Commons, from a seat in the front of the Strangers' Gallery, was a stern but elegantly dressed figure, who surveyed it all with a tense, unblinking eye. He had also been a victim of Little Cocking George Onslow at one time during that choleric Member's campaign against the Press; only days before the Lord Mayor was sent to the Tower, this man had himself been let out of prison, where he had been sent for reporting the House of Lords. He was Memory Woodfall, one of the most extraordinary men, out of a long list of extraordinary men, who have reported political events at Westminster.

William Woodfall came from a family of printers and journalists, and although he at first tried his luck as an actor, in 1769 he became editor, reporter and printer of the Whig newspaper, the *Morning Chronicle and London Advertiser*. At the time, of course, reporting Parliament was strictly forbidden, and Woodfall learnt this to his cost when he was sent to Newgate prison for a month, and fined £100, because he had reported a case which was being heard in the House of Lords. He appealed against the sentence; he was, he said, 'conscious of neither wantonly or wilfully offending their Lordships, and entertaining the highest Idea of their Lordship's (sic) Mercy and Humanity, most humbly prays an immediate enlargement from his present dangerous confinement; and, as in duty bound, will ever pray.' Their Lordships let him out, on payment of his £100 fine and his fees to Black Rod.

Memory Woodfall got the nickname by which he was known all his life because of his ability to sit in the Strangers' Gallery and, without taking a single note – notetaking was, and still is, strictly forbidden in the Strangers' Gallery – return to his office near Fleet Street to dictate column after column of the speeches he had heard. He would sit in the stuffy, cramped gallery for hours on end, with his hands resting on the amber top of his cane, peering intently at whoever was speaking. He was a rather forbidding, but dandified figure: 'dressed in a suit of brown dittos with salmon-coloured silk stockings', recalled a contemporary, 'gold buckles, a tie wig and an amber-headed cane'.

For twenty years, Woodfall slaved on, night after night, listening to debates and then transcribing them for his paper from his photographic memory. He became something of a national figure. When an awe-struck provincial visitor was brought to the House, he asked: 'Which is Memory Woodfall and which is Mr Speaker?' When Woodfall went to Dublin to report the Irish Parliament he was followed through the streets by a curious crowd. He had an odd habit of keeping himself going on hard-boiled eggs; he kept a supply of them in his coat pockets, and periodically took one out and cracked it in the rim of the hat and then peeled it into the crown. In later years he became rather ponderous and heavy-handed towards his fellow journalists and, to get their own back, they once slipped a raw egg into his pocket with the inevitable, and messy, results.

Great politicians looked to Memory Woodfall for judgements on their speeches and their ability. After his maiden speech, Sheridan asked Woodfall how he thought it had gone. 'I think it is not your line', Woodfall told the great playwright. 'No, Sheridan, you had better stick to those pursuits you are much more fitted for.' Sheridan, much distressed, banged his forehead and said, 'It is in me, and by God it shall come out.' It did. Seven years later, during one of the great debates on the impeachment of Warren Hastings, Sheridan made a speech of such overwhelming power that the House adjourned to recover from the spell laid upon them by 'the wand of the enchanter'. Woodfall was unenchanted; Sheridan spoke for over five hours, although Woodfall's report made it appear as though the speech had lasted only half an hour.

Opinions about Woodfall's real ability were mixed, presumably depending on whether he flattered you or not. Mrs Tickell, Sheridan's sister-in-law, thought Woodfall 'ought to be tossed in a blanket', but Anthony Storer, MP, thought Woodfall reported debates 'almost always faithfully'.

Woodfall was, in fact, only one of the memory men who reported Parliament, although he was by far the most successful and famous of them all. Almost equally famous was William Radcliffe, who owned the *English Chronicle*. He, it was said, had the extraordinary ability to come away from the Commons and go to the printers and there stand between two compositors, dictating alternately to each a sentence from entirely different speeches, and this without any hesitation or confusion between the two.

Both these paragons, however, were eventually outstripped by progress when, with the changing of attitudes in the Commons and the judicious spreading of heavy bribes around the Gallery attendants, newspaper competitors were able to get reporters into the House in relays, so that they could then hurry back to their offices in time to bring out full accounts of the debates next morning. Although Woodfall had been the first journalist to publish his reports on the following day, his methods meant that times of publication were uncertain, and instead of papers appearing in the early morning, they were sometimes delayed until late afternoon. Woodfall died in 1803, at the age of fifty-eight; he was buried, appropriately enough, in the Parish Church of the House of Commons – St Margaret's, Westminster.

Woodfall's death came too early for him to participate in the great battles between the Press and the Irish liberator and fiery orator, Daniel O'Connell. These battles went on for years, with the Irishman always complaining he was either under-reported or misreported, and the reporters claiming they had reported him correctly or that he was unreportable. O'Connell constantly complained to the editor of *The Times*, and to other papers, of 'gross misrepresentation', and in 1835 wrote furiously, 'The reporting in the newspapers is scandalous. I made a speech last night which was more cheered than any, I believe, I ever made. The report is in a few insignificant lines.' When he complained of incorrect reporting, the journalist responsible said his notebook had got wet in the rain on the way back to his office. 'That', retorted O'Connell, 'was the most extraordinary shower of rain I ever heard of, for it not only washed out the speech I made from your notebook, but it also washed in another and an entirely different one.' Eventually, the journalists had had enough of the Irish liberator's constant complaints, and they imposed a reporting ban on him. 'We . . . feel it our due', they wrote, 'to our honour and character thus publically to repel, as far as we are concerned, with the utmost scorn and indignation, the false and calumnious charges which had been brought by Mr O'Connell against the reporters of the proceedings of Parliament.' O'Connell retaliated by 'spying Strangers' in the Chamber – a device to have all non-Members, including journalists, excluded from the House. Politicians, however, quickly realised that they could not do without the journalists; if there was no one to report their speeches, the speeches were hardly worth making. 'For the first time within my recollection', noted one MP, 'Members kept their word when, on commencing their orations, they promised not to trespass at any length on the patience of the House.'

By the 1830s journalists were fully established in Parliament. The Lords were the first to recognise them officially, although it was done in a slightly shame-faced way. That courteous act of the Lord Chancellor's, when he picked up a reporter's notebook, had already given journalists in the Lords a tacit approval, but public interest in politics was such that real provisions had to be made to keep the nation informed. For the debates on the Catholic Emancipation Bill of 1828 and the Reform Bill of 1831 the Lords ordered extra accommodation for the public to be built in their Chamber, with the clear, although unwritten, understanding that the front row of the new seats would be reserved for the Press. The new Gallery was opened on 6 December, 1831, and even *Hansard* had earlier allowed itself one of its extremely rare comments: 'The erection of this Gallery is an epoch in the history of the House of Lords. In it, by their Lordships' approbation, was accommodation for the reporters of the Public Press, though according to their Lordships' Standing Order it still remains a breach of their privilege to report their debates.' There were, however, limits to their Lordships' enthusiasm for the Press. When Lord Campbell became the Lord Chancellor in 1859, he tried hard to forget the fact that he had once been a reporter in the Press Gallery. He was, in fact, one of many lawyer-reporters who have worked at Westminster. Lawyers working in the Law Courts in Westminster Hall found it convenient to pop round to the Houses of Parliament and do a little journalism to supplement their meagre fees. The Benchers of Lincoln's Inn thought this very degrading. In 1807 they decreed that, 'No person who has written for hire in the newspapers shall be admitted to do exercises to entitle him to be called to the Bar.' This pomposity was rightly ignored.

The Commons took a little longer than the Lords to provide for the Press. The Great Fire of October 1834, solved all the problems of accommodation that they had endured in the old Chamber, so when MPs built themselves a temporary Chamber, they put in a small Reporters' Gallery above the Speaker's chair. There the reporters sat for the first time on 9 February, 1835, although, noted *The Times*, 'we regret to say that some of the reflux from the (Strangers') Gallery found their way to what had been intended exclusively for the Press, to the great annoyance and inconvenience of the reporters.' Still, the Gallery was above the Speaker's chair, which meant that MPs would automatically turn towards the reporters when they made speeches, and this was a great improvement.

Presumably among those annoyed and inconvenienced reporters who could not get into their own Gallery were men from *Hansard*, a name which has now become synonymous with total accuracy in parliamentary reporting. *Hansard* had begun over thirty years before the opening of the Commons Press Gallery with William Cobbett's *Political Register*, which he eventually sold to Thomas Curson Hansard, son of Luke Hansard, the printer to the House of Commons. In 1829 the *Political Register* became *Hansard's Parliamentary Debates*, and continued as an entirely private undertaking, compiled mainly from newspaper reports,

The Press Gallery, House of Commons It has always been, and theoretically still is, strictly against the rules of the Commons to report its proceedings. Eighteenth-century resolutions said it was 'a high indignity to, and a notorious breach of the privileges of this House' to report its debates, and although these resolutions have never been rescinded, the House has now agreed not to proceed with them. Some 250 journalists now work regularly in the Press Gallery with their own offices, library, dining room, bar and other facilities, to which MPs may come only as guests. Parliamentary reports have immunity from legal action by people outside the Commons, provided the reports are fair and accurate accounts of what has been said

until 1855, when the Stationery Office was ordered to subscribe to a hundred copies for distribution to government departments at home and in India and the colonies.

Financially, however, *Hansard* was in a mess, and continued to be so, in spite of Treasury subsidies, until it was eventually taken over by the government in 1908. Debates in the Lords began to be separately published in 1909, and were also taken over by the Stationery Office in 1920. The two *Hansards*, Lords and Commons, still have an entirely separate staff of editors and reporters. They do not claim to be a totally verbatim report of every word that is said in either House, but a full and accurate account of the proceedings.

Like its finances, the name of *Hansard*, the name by which it is known all over the world, has varied over the years. In 1892, the title *Hansard* was dropped, and the daily publication became known as the *Authorised Edition*. In 1909 it became the *Official Report*, but in 1943 the word

Hansard was restored and added, in brackets, to the title page. It is there still.

Hansard reporters, who write shorthand at speeds of some 250 words a minute, are not, incidentally, the official shorthand writers to the Houses of Parliament. That title belongs to the firm of Gurney's who supply shorthand writers to select committees and private bill committees. On 18 May, 1813, the Commons decided that: 'The Clerk of the House do appoint a shorthand writer who shall by himself, or sufficient deputy, attend them when called upon to take minutes of evidence at the Bar of the House, or in Committee of the same', and W. B. Gurney was appointed to both Commons and Lords. Gurney came from a family of shorthand writers; his grandfather was the first shorthand writer at the Old Bailey and had taken notes during the trial of Warren Hastings. Those notes still exist. Gurney's, too, still have the duty of attending at the Bar of the House to report the proceedings if anyone is brought before the Commons accused of breach of privilege.

There have been few changes in the reporting style of either *Hansard* or Gurney's in recent years, although both have made use of modern technology in preparing their reports. For newspapers and broadcasters, however, there have been many changes in post-war parliamentary reporting. Where Parliamentary Correspondents were once the great figures of the Press Gallery, now it is the Political Correspondents who dominate political news, and proceedings in the Chamber are largely ignored unless they happen to be noisy or particularly important. The Political Correspondents – the Lobby men – are journalists who specialise in obtaining, and explaining, the background of politics; although this is often done through a system as formalised and predictable as the procedure of the Commons itself. Regular, off-the-record briefings are held for Political Correspondents every morning and afternoon by officials of 10 Downing Street; and with the Leader of the Commons and the Leader of the Opposition every Thursday afternoon. There is also a special House of Commons Bar – Annie's Bar, named after a famous pre-war barmaid – which is set aside so that journalists and politicians can meet and gossip on non-attributable terms. Lobby journalists are also allowed to stand in the Members' Lobby immediately outside the Commons Chamber, to waylay politicians as they go in and out of the House, and they also have many informal contacts with Members and Ministers.

This system is not without controversy, for many people are concerned about both the good and the harm it can do to the parliamentary process. It has grown up over the last century and *The Times* was the last major paper to have a Lobby man, Ernest W. Pitt appointed in 1891. Since the Lobby system is based on secrecy – its advocates use the word 'confidentiality' – it is open to manipulation by governments and parties, and both politicians and journalists complain they are being used by each other; yet neither side is willing to give up the system. The well-placed leak is of enormous advantage to both politician and journalist; it furthers the politician's cause and it establishes the journalist's authority and credibility. Both sides use each other in a carefully defined and clearly understood way – even if it is not too clearly understood by readers and viewers.

Lobbying is, however, a well-established practise. In 1859, Queen Victoria complained to Lord Granville that: 'The Queen is much shocked to find the whole conversation with Lord Granville yesterday and the day before detailed in this morning's leading article in *The Times*. What passes between her and a Minister in her own room in a confidential intercourse ought to be sacred . . .'

Queen Victoria would, perhaps, have approved of the number of women political and parliamentary journalists who now work in the Press Gallery. For many years women enjoyed the distinction that all MPs still enjoy – they were not allowed in the Press Gallery except as guests. In 1890, the *Women's Penny Paper* wanted Miss Julia Blain, representing a paper that was 'written by women for women', to work in the Gallery. The Serjeant-at-Arms replied that it was quite impossible for him to admit her. The Speaker supported him. Admitting Miss Blain would, said the Serjeant, lead to 'consequences which at present it is difficult to conceive', and 'the outcry would be terrific'. The Press Gallery Attendant, Woodraft, had the last word on the subject of admitting women: 'I would not have them here. There would be too much play going on.'

Ladies, of course, are now an established presence in the Press Gallery. Nevertheless, both ladies and gentlemen of the Press are still there strictly against the rules, for those thunderous resolutions which say it is a high crime for the Press to intermeddle with Parliament are still, theoretically, in operation. In 1971 the House did finally decide that, although they would not actually enforce the rules, neither would they scrap them. Journalists, therefore, remain part *of* Parliament, but not *in* Parliament. It is a compromise both sides find works very well indeed.

Particular Parliaments

Mad Parliament
Summoned to meet at Oxford on 11 June 1258. So called by the supporters of Henry III, although it drew up the very sensible Provisions of Oxford, which imposed controls on the King's actions and spending.

Model Parliament
Met on 13 November 1295, under Edward I. It settled the general principles of Parliament which have been followed ever since. Elected knights, citizens and burgesses were called to attend, together with lower clergy, who sat with the lords to advise the King.

Black Parliament
A Scottish Parliament that met at Scone in 1320. So called because of the savage punishments inflicted on people involved in the conspiracy of Sir William de Soulis.

Parliament of White Bands
Met at Westminster on 15 July 1321, when a discontented faction wore multi-coloured clothes with a white band across their chests.

Good Parliament
It met in 1376, and is so called because it took measures against the corruption at Edward III's court, and especially against his mistress, Alice Perrers.

Merciless Parliament
Met on 3 February 1388, and ordered the judicial murder of a number of Richard II's supporters when he had tried to regain control of the government. People who approved of what it did called it the: Parliament That Wrought Wonders.

Shortest Parliament
Met on only one day – 30 September 1399, and deposed Richard II.

Unlearned Parliament
Met in 1426; the Lord Chancellor, Beaufort, illegally inserted in the writs of summons a clause that no lawyer should be elected.

Parliament of Bats
A Parliament of 1426, when the Members carried bats and clubs because

they had been stopped carrying more dangerous weapons. Also known as: *Club Parliament.*

Reformation Parliament
Sat from November 1529 to April 1536, and enacted Henry VIII's Reformation measures. It ended church domination of Parliament, and the Commons emerged, for the first time, as the more powerful of the two Houses. Known to Catholic supporters as: *Black Parliament.*

Running Parliament
A Scottish Parliament that met in 1536; so called because it met at intervals and not consistently.

Reconciliation Parliament
Called by Mary I on 12 November 1554, to reconcile England with the Church of Rome. It scrapped all the ecclesiastical laws which had been passed by Henry VIII's Parliaments.

Red Parliament
A Scottish Parliament that met at Perth in 1606. The King, James VI, ordered the lords to wear red robes.

Addled Parliament
Called by James I on 5 April 1614, to try to raise money. Neither Commons nor Lords could agree on how it should be done, and no legislation was passed. Hence the name.

Short Parliament
The Parliament called by Charles I in 1640, before the Long Parliament which was called the same year. Charles demanded money for his war with Scotland, but the Commons refused to grant it. After three weeks, Parliament was dissolved.

Long Parliament
The last Parliament of Charles I. It first met on 3 November 1640, and was finally dissolved on the Restoration on 16 March 1660. In 1653 Cromwell and his army expelled the MPs from the Commons chamber because, he said, they were trying to perpetuate their own powers.

Parliament of Nominees
Called on 4 July 1653 by Cromwell it consisted of 140 Members, nominated as being of 'devoted zeal for the cause of God'. It was also known as the *Barebones Parliament* after one of its more fanatical Puritan members, Praise-God Barebone. It was more sedately called the *Little Parliament* because of the shortness of its life. It resigned in less than six months; on 12 December 1653.

Rump Parliament
The final part of the Long Parliament. It met on 23 April 1659 with only 42 members, but the numbers later increased to 91. It was the Rump Parliament that paved the way for the Restoration of 1660.

Convention Parliaments
The first, in 1660, restored Charles II to the throne. The second, in 1689, offered the Crown to William and Mary.

Drunken Parliament
A Scottish Parliament that met at Glasgow on 1 October 1662. Only one of its members was sober on the first day's sitting. It sat for only eight days.

Cavalier Parliament
The second Parliament of Charles II; it met for seventeen years: from 8 May 1661, to 30 December 1678. It is the longest consecutively sitting Parliament, and it undid much of the legislation of the Long Parliament. Because of its long life it is also known as the *Pensionary Parliament*.

Oxford Parliament
Met at Oxford on 21 March 1681. Charles II held it there to show his displeasure with the City of London.

Unreported Parliament
The Parliament of 1768 to 1774. Particularly rigid rules were enforced to exclude Strangers – including, of course, journalists – from both Houses. One MP, Sir Henry Cavendish, did, however, take shorthand notes of many of the main Commons speeches.

Bibliography

An Encyclopaedia of Parliament Norman Wilding and Philip Laundy
  (Cassell, 1970)
Bedlam Anthony Masters (Michael Joseph, 1977)
Black Rod Maurice Bond and David Beamish (HMSO, 1976)
The British Parliament COI Reference Pamphlet 33. (HMSO, 1980)
Ceremonial and the Mace in the House of Commons Sir Peter Thorne
  (HMSO, 1980)
Curiosities from Parliament Stanley Hyland (Allan Wingate, 1955)
English Constitutional History S.B. Chrimes
  (Oxford University Press, 1978)
Erskine May: Parliamentary Practice 19th Edition. Edited by Sir David
  Lidderdale, KCB (Butterworths, 1976)
Great Parliamentary Occasions J. Enoch Powell MP (Herbert Jenkins,
  1960)
Historic Parliamentary Documents Maurice Bond OBE (HMSO, 1960)
The History of the King's Works, Vols I – VI General Editor, H.M.
  Colvin (HMSO, 1976–1982)
The Houses of Parliament Edited by M.H. Port (Yale University Press,
  1976)
The Houses of Parliament Sir Bryan H. Fell, KCMG, CB and K.R.
  Mackenzie, CB Thirteenth edition revised by R.B. Sands (Eyre and
  Spottiswood, 1977)
The House of Commons at Work Eric Taylor (The Macmillan Press
  Ltd, 1979)
The Journal of the House of Commons House of Commons Library
  Document No. 7. (HMSO, 1971)
The Life and Works of Sir Charles Barry, RAFRS The Rev Alfred Barry
  D.D (John Murray, 1867)
The Lord Chancellor Maurice Bond and David Beamish (HMSO, 1977)
Mid-Victorian Masterpiece Sir Barnett Cocks (Hutchinson, 1977)
The Mother of Parliaments Harry Graham (Methuen and Co. Ltd, 1910)
The Officers of the House of Commons, 1363–1965 Philip Marsden
  (Barrie and Rockliff, 1965)
Parliamentary History, Libraries and Records Edited by H.S. Cobb
  (House of Lords Record Office, 1981)
Parliament House Maurice Hastings (The Architectural Press, 1950)
Parliament Past and Present Arnold Wright and Philip Smith
  (Hutchinson, 1902)
Parliament. Its Romance. Its Comedy. Its Pathos Michael MacDonagh
  (P.S. King and Son, 1902)

The Press Gallery at Westminster William Barkley and Guy Eden
(Press Gallery, 1975)

Pugin. The Portrait of a Mediaeval Victorian Michael Trappes-Lomax
(Sheed and Ward, 1932)

Pugin. An Illustrated Life of Augustus Welby Northmore Pugin John
Glen Harries (Shire Publications Ltd, 1973)

Questions in the House The Clerks of the Table Office (HMSO, 1979)

The Reporters' Gallery Michael MacDonagh
(Hodder and Stoughton, 1924)

Royal Westminster Penelope Huntins (RICS, 1981)

The Seventh Centenary of Simon de Montfort's Parliament, 1265–1965
(HMSO, 1965)

Saint Thomas More E.E. Reynolds (Catholic Truth Society, 1980)

The Times October, 1834, 1885

The Story of Big Ben Alan Philips (HMSO, 1971)

The Victorian Underworld Kellow Chesney (Pelican Books, 1979)

Westminster Hall Hilary St George Saunders (Michael Joseph, 1951)

Picture Credits

The BBC would like to thank the Lord Chairman of the Committees, House of Lords and Speaker of the House of Commons for their kind permission in allowing the BBC photographers access to the Palace of Westminster. Picture research (except for work by BBC photographers) by Vanessa Whinney. Page numbers in bold type denote colour photographs.

By Gracious Permission of Her Majesty the Queen/Windsor Royal Library: p. 24, 28, 154, 161; Associated Newspapers: p. 165 *right*; BBC Hulton Picture Library: p. 100, 113, 121, 122, 148, 165 left, 166, 175, 198, 204, 247; The Late Monty Bernard (Photo Eileen Tweedy): p. 85 *below*; Boston Public Library: p. 41 *above*; British Architectural Library/Royal Institute of British Architects: p. 78 *below*, 79, 86 *above*, 116; British Library: p. 12, 37 *below right*; British Museum/Fotomas Index: p. 58 *right*, 223; Chris Capstick: p. 219 *above*, 222; Philip Carr: p. 33, 35, 81, 83, 89, 90, 92 *above*, 95 *below right*, 96, 132, 133, 142 *below left* and right, 143 *above right and left*, 212 *below left*, 213 *above left and right*, 220; Tully Chaudry: p. 41 *centre left and right*, 43 *top left, centre and right*, 48 *above*, 82, 86 *below left and right*, 87 *centre and below left and right*, 91, 92 *below*, 93, 94, 95, 129, 130 *above left and below left and right*, 134, 135, 136, 137, 138, 139, 140, 141, 142 *above*, 143 *below*, 144 *above*, 209, 210, 211, 212 *above and below right*, 213 *below left and right*, 214, 215, 218, 219 *below left and right*, 221; Crown Copyright/Permission of the Controller of HMSO: p. 15, 48 *below*, 61, 76 *right*; Dean and Chapter of Westminster Library: p. 65; Dickens' House: p. 240; Fotomas Index: p. 29, 40, 144, 186; Guildhall Library, City of London: p. 31; Michael Holford: p. 8 *below*; The Honourable Society of the Inner Temple/E.T. Archive: p. 18, 36 *above right*; House of Lords Record Office: p. 98–99, 118; Huntington Library and Art Gallery, California: p. 36 *above left*; *Illustrated London News* Picture Library: p. 106 *right*, 171, 172, 173, 180, 227, 229, 245; Peter Jackson (Photo Eileen Tweedy): p. 26, 34, 43 *below*, 46, 47 *above*, 58, 64 left, 78 *above left and right*, 101, 126, 130 *above right*, 131 *below*, 146, 147, 195; Mansell Collection: p. 106 *left*, 182; Roy Miles, Fine Paintings, London: p. 84 *above left*; Museum of London: p. 38 *below*, 39 *below*, 47 *below*; National Monuments Record/Peter Jackson: p. 21; National Portrait Gallery: p. 43 *centre*, 76 *left*, 224, 230, 236; The National Trust: p. 189; Palace of Westminster (Photo Godfrey New): p. 36 *below*, 38 *above left*, 39 *above*, 42, 44, 45, 84 *above right and below*, 85 *above*, 88 *below*; Public Record Office: p. 80; The Syndics of Cambridge University Library: p. 8 *above*, 37 *above*; Sotheby's: p. 236 right; Victoria and Albert Museum (Photo Sally Chappell): p. 87 *above left, centre and right*, 88; Westminster Library: p. 104, 111; Westminster Library (Photo Godfrey New): p. 37 *below left*, 40 *below*, 68; Les Wilson: p. 38 *above right*, 216, 217

Index

Italic figures at the end of entries refer to illustrations.